D0982497

Academia from the Inside

"As this era of social reckonings has made clear, all of our major institutions—especially education—stand in urgent need of transformation if we are to create a world that works for everyone. Here's a blueprint for that transformation. Written by a collective of dedicated and experienced educators, the essays in this volume offer much more than a hopeful vision. Instead, they tell embodied stories of personal agency that move from reclaiming our identity and integrity as educators, to creating community with colleagues, to taking action together. Transforming academia 'from the inside out' is a route to the kind of change that matters and that endures. This book will take us closer to that goal."

—Parker J. Palmer, *author of* The Courage to Teach, A Hidden Wholeness, *and* Healing the Heart of Democracy

"Like rain in the desert, these essays create the conditions for new life in academe. They provide scenarios in which students and professors can thrive, not only as scholars, but as whole human beings, using resources such as mindfulness meditation, communities of support, and the natural environment. An exciting cross-disciplinary showcase for the integration of mind, body, and spirit in higher education."

—Jane Tompkins, *author of* Reading through the Night *and* A Life in School

"This book is an inspired and honest exploration of the ways today's educators are enlivening their classrooms, invigorating their institutions, and enriching their own journeys as educators and people. Through engaging first-person narratives, Hall and Brault demystify the life of the individual in academia and illuminate the many ways one can bring one's whole self to the practice of teaching."

—Susanna Space, *Essayist and Nonfiction Grantee, Barbara Deming Memorial Award for Feminists in the Arts*

Maureen P. Hall · Aubrie K. Brault
Editors

Academia from the Inside

Pedagogies for Self and Other

Editors
Maureen P. Hall
University of Massachusetts
Dartmouth
North Dartmouth, MA, USA

Aubrie K. Brault
University of Massachusetts
Dartmouth
North Dartmouth, MA, USA

ISBN 978-3-030-83894-2   ISBN 978-3-030-83895-9   (eBook)
https://doi.org/10.1007/978-3-030-83895-9

This Palgrave Macmillan imprint is published by the registered company Springer Nature
Switzerland AG
The registered company address is: Gewerbestrasse 11, 6330 Cham, Switzerland

CONTENTS

NOTES ON CONTRIBUTORS

Elizabeth Bifuh-Ambe is an Associate Professor at the University of Massachusetts, Lowell. She was born in Cameroon, West Africa where she got a Post Graduate Diploma in Education. When she accompanied her husband to Niger, she taught at the American School of Niamey, while also serving as a part-time UNICEF consultant. It is in this role that she became aware of the low literacy rates of children in parts of Sub-Saharan Africa, and across the globe. She developed a passion for literacy learning, and went back to school in the USA, where she acquired a Ph.D. in Reading, with the hopes of being a part of the change needed to bring about equity in literacy learning for underprivileged populations. Her teaching, research, and professional activities are focused on closing the achievement gaps that exist among learners in school settings in the USA and globally. She is married, with four children.

Aubrie K. Brault From 2015 to 2017, she refined her graduate thesis and portfolio work to consider the intersectionality of learning and design. She has long since been interested in how concepts and materials can be digitally constructed to meet learning objectives and how users experience them. She had the privilege of making this her career for the last four years as an instructional designer at a healthtech company. Through her promotion to senior instructional designer, her job involves designing and developing both mobile and desktop training solutions for clients to learn their software that ultimately runs different components of their health-care practices. In this role, she is a curriculum strategist and designer, content developer, scriptwriter, and demo video producer. Outside of her healthtech career, she has written for publications such as *Ubiquity* and UMassD Magazine. She is also one of the original co-founders of the first food pantry responding to food insecurity within the UMass Dartmouth's community, now known as "Arnie's Cupboard."

Agnes B. Curry is a Professor of Philosophy at the University of Saint Joseph, Connecticut, where she also directs the undergraduate Core Curriculum program. As a bit of a generalist, she has published on topics in Continental philosophy on thinkers ranging from Luce Irigaray to Karol Wojtyla (Pope John Paul II), the creation and reinforcement of values in popular culture narratives, the recuperation of Indigenous philosophical perspectives, and contemplative practices in engineering education. When she is not teaching, she can be found digging in the earth and planting things, wandering the snatches of forest she is so privileged to live near, or serving as a Spiritual Director/Companion through the Spiritual Life Center in West Hartford, Connecticut. She is married and has a college-aged son, stepdaughter, and three grandchildren.

Justine A. Dunlap is a Professor of Law at the University of Massachusetts School of Law, where she teaches Civil Procedure, Family Law, Family Law Practice, and Access to Justice. She started her legal career as an attorney at the Legal Aid Society of the District of Columbia. She transitioned to full-time law teaching 14 years after law school. She loves both lawyering and teaching and hopes to impart her enthusiasm to her students. She lives in Providence, Rhode Island, where she serves on the board of Sojourner House, a direct service agency supporting survivors of intimate partner violence and sexual assault. She has a meditation practice. She is the mother of a teenager and the daughter of a nonagenarian. She is also the daughter of a college professor.

Maureen P. Hall is a Teacher, Educator, and Professor at the University of Massachusetts Dartmouth, and her work focuses on the intersections between and among literacies, Social Emotional Learning (SEL), and Teacher Leadership. She has published more than 19 articles in peer-reviewed journals, along with many edited chapters, and her books include *Transforming Literacy* (Emerald Publishing, 2011) with Dr. Robert P. Waxler, and, *The Whole Person* (Rowman & Littlefield, 2019) with co-editors Drs. Jane Dalton and Catherine Hoyser. Her spiritual education home is in northern India at Dev Sanskriti Vishwavidyalaya

(DSVV), a place she first visited when she was a Fulbrighter in India over 2010–2011. She derives great joy from her collaborative work with colleagues and students both near and far, and, after taking refuge in northern Vermont during this pandemic, she now understands how the "wilds of nature" sing to her soul and keep her *academic forest biome* healthy and strong.

Danielle C. Johansen holds a Master of Arts in Teaching, currently works as an inclusion special educator, and is actively pursuing a special education administrator's license. She worked with students with severe disabilities for six years before transitioning to working with students with mild to moderate disabilities. Prior to becoming a special educator, she spent four months teaching an English Communications course to university professors at Dev Sanskriti Vishwavidyalaya in northern India. She is married with three children: a two-year-old son, a four-year-old daughter, and a thirteen-year-old stepson. Their pack also includes: a black lab rescue, a bichon mix, a cat, three glowfish, and a tarantula. They spend a lot of time as a family outside, and especially enjoy kayaking, going to the beach, and cruising the local river on their skiff during the summer months in their seaside hometown of Westport, MA.

Libby Falk Jones is a Poet, Writer, Photographer, and Teacher with a higher education career spanning five decades. She has published three poetry collections and several creative nonfiction essays as well as book chapters and essays on pedagogy, faculty development, writing centers, and contemplative education. Her photography has been exhibited in various Kentucky galleries and as part of Art as Healing projects at several hospitals in Kentucky and Louisiana. She has made presentations and led workshops on creative and contemplative pedagogies at Association for Contemplative Mind in Higher Education, Conference on College Composition and Communication, and American Educational Research Association, as well as at various colleges and universities. She is currently working on a new poetry collection and a book on contemplative writing and seeing, as well as co-leading "Coming of Age," a project supporting writing and creative work of Kentucky women over 60.

Narelle Lemon is an Associate Professor in Education and Associate Dean Education in the School of Social Sciences, Media, Film, and Education at Swinburne University of Technology in Melbourne, Australia. She is trained in the disciplines of arts, education, and positive psychology. Her portfolio approach to research is focused on participation and engagement. She explores this through a variety of avenues including social media use for learning and professional development; creativity and arts education; and positive psychology specifically aimed at mindful practice and productive self-care strategies. She podcasts, blogs, grams, and tweets at @rellypops and www.exploreandcreateco.com. Away from academia she volunteers as Chair for Action for Happiness Australia. She also knits, makes, hikes, camps, rides, and embraces nature at any given opportunity. She is also fond of green tea and her adventures can be followed on Instagram at #greentearefillsrequired.

Kath McLachlan is a Senior Research Fellow at Macquarie University in Sydney, Australia. From 2013 to 2021, she led the successful development, implementation, and scalability of Macquarie's Work Integrated Learning Program, PACE (Professional and Community Engagement) in the Faculty of Human Sciences. A core focus of her teaching, research, and community engagement is in reflective and contemplative practices, as a critical aspect of learning and teaching, and professional practice. As a child she felt a strong connection to nature and is actively involved in teaching and researching on nature-connection and sustainability. As the mother of a beautiful daughter who is no longer with us, she believes it is our responsibility to steward the earth and leave a better legacy for our children. Through our darkest hours and our pain, we learn that love is a give story.

Paul Moerman is a Dancer, Actor, and Literary Translator educated at Stockholm University of the Arts and Valand Academy in Gothenburg, a Lecturer at Södertörn University in Stockholm and a Doctoral Student of Art Education at the University of Jyväskylä in Finland, formerly a Civil Engineer and Architect, trained at Ghent University and the Royal Institute of Technology in Stockholm, working in Belgium, Sweden, and the USA. Alongside his artistic career, he had taught dance, drama, and creative writing, from pre-school through higher education, also integrated in language, math, sciences, and philosophy teaching. His research in dance *as* education focuses on the relational, the entwinement of esthetics and ethics, and the arts as spaces for new beginnings. Shifting perspectives, as stage artist and spectator, architect and redecorator, scholar and student, friend and father, allows for multiple dialogue and a sense of the self's littleness, trying to be at home in a big, wonderful, and challenged world.

Aminda J. O'Hare, Ph.D. is the Director of Neuroscience and faculty in the Department of Psychological Sciences at Weber State University in Ogden, UT. She specialized in teaching topics in affective and cognitive neuroscience both in the classroom and in her research lab. The CAPES Lab (Cognitive and Affective Psychophysiology and Experimental Science Lab) is particularly interested in how training in mindfulness practices alters emotion-cognition interactions in the brain. She advocates for incorporating practices of well-being and healthy habits of mind into higher education for all participants in campus communities. She loves the outdoors, being in the mountains, spending time with her husband, and being with her dogs and cats.

Billy O'Steen Throughout his 30 years in education, his teaching and learning contexts have included community projects, Outward Bound courses, whitewater rafts, and university classrooms. Probably his most genuine alignment of his philosophy with his practice occurred when he created a middle school that was located in a house and had bean bags and couches instead of desks. His Ph.D. was an extension of that in his research of the effects of a middle school program that used activities like canoeing and hiking as ways to teach the core subjects. He applied all of these experiences in creating a service-learning course at the University of Canterbury in response to the devastating earthquakes in Christchurch, New Zealand in 2010 and 2011. This work was recognized through his receipt of a Teaching Award. Ten years later, his wife and two college-aged daughters had stayed there and had been contributors to the city's recovery.

Bronwen Wade-Leeuwen   is an Arts Educator, Researcher, and Teacher (ART-ographer). For the past two decades, she is working as an academic and project officer at Macquarie University in the School of Education and Environmental Sciences. Her specialty area is STEAM/STEM education and her Ph.D. was in how to foster creativity in teacher education. She teaches STEAM education in schools and works closely with teachers on professional learning to recognize different levels of creativity and reflection. Additionally, she is an ADOBE Education Leader (AEL) teaching digital literacy programs in schools and higher education. As an exhibiting artist, she has held numerous shows in Singapore, Hawaii, Malaysia, Taiwan, and Australia. She is a proud mother of four children, two boys, her niece, and nephew.

Steven Willis is a Storyteller who uses his poetic and theatrical background to embark on the daunting task of creatively articulating African-American culture. With art heavily influenced by urban life and religion, he mixes elements of hip-hop poetics and theatrical performance with formal teachings and anthropology, and political theory to help express his eclectic personal narrative. He is a contributing writer to the *Breakbeat Poets Anthology*, NYU's National Council for Teacher of English Journal, a three-time individual World Poetry Slam finalist, and a former resident poet of the Nuyorican Poets Cafe. He received his MFA in acting from the University of Iowa in 2021 and has just entered the MFA program and Iowa Writers' Workshop for Poetry.

LIST OF FIGURES

CHAPTER 1

Foreword/Introduction

Maureen P. Hall, Aubrie K. Brault, Libby Falk Jones, and Steven Willis

FOREWORD

Where I'm From

By Steven Willis

I'm from a family full
of fast and slick talkers.
I'm the elegant one.
Born to speak to police,
or give the funeral speech.
If my brother is ever found

M. P. Hall (✉) · A. K. Brault
University of Massachusetts Dartmouth, North Dartmouth, MA, USA
e-mail: mhall@umassd.edu

L. F. Jones
Berea College, Berea, KY, USA

S. Willis
University of Iowa, Iowa City, IA, USA

1

dead in street,
it'd be up to me
to address the newscasters in grief.

Grandma says my voice is anointed,
I'm destined to preach.
Cousin say I got flow,
sound best of beats.
All I know
is from the moment I learned to speak
my voice never belonged
to me.

Steven Willis c. 2018
Dedicated to my 7th graders in Brooklyn

It was exactly 24 hours after I graduated from undergrad that my mentor dropped me off in Brooklyn to start my life as an artist. Somehow my best friend Anthony convinced me it was a good idea to stay with him in a single room he was renting in a brownstone right off Myrtle Ave. in Clinton Hill, Brooklyn. Myrtle Ave. at one point was known as Murder Ave. by Brooklyn natives for its high murder rate during New York's drug peak, but had since drastically mellowed. By the time I arrived in 2015 the seeds of gentrification had already taken root. The Starbucks, the Chipotle and the grocery store that was to be finished by the fall were in full bloom. "It's just until I get on my feet," I smiled, pulling a large suitcase and bin of books from the car. "Of course," he nodded.

In my mind it wouldn't take more than a summer. I was an ambitious spoken word artist slamming nightly at the Nuyorican Poets Café, and was certain I would be discovered in no time. If my big break didn't come on stage it would be from one of my poetry videos online.

I had the whole thing figured out. I had calculated with some made-up statistics in my head (math was never my strong suit) that a million views would generate about a hundred thousand dollars in income in visibility, from shows and appearances. This calculation was something I believed and recited to everyone my first summer in NY with the hubris and ignorance of a person growing up in the generation of viral sensations. (For the record, I have over a million views collectively on my videos on YouTube, still waiting on the hundred grand though.)

The set-up at Anthony's was less than ideal. The old, rugged, three-story brownstone was in great need of repair and the only justification for its rent price was it was just a few houses down from the famous Walt Whitman home on Ryerson. On every first date I had that summer I would stroll pass the house and mention its famous former tenant. When I arrived at my doorstep a few moments later I would turn with a smile saying, "Now two famous poets live on this street." The line worked more times than it should have.

Like most living arrangements in Brooklyn the house was habited by "boarders." This is code for roommates who share everything but conversation. You share the bathroom, the fridge, the utilities, and the same disdain for the G train. Exchanging nothing more than a "yo" as you pass each other through the small corridor. Occasionally, if you are lucky, you will be greeted by a passive aggressive note about the air conditioning or the hair you left in the drain. This is adulting the New York way.

Anthony had two roommates (I think there was a third guy who never left his room on the top floor), a photographer from Algiers who did mostly black and white nude photos and city landscapes (an odd mix I know). The other was a documentary filmmaker (let's call her House Mother since she was the one whose name was on the lease and had direct contact to the landlord) who on her off-days doubled as despiser of all things Steven Willis. Each morning commenced with me waking up flat on the floor staring at the ceiling (compliments to the air mattress with a hole in it) or the occasional whisper of Anthony to his girlfriend "we can, it's ok he's asleep" Again, the set-up was less than ideal.

House Mother was notoriously known for keeping strange company (I think I saw Afrika Bambaataa in my kitchen once). Her friends shifted by the season, mostly centered around whatever film she was making at the time. Though the house was rarely clean and arguably unhabitable, that didn't stop her from holding big barbeques after wrapping a filming in the house's spacious (by New York standards) backyard. The only consistent face at these gathers was John, a romantic interest of House Mother's who had seen many artists come in and out of the brownstone over their eight years of dating. "Why don't you just open an orphanage?" I heard him say to her once. "They just keep getting younger."

He didn't have much love for the artist type but had respect for the "balls" it took to go at it full time so he opted to indulge in a few laughs. Once he asked me what I was doing to supplement income between gigs.

Shit. Dude I'm broke.

This was his chance to offer what he would do the best the rest of the summer. Offer unsolicited advice.

> *Well, There have always been 3 options for employment for the artistic types
> like yourself.*
> *What's that?*
> *Well it's the three c's.*
> *Crack,* (the rappers had a strong corner on that market. Not for me.)
> *Coffee* (this is what I would try. Working at a savory pastry shop in Windsor
> Terrace that Anthony was manager of. I quit mid-shift one morning and
> fled to Massachusetts to stay with my then-girlfriend for a few days. A
> move that almost cost Anthony and me our friendship.
> *or, other people's kids.*

I stared at him. Not because *kids* wasn't a word that started with a C,
but because he was onto something. He was right, I could be a teaching
artist.

Teaching artists work is quite possibly the number one legitimate
source of steady income for many full-time artists in New York City.
The average teaching artist gig pays about $50 to $75 a class and greatly
rivals minimum wage jobs if you can get something consistent. Same pay
for what is a fraction of the work, and for those with even a smidge
of patience for children—it's a solid gig. For one it allows the artist to
make money by doing their craft, maintaining some sense of dignity that
a bar or restaurant doesn't give as you smile for tips. Two, the freelancer
schedule allows the flexibility to travel or perform late nights. A waiter
might need someone to cover their shift to take a last minute gig, but a
teaching artist is done by 3, at latest 6, for most after-school gigs, more
than enough time to freshen up and hit the late night venues.

Shortly after the barbeque conversation, I began freelancing with a
few orgs around the city. The most steady go was a gig with Urban Word
NYC, a youth literacy org based out of Manhattan; it is the home of the
New York Youth Slam Team and the parent organization to the National
Youth Poet Laureate program. (Yes I've met Amanda Gorman.)

I wish I could say my career as an educator started differently. That
it was the result of some great passion to make a difference or help
others. But the truth is jobs with children, i.e., teacher's aides, daycares,
after school programs, or even the charter school system, serve as one
of the only consistently-available jobs for young people straight out of
college. This is especially true for people of color. Most schools salivate
at the thought of having young people of color in the classroom for any
reason—especially young Black men. Too short for the NBA, and too
thin for the NFL, it was in Education I felt the most commodified for

my race and gender. To add to this I was an artist. A poet at that, and making steady money was a necessity.

I worked my way up the ranks quickly. Half for my passion and dedication and the other half for my willingness to "traverse the land"; that is, I was willing to travel to any part of New York City to take a gig. While a true New Yorker has hard set rules about when, how far, and for how much they leave their home borough, I, a Chicago kid, had no such distinctions and would find myself as far as Coney Island to Pelham Parkway in a single day.

At the height of my teaching artist work I was spending an average of 22 hours a week on trains trekking between the Bronx, Brooklyn, and Queens. The average trip from my home in Brooklyn to the Bronx was 90 minutes. The average time I spent in a classroom with students for instruction was 35.

As a teaching artist, you stand in the middle of a warring system between the academy and the arts. It's no secret that art and music teachers are becoming less and less prevalent in public schools, and oftentimes a $75 an hour teaching artist is meant to fill that void. Paying me for one hour a week beats having to pay a teacher's salary, but without that protection, a teaching artist knows they are one budget cut, one reallocation of funds, one less generous donation away from not being there. This causes us to keep it simple and not rock the boat. One or two simple workshops that keep the kids engaged and smiling, then move on. If the average teacher is underpaid and underappreciated, a teaching artist is totally expendable. There is no tenure track, no student loan forgiveness after 10 years. Most of us lack the bachelor's and master's degrees held by the fresh-out-of-college homeroom teachers we report to who are in well over their heads. What I remember most are their eyes, thankful each time I arrived to take their class, giving them a much needed prep period before math or a chance to eat. That's the flip side of this for teaching artists. For what we lack in job security and academic standing, we possess in soul.

In 2016, I would received a promotion and become a part of the Urban Word staff officially, given the title Mentor in Residence. I was half employee, half freelance artist. While I was free to work for other orgs, I was required to teach for Urban Word at least 10 hours a week. This meant I was to take the more lucrative and longer-tenured teaching jobs they got from the DOE.

In the over 200 schools I have taught in through this time, I am convinced that academia is aware that it is a soul-zapping process. Nothing gives it away more than the response I get when I ask a principal what they hope the students get out of my visit to their school. "We just want to give the kids a chance to be themselves," proof they are aware that in order to excel in academia children must separate self from student. And for one day a semester, usually right before standardized testing begins (or right after), a teaching artist like myself arrives to make a child feel whole again.

By 2018, I was exhausted. I knew I wouldn't be in teaching much longer (so I thought) and began flirting with options of grad school. At the time, I was appointed for a 10-week stay at a middle school in Sheepsheads Bay on the far end of Brooklyn. It was week 7, and I was already out of ideas. I had filtered through all my good and safe workshops four weeks ago and was basically winging it.

As I boarded the B44, "I have no clue what to do with these kids," I texted Anthony, who by this point was living in DC with his soon-to-be wife. I was living in an apartment in Bedstuy with 6 roommates (3 couples) but I had my own room. "Hey man hit them with Where I'm From," he responded. I sighed. Where I'm From is the workshop that every teaching artist knows. It's so famous that if you were to google it now, you'd find millions of student poems and essays.

It's based on a poem with the same title by George Ella Lyon. It prompts students to become distant observers to their neighborhoods. It's a great workshop for beginners. It asks students to engage with their senses and helps define community and identity. A good teaching artist will pair it with something that really resonates with kids to help the images land.

If I'm in the Bronx, Wille Perdomo's, Where I'm From is a good fit. If I'm in Brooklyn, I pair it with Jays Z's, Where I'm From In My Life Time Vol. 1. If you are in Houston, I suggest skipping George Ella altogether and going straight to Scarface's My Block. I swore I would never do the workshop, having had to suffer through a thousand versions of it myself as a youth poet, but void of another idea I caved.

The students were particularly antsy this day, no doubt a result of the weather warming and summer near. I explained the Where I'm From assignment and prompted the students to think about what they see, taste, smell, and hear in their neighborhoods. Sirens, cop cars, bodegas, chopped cheeses were some of the answers. They seemed to get it. As folks began to work I was approached by a student.

"Mr. Steven, can I write about where I'm *from?*" she asks staring at me. "Yes," I said passively-aggressively, "That's the assignment." Suddenly her eyes began to water.

I can write about where I'm from, even if it isn't there anymore?

Confused, I stared at her, before I remembered that in a previous class this student mentioned they were from Yemen…and still had family in the region. No doubt she had heard about the upticks of violence there, and had family in harm's way. "Oh sweetheart," I said grabbing her shoulder, "of course you can write about Yemen. In fact you have to." For the first time in my career, I asked to be excused, walked to the bathroom and cried. I was snapped back into my body. Here I am casually going through this workshop asking my students to tell me where they are from, forgetting traumas attached to lives and the identity they carry outside the classroom.

Despite public schools sitting in the middle of most under-resourced neighborhoods (and being punished for it in funding and stigmas like inner city school), they are often seen as a foreign entity, an adversarial force for student and parents alike. A clash of culture differences and immediate priorities.

A teaching mentor of mine once described school for children in under-resourced communities as "unconsensual contact." "Unconsensual" in the idea that that they are forced by law to be here when they would rather be anywhere else. Playing video games, playing basketball, helping a sick grandma, or watching over younger siblings, or working to help ends meet. School is just a major timesuck away from more immediate lucrative and emotional needs.

Present in my student's question was not only that by the time she finishes this poem where she was from would be gone, but also would I even care to listen? Was that version of her appropriate to bring to this space? She was asking if her full authentic self was allowed in this academic space. If her fear, her anger, her frustration could be present in an environment that has been less than welcoming to her in every façade. To every teaching artist, and educator on every level, I ask that you remember. We are asking much more of students than just to engage in assignments. We are often asking them to dive into the source of their insecurity and pain, and sometimes due to time constraints, we ask them to do this without ever creating an environment of safety or even acknowledging their humanity.

I never once considered the intimacy of the question "Where are you from?" or any of my poetry workshop prompts and began to question what had I done to even feel I am owed their answer and participation. The answer is arrogance, and over time absorbing the culture of academia that says "I" is unprofessional. That we should speak and be academic, which is to say outside of ourselves. Being yourself is mere extracurricular. There is no "I" in "student" after all. I resent this. Giving the "students" the opportunity to express and be themselves should not be a luxury in the curriculum, nor seen as pedagogically radical. Instead, it should be the entire basis of education.

Which means the most important pedagogical framework for teaching is one that encourages cultivating spaces of trust, intimacy, authenticity, and support. How can we drastically shift the world of education where this is possible?

The core of *Academia from the Inside* moves to answer this question, and addresses the issues in academia that create them, offering new imaginings on how they can be rectified. Maureen Hall and the group of educators in this volume appeared in my life as I began to question my own scholarly journey—a month before finishing my first master's program at the University of Iowa in theater and a few months away from entering the Iowa Writers' Workshop for Poetry. It was a great relief to know a group of others were too thinking of ways of how they could better bring themselves and their students into the classroom. Each strategic framework in the book offers a new way to approach scholarly communities with teachers and with students to better serve the self that lives in each.

What is also valued is the single story. In a way, each writer has written their own Where I'm From (education edition) purposely leaning into the use of I and other first-person pronouns, shunning the traditional approach to academic writing. Teachers have turned the dreaded reflection framework on themselves and asked, "What have I learned?" What emerges are the same themes of authenticity, community, and humanity that were present in my student asking if she could really tell me where she is from. Revealing students and educators both are struggling with the oppressive omnipresence of the academic mold. My story and others you will read, though different, all bring us back to the same place of asking what is a better way? It's about time that we all recognize that the issue in inner city schools is the same issue present in the ivory tower, and that is the archetypal student or scholarly educator is archaic and does not address the complexities of human needs, desires, or interests. What you will find in the pages of *Academia from the Inside* is a radical shift from traditional expectations—a new educational avant-garde grounded in new strategies aimed at dismantling the scholarly severance that divide us from ourselves as educators and each other and erasing the academic monoculture that erases the diversity of our students.

Steven Antoine Willis, MFA
Iowa City, Iowa
June 2021

Introduction to *Academia from the Inside*

Maureen P. Hall, Aubrie K. Brault and Libby Falk Jones

Academia from the Inside: Pedagogies for Self and Other invites readers to explore how fourteen different experts in their respective fields create deeper meaning in their profession and work with students through thinking, in multiple ways, about the self who teaches, the self who learns, and the ways these selves interact within the academy. This book brings into dialogue the ideas of educator Parker Palmer with ancient Indian ideas and philosophies as practiced by medical doctor and educator Dr. Chinmay Pandya. In the United States, Parker Palmer, a writer, teacher, and activist, has explored spirituality in education through his long career. Author of several widely-read books, including *The Courage to Teach* (2017), he is founder and Senior Partner Emeritus of the Center for Courage & Renewal. In 1998, he was named one of the 30 most influential senior leaders in higher education and one of the 10 key agenda-setters of the past decade by the Leadership Project, which involved a national survey of 10,000 educators. Like Palmer, Pandya's work at a university in northern India connects to spirituality in urging all humans to go deeply in search of identity and purpose of existence in the global consciousness. Pandya's work, less well-known in the West, has an international reach.

Dr. Chinmay Pandya, Pro Vice Chancellor of Dev Sanskriti Vish-wavidyalaya (DSVV), views himself as the torchbearer of his grandfather's legacy and vision of the university. As part of maintaining this legacy, Pandya has been instrumental in creating and sustaining more than 60 international collaborations between DSVV and other universities around the world. DSVV is connected to the larger organization of the All World Gayatri Pariwar (AWGP) movement, which has more than 100 million members worldwide and thousands of global centers for social reform. Palmer's Western ideas are palpable through many of the chapters in this book; the Eastern philosophies and practices of Pandya are detailed in Chapter 13.

The ideas and spiritual journeys of these two key educators provide a framework for understanding the concepts and practices explored in this book—a new way of understanding the inside of academia: *embodied education*. Embodied education refers to learning and living experiences that bring us closer to understanding our true selves. It is the intersection of East and West, the point where the ideas of Parker Palmer and Dr. Chinmay Pandya meet. Whether this understanding of self plays out in academia or in our personal and home communities or both, we all have the possibilities before us to develop our consciousness. In many ways, the work of this book provides a thoughtful unstitching of the academy as it is currently known, an unstitching that opens new opportunities for awareness and new learning in educational spaces.

Embodied education calls for cultivating our understanding of ourselves as teachers and as human beings. The journey and routes to self-knowledge do not end, in part because we continue over time to move through and make sense of our life experiences—even the simplest of them. One resonating element in these essays is the concept that teachers are also students, with continuous opportunities to learn about themselves and about their students' needs.

The ways the concept of embodied education can grow from a teacher's reflective practices is illustrated in the journey of contributor Aubrie Brault. Critical feedback from her students compelled Brault to change her teaching approaches and curriculum design. By making the conscious decision to listen to this feedback and reflect on it, Brault allowed students to be heard. She began to use new approaches designed to improve the whole classroom environment, approaches that helped her engage more comfortably with students and make connections between students' lived realities and the curriculum.

This opening up of oneself to students is just the kind of vulnerability that Palmer suggests we can leverage to grow as teachers. Brault deepened her knowledge of herself as a teacher and as a person, finding ways to bring her true self into the classroom. Students sensed this new authenticity and responded positively. While Brault still faced fears and had challenging days, she began to understand responsive teaching as embodied education. By staying connected to her emotions and paying attention to her senses, she gained self-confidence. From an Eastern perspective, her awareness expanded by learning through and inhabiting her true self.

ISSUES IN ACADEMIA THAT INSPIRED THIS BOOK

The notion of an inside perspective on academia initially grew from conversations that Hall and Brault had about their experiences in the academy. Through linking themselves together in conversation(s), they recognized that their identities as teachers had often been minimized and disregarded. Through further conversations, they realized that this was happening to other teachers and in the academy as a whole.

In this book, readers are given access to truths that may often have been unarticulated or hidden. Academic culture, as Palmer characterizes it, views the teaching self as "not a source to be tapped but a danger to be suppressed" (2017, p. 18). Palmer calls on teachers to re-examine and reconnect to themselves, their subject(s), and their students. He asks teachers to recognize the issues of fear and disconnection as real hazards of higher education teaching. This book responds to Palmer's call by illuminating lived experiences in the academy and creating a kind of "truth-telling" zone. That these essays are insiders' views is significant: authors mine their own academic histories and practices for insights that can help teachers everywhere.

The truth-telling from these authors also affirms the work of Brazilian educator Paulo Freire's notion, "There is no teaching without learning" (2018, p. 31). Inviting students and teachers to look for, and include in their classes, deeper, more personal, and insightful means of constructing knowledge provides an alternative route that challenges the "banking concept" of teaching and learning that Freire argues against.

But looking into ourselves is only one part. We are made to be who we are through our interactions with one another in the world. Freire underlines that teaching and learning are complex human activities. One goal of this collection is to show how education might change if it were humanized. Humanizing education requires educators to humanize themselves first, and, through reflection, to realize and actualize both independence and interdependence. Each chapter in this work strives to answer this question: How do teachers conceptualize their inwardness and how does this inwardness translate into the spaces of teaching and learning?

Tobin Hart emphasizes the importance of inwardness, in terms of how knowing one's self is vital to education. Hart refers to this knowledge as part of "interiority." He argues that "developing interiority may be most valuable not simply as an adjunct to knowledge acquisition but as central and essential to the process of deep and lifelong learning" (2008, p. 247). Like Palmer, Hart stresses that *who* we are is central to teaching.

PARKER PALMER'S MODEL
OF ALTERNATIVE EDUCATIONAL REFORM

In *The Courage to Teach*, Palmer argues that good teaching "cannot be reduced to technique; it is the identity and integrity of the teacher" (2017, p. 10). To help teachers focus on this genuine center of good teaching, Palmer calls for creating a "Community of Truth," which puts the subject at the center and empowers the students as creative knowers who actively shape the learning experience(s) for themselves and others. Such a community encourages individual development that then becomes the basis for broader institutional change.

Palmer outlines four stages of his Alternative Educational Reform Model:

Stage 1: Isolated individuals make an inward decision to *live divided no more*, finding a center for their lives outside of institutions.

Stage 2: These individuals begin to discover one another and form *communities of congruence* that offer mutual support and opportunities to develop a shared vision.

Stage 3: These communities begin *going public,* learning to convert their private concerns into the public issues they are and receiving vital critiques in the process.

Stage 4: A system of *alternative rewards* emerges to sustain the movement's vision and to put pressure for change on the standard institutional reward systems (pp. 172–73).

Academia from the Inside stands as a collective enactment of Palmer's model. The work of this book has brought educators across disciplines and continents together to live the model's four stages.

This book began with Hall's and Brault's realization that in academia, they were *living divided no more*. They then invited other educators to reflect on and interrogate their own experiences in academic life. These educators suggested others who had made this commitment to wholeness. The final group of this book's contributors includes scholars from the United States, Australia, New Zealand, and Sweden, representing a wide variety of fields, including English, Art Education, Teacher Education, Dance Education, Philosophy, Neuroscience, and Law. While all contributors have chosen to inhabit and explore their own truths and evolving identities as teachers and learners, the collection reflects variety in focus and research methodology. Some chapters show pedagogical interventions created for the classroom, while others document authors' lives in academia as personal narratives. Other chapters do both of these things because teaching and learning are inextricably connected.

This book's move toward enacting Palmer's second stage, creating a *community of congruence*, began when Hall and Brault read through contributors' chapter proposals and realized that formative dialogue among the group would be valuable. While chapters were in process, over the months in which COVID-19 continued to ravage the world, Hall and Brault organized three virtual workshops to connect the writers to one another and to the book's purpose.

In the first Zoom workshop, held in July 2020, contributors introduced themselves and shared the focus of their chapters. As they explored surprising connections across fields, space, and time, they realized that a supportive community was available to them as they engaged in reflection and writing about their experiences inside academia.

In addition to connecting contributors, the first Zoom meeting yielded a list of emerging themes of the book. After distilling the list into four salient themes, Hall and Brault invited contributors to create a 500-word vignette on one of the themes. Vignettes were shared in advance of a second Zoom meeting in December 2020, which then included small-group conversations about specific similarities and differences among experiences and approaches. At the conclusion of this second meeting, contributors affirmed their excitement at gaining new ideas about their work and its meaning.

A third Zoom call occurred some four months later, after Brault and Hall had provided one or more rounds of formative feedback on contributors' chapters. Each contributor was matched with a chapter partner and invited to exchange chapters in advance of the meeting. In the late-April 2021 Zoom, partners met in breakout rooms to share feedback and responses to particular questions authors had posed. Some authors provided written feedback for their partners before or after the conversation. An additional outcome was contributors' recognizing that pandemic-caused stress and isolation had accentuated the importance of this growing community of congruence. In light of the pandemic's impact on contributors' lives and writings, the group decided to include in their chapters some commentary about their experiences of the past two years.

Palmer's third stage, *going public*, is happening with the appearance of this book. Publication opens up the work to critique, application, and extension by others across academia. Telling and reflecting on personal academic stories is a courageous act, as Palmer affirms. We hope that readers at all stages of their academic careers—from those entering graduate school to those nearing retirement—will gain new understandings of the opportunities, benefits, and challenges of living an academic life. Our goal is to spark dialogue that can lead us all to even fuller understandings.

Finally, the writing of this book has tapped into a system of *alternative rewards*, Palmer's fourth stage. One reward contributors have shared has been the knowledge that others in academia are walking a similar path. For example, in an email, contributor Agnes Curry thanked the editors for their efforts "to foster a more humane, less-sundered academia and for being supportive of my chapter topic." Other contributors have thanked their chapter partners for their helpful responses. Additionally, contributors have affirmed the learning they have experienced during their writing and revising, as well as their learning from reading one or more others' chapters. Contributor Libby Falk Jones noted that extensive work was involved in drafting and revising her chapter, as well as in reading and responding to another's chapter, but added that "it's been a labor of love." Understanding the work's intrinsic value is a reward that bolsters contributors' motivation, commitment, and satisfaction as contributors continue to move through their teaching experiences.

The collaborative writing model emerging from this project, a reward in itself, is one that could be replicated to bring together other groups of international academics from a range of disciplines in academia to write about and learn from sharing their experiences. And ultimately, such collaborations and investigations such as this book are first steps, as Palmer claims, to effecting change in the academy.

Emerging Themes and Overall Structure

Dialogue within this book's community of congruence has not only supported individual members' deepening of their reflective work, but has also helped to identify three central facets of embodied education around which these essays are grouped. These themes include Pursuing Authenticity, Creating Creative Community, and Humanizing Education. These themes provide a map for navigating this book's exploration of the inside of academia.

Pursuing Authenticity

The chapters in this section demonstrate this first theme of Pursuing Authenticity in a range of ways. The idea of authenticity refers to self-awareness and awakening the inner self, then moving outward in those truths. The first four chapters in this collection examine the concept and practice of authenticity.

Turning inward, trained cognitive-affective neuroscientist and professor Aminda O'Hare guides readers along part of her own journey. In Chapter 2, "Risking Being Yourself: Owning Your Identity Within the Academic Framework," O'Hare shares critical points of her career where she found herself asking where she both wanted, and needed, to invest her efforts in academia. In reflecting on her academic identity, O'Hare comes to recognize how being part of a community of faculty and staff scaffolded her to pursue authenticity in her professional career—as a researcher, an engaged citizen of the academy, a community builder, and a socio-emotionally driven instructor.

In Chapter 3, "Living Divided No More: Cultivating My Own Biome in Academia," teacher-educator Maureen Hall takes Palmer's model for alternative educational reform and applies it to her own life in academia. Hall shows how Palmer's philosophy has informed her approach to teaching in the past and continuing today. Through this reflective analysis grounded in research, Hall illustrates how she has innovated what she calls her *academic forest biome*. Weathering the pandemic in northern Vermont, immersed in the changing deciduous forest, helped her understand how biomes can translate into academic life. These efforts to make new meaning have helped her to step more authentically into her own teaching practices and identity.

In Chapter 4, "A 'World in Between': A Reflection on Teaching and Learning," former English instructor Aubrie Brault explores a different path toward authenticity. She recounts her experience in a teaching fellowship whose program structure and resources created a unique system of community that enabled her to find her true self. Her experiences in academia, she found, not only shaped her teaching education but also empowered a personal sense of confidence, identity, and authenticity in the classroom. Brault also reflects on the duality of being both a graduate student and a professor. Ultimately, her chapter explores the ways in which she disrupted a culture of silence in herself, and, in Freire's terms, offers a problem-posing education and route to authenticity.

In Chapter 5, "Embracing Otherness in the Self that Teaches," Professor Elizabeth Bifuh-Ambe invites readers to consider the influence and impact the academic environment can have on one's identity. As a first-generation Black woman who came from Africa and entered U.S. higher education, she has found the courage to transcend the difficulties of being "othered" and the grace not only to belong, but to thrive in academia. Through examining her own experiences, she exemplifies just how much academia can shape our drive and capacity for feeling welcomed as well as for our capacities to grow authentically.

In this book, pursuing authenticity can be thought of as the next step beyond engaging in reflection. Authenticity begins when action is created by new awareness; contributors remind us that we are each a point of agency (in relation to the resources available to us) in and for ourselves and our students, as well as for the larger academy. Pursuing authenticity in academia can be fraught with challenges and fears, but through the power of self-knowledge, teachers can emerge and act in their true identities.

 Creating Creative Community

Creating Creative Community, as a theme, involves cultivating an environment where learners feel safe to share ideas and where teachers' and students' imaginative capacities are valued. The space for learning becomes a generative space, where teacher and students can be knitted together, often in magical ways. Four chapters probe ways in which community can be enacted and experienced.

In Chapter 6, "'Going Out into the World to Find Wonders': Nature as a Source of Generation, Regeneration, and Community," English professor Libby Falk Jones argues that spending unstructured time in nature feeds students' creativity in writing and visual arts and leads, in turn, to creating community within the class. Outdoors in solitude and silence in her Contemplative Writing classes, students journaled on their observations, thoughts, and feelings, as well as on course readings. In sessions together, students shared writings and took turns leading the group in writing exercises designed to deepen thinking and bring interconnections to light. From her own reflections and poems, as well as comments from students made during post-course interviews, Jones shows how these practices created imaginative synergy and a strong self of self as well as an awareness of other.

In Chapter 7, "The Self Who Teaches and Learns: Sharing the Space After a Disaster," community-engaged scholar and professor Billy O'Steen chronicles the teaching and learning experiences he created through service-learning to respond to a natural disaster. In 2010 and 2011, the city of Christchurch in New Zealand suffered intense earthquakes that caused significant damage and loss of life. O'Steen created a Student Volunteer Army (SVA) through which students earned college credit by working to rebuild the city of Christchurch and by reflecting on those community-engaged learning experiences. O'Steen's work in academia showcases how pedagogical innovation can create a meaningful curriculum while simultaneously addressing a community's particular issues and needs.

In Chapter 8, "Holding the Space: Being Curious as a Teacher Educator with Pre-service About Self-Care," writer and teacher educator Narelle Lemon illustrates how frequent in-class reflections with her pre-service teachers led to a poetry practice in which they deeply explored questions of meaning for their lives and work. This practice allowed pre-service teachers the rare opportunity to answer hard questions, to disrupt silence and confront experiences often dismissed, and to embrace new ideas about how one desires to and can be within the profession of teaching. Lemon argues that teachers must work to be in community with themselves first and then to cultivate community with students, creating safe spaces for teaching and learning.

In Chapter 9, "Dancing with the Other: Esthetic Experiences and Ethical Responsiveness," university lecturer and doctoral student Paul Moerman posits the idea that more spaces are needed in education and in academia for dance, imagination, and intercorporeality. The goal of dance, Moerman argues, is to shift focus from self-expression to responsiveness to otherness. Exploring self-knowing through others leads students to discover common ground, which then leads to a consideration of humanism, democracy, and coexistence that opens ideas in a challenged world and calls upon us all for dialogue, for survival. Drawing on his workshops for preschool children, elementary school pupils, and teachers, Moerman shows how the shaping of educational relationships and education can be a communal space for becoming.

Through different pedagogies, spaces, practices, and resources, the diverse scholarship of *Academia from the Inside* demonstrates, as O'Hare notes in her chapter, "how grass-roots approaches to building communities of care and support within academia can create environments of personal growth and resiliency."

 Humanizing Education

Humanizing education as a theme refers to teaching to and from the whole person—a concept in which pursuing authenticity and creating creative community are also grounded. For Steven Willis, author of the Foreword, humanizing education emerges as a central take-away from this book. To get there, Willis examines his own journey into the teaching profession as a Teaching Artist, working within the classroom as well as afterschool programs in the New York City Schools. There he found that pedagogical approaches that involve the self are few and far between, and yet are often the only opportunity for students to bring their full and authentic selves into the classroom space. These opportunities, he writes, "should not be considered a luxury in the curriculum...[but] should be the entire basis of education." Willis characterizes the chapters in this book as "a radical shift from traditional expectations, a new educational avant-garde grounded in new strategies aimed at dismantling the scholarly severance that divide us from ourselves as educators and each other" (p. 3). These final four chapters offer analysis and/or intrinsic insights to demonstrate the impact of humanizing education for the self and others.

In Chapter 10, "'The Wound Is Where the Light Enters': Bringing Our Impure, Journeying Selves into Our Teaching," philosophy professor Agnes Curry examines what she calls the "courage of vulnerability." First practicing that courage on her path to becoming a teacher, she goes on to argue that practicing courage serves to humanize education. She recounts her own continual growth as an educator as it has pushed her to be more forthright in naming for her students the catalysts for her passion to teach. Her journey, she notes, has brought both risks and rewards.

In Chapter 11, "Who Am I?: Relational Pedagogies for Fostering Creativity and Reflective Practice," teacher educator and artist Bronwen Wade-Leeuwen teams up with practitioner and educator Kath McLachlan to build and practice a transformative learning model for teachers. Through case studies and model diagrams, Wade-Leeuwen and McLachlan show how an inquiry-based arts learning framework can help participants move through levels of participation and reflection. During their workshops, teachers were encouraged to use imagination in exploring creativity and innovation—an opportunity to freely express themselves within an academic framework. In return, this expression offered teachers the possibility for transformative ways of thinking, interacting, and being.

In Chapter 12, "Law School: Imbuing It with Both Rigor and Support," law professor Justine Dunlap illustrates how the complex study of law is an example of education that requires thoughtful support for law students as they shape their professional identity and adjust their way of thinking to do this work. Dunlap looks at her experience as a law student and now as a law professor who is aware of the damage that law school can do to its students. Dunlap examines the dominant methods of law teaching, the grassroots humanizing legal education movement, and recent efforts for legal education reform. She shares how she came to adapt humanizing practices, which she believes are essential to the well-being of students. Her pedagogical approaches grow directly from her desire to be authentic and to support students as they learn to become lawyers.

In Chapter 13, "Embodied Education at Dev Sanskriti Vishwavidyalaya: Narratives from the Field on How a University in northern India Is Transforming Students," English educator Danielle Johansen and Maureen Hall describe the unique philosophy and vision of Pandit Sriram Sharma, and the ways his grandson Dr. Chinmay Pandya maintains these visions as pedagogical structures at a university in northern India. To capture the essence of DSVV's educational approaches, Johansen's and Hall's chapter draws upon their own lived experiences at DSVV, interviews with Pandya, as well as reflections from other professors and students who have visited at the university and participated in various aspects of its spiritual education, including yoga, ceremonies, and rituals.

This collection speaks to Freire's definition of humanization as the contributors of this work, and some of their communities, were able to engage in "the process of becoming more fully human as social, historical, thinking, communicating, transformative, creative persons who participate in and with the world" (as cited in del Carmen Salazar, 2013, p. 126).

CONCLUSIONS: JOURNEYING TOWARD EMBODIED EDUCATION

Academia from the Inside: Pedagogies for Self and Other offers readers insight into how different faculty create deeper meaning in their profession through thinking, in some way, about the self who teaches, the self who learns, and their various experiences within the academy. This book's work helps to counteract the danger that higher education institutions will become "soulless" places, where students—and, we argue, teachers— are viewed as a "brain on a stick" (Lewis, 2006, p. 100). To counteract the dehumanization that ultimately damages society as a whole, teachers must assert their full selves as teachers and as learners. To the process of dehumanization, *Academia from the Inside* provides a needed response. The dynamism of the individual contributors adds to the dynamism of the group.

In examining embodied education, the essays in this collection show that subjective, as well as objective, knowledge is valuable in academia. The academy often puts objectivity on a pedestal, though objectivity is part myth. In this book, subjective truths are shown to be powerful, suggesting that academic culture, norms, and institutional rewards should be responsive to change.

In celebrating the notion that all teachers are learners and all learners are teachers, this book builds on the work of important scholars and also creates new scholarship. These collective voices make clear that pedagogies for self and for other are needed today. A new trajectory in and for the academy needs to be embraced, one that reaches toward wholeness. From an appreciation of interconnectedness across disciplines and continents, wholeness can grow.

References

del Carmen Salazar, M. (2013). A humanizing pedagogy: Reinventing the principles and practice of education as a journey toward liberation. *Review of Research in Education, 37*(1), 121–148.

Freire, P. (2018). *Teachers as cultural workers: Letters to those who dare teach.* Routledge.

Freire, P. (2000). *Pedagogy of freedom: Ethics, democracy, and civic courage.* Rowman & Littlefield.

Hall, M. P. (2019). Embodying deep reading: Mapping life experiences through lectio divina. In J. E. Dalton, M. P. Hall, & C. E. Hoyser (Eds.), *The whole person: Embodying teaching and learning through lectio and visio divina* (pp. 11–21). Rowman and Littlefield.

Hart, T. (2008). Interiority and education: Exploring the neurophenomenology of contemplation and its potential role in learning. *Journal of Transformative Education, 6*(4), 235–250.

Jones, L. F. (2019). Reading the word, the self, the world: Lectio and visio divina as a gateway to intellectual and personal growth. In J. E. Dalton, M. P. Hall, & C. E. Hoyser (Eds.), *The whole person: Embodying teaching and learning through lectio and visio divina* (pp. 49–60). Rowman and Littlefield.

Lewis, H. R. (2006). *Excellence without a soul: How a great university forgot education* (pp. 1995–2003). PublicAffairs.

Palmer, P. J. (2017). *The courage to teach: Exploring the landscape of a teacher's life.* Wiley.

PART I

Pursuing Authenticity

CHAPTER 2

Risking Being Yourself: Owning Your Identity Within the Academic Framework

Aminda J. O'Hare

[handwritten annotations: "practice", "communities of mindfulness", "Role of mindfulness"]

"…because at the end of my rough road, I see
   that I was the architect of my own fate,
   that if I extracted honey or gall from things
   it was because I instilled them with a gall or honey flavor:
   when I planted rosebushes, I always harvested roses."
   Amado Nervo, En paz. (In Peace—translated)

I never intended to research the effects of mindfulness practices on cognition, emotion, and learning. I never intended to incorporate mindfulness into my pedagogy. And, I certainly never intended to guide other faculty and staff through their own personal practices with mindfulness and how to use it in their own teaching. As a trained cognitive and affective neuroscientist starting my first academic position as a tenure-track professor, I was focused on starting my first lab, prepping my courses, and keeping my

A. J. O'Hare (✉)
Weber State University, Ogden, UT, USA
e-mail: amindaohare@weber.edu

© The Author(s), under exclusive license to Springer Nature
Switzerland AG 2021
M. P. Hall and A. K. Brault (eds.), *Academia from the Inside*,
https://doi.org/10.1007/978-3-030-83895-9_2

25

head down. This is advice that is commonly passed on to junior faculty. It promotes self-preservation and productivity, but it does not promote the integration of your professional self with your personal self.

For me, entering academia consistently challenged me with conducting myself in ways that best suited the expectations of my administrators and senior faculty versus in ways that best suited my personal growth and well-being. As I continue to move through different stages of my career, I have become more adept at aligning my personal interests with my scholarship, service, and teaching. This process has not always been smooth, as it has often taken me against the expectations of academics higher up the hierarchy. Nonetheless, I have found myself in a position now where I can be my whole self at work—something by and for which I am continually gratified and grateful.

A year into my first faculty position, I decided to embark on a collaborative mindfulness project with a colleague, perhaps heady with the newfound academic freedoms of being my own principal investigator (PI). After designing the project and gaining institutional approval, the feedback I received from my department chair was, "Be careful what you waste your time on." This was not the first nor the last time I would be told by others that I was not doing academia the right way. This project also marked the beginning of the development of my identity as a professional that was constructed from within, rather than from outside expectations.

Universities tout academic freedom—the ability of scholars to study topics of their own choosing. Yet, most pressure on faculty in academia is to publish and get funding, and some areas are considered more publishable and fundable than others. With this emphasis, "passion projects" are often frowned upon, and spending time pursuing projects that are not directly related to data, manuscripts, and, above all, grants is given little value by most university administrators, especially those at research-focused institutions.

In this chapter, I will discuss how a community of faculty and staff was formed around mindfulness at my university, and how the support and value of my work by individual colleagues allowed me to develop into my professional identity as a researcher, community builder, and socioemotionally driven instructor. This chapter will explore how grassroots approaches to building communities of care and support within academia can create environments of personal growth and resiliency and propose that this model leads to secure scholars who flourish.

There is an institutionalized culture of stress that is prevalent within our colleges and universities. Parker Palmer (2002, p. x) described the challenges of academic environments as follows, "...cultivating community is a complex challenge in the midst of an academic culture infamous for its individualism, judgmentalism, and competitiveness." Most research on mental health in academia is focused on the well-being of students, which is of course warranted, but there is a lack of large-scale research on the constants of a university, the faculty and staff. Most of what we know about the impact of academic environments on the well-being of faculty and staff is anecdotal (Lashuel, 2020), but one review of academics in the United Kingdom concluded that they experience less job satisfaction and extremely low levels of psychological health compared to other professionals and community samples (Kinman, 2001).

From my own personal experiences with academia, elevated levels of stress, negative affect, and low job satisfaction among my peers have been my perception as well. Academia is a unique area of the job sector in many ways. Among those is the culture of continuous work. It is not a field where there are often tangible endpoints to tasks—there is always the next grant to write, study to design, dataset to analyze, literature to review, assignments to grade, and classes to create, modify, update, etc. It is up to individual academics to determine how long they work and when.

As such, academia has created a culture where working constantly is considered the norm, despite most faculty being on nine-month contracts, and the longer, harder hours you work the more elite you are. We see this reflected in the broader mental health of Americans versus the rest of the world. A culture that does not value work-life balance and intrinsic work value is a culture that produces mental illness (Dinh et al., 2017; Pega et al., 2021).

Research has long supported that individuals are more creative and produce higher quality work when driven by intrinsic motivation (e.g., Cerasoli et al., 2014). In other words, when you inherently are rewarded by your work, rather than being driven by extrinsic factors, you do better work. Academics can also embrace this model for being both professionally and personally rewarded through their interactions at work. A meta-analysis of research on faculty in Nursing programs has supported this idea, finding intrinsic motivation to be one of the strongest predictors of job satisfaction (Gormley, 2003).

There are many academics who do thrive in the competitive, publish-or-perish culture of academia. Nonetheless, the intention of this chapter is to tell my own story as an example to other academics, who may be starting their careers or finding frustration with their careers, of how I was able to align my personal values and interests with my academic life. This chapter is for academics who are interested in a different model of success. This is my own story of how I found my way to be whole and happy in my career by risking being myself.

When Academics Stop to Reflect

"You can't stop the waves, but you can learn to surf" (Kabat-Zinn, 2013).

This is a common saying of Dr. Jon Kabat-Zinn, the developer of mindfulness-based stress reduction (MBSR) therapy. It refers to the inability to control the stresses of life, but the ability to develop coping strategies and resiliency to better navigate those stressors. I did not learn how to surf until I was a postdoctoral fellow.

At the time, I was struggling with my own stress and anxiety as I figured out my identity as an academic. I had started my first position as a Ph.D. in a hyper-competitive lab where trainees were pitted against each other for authorship and favor. Lab meetings were highly stressful events where lab members were ridiculed for any perceived shortcomings in their work. I was once chastised for not being in my office when the PI was looking for me. I was in the bathroom at the time and endured the jokes made at my expense about getting paid to use the restroom.

I was not prepared for this kind of environment and quickly started experiencing psychosomatic manifestations of my stress. I developed an ulcer, struggled with insomnia, and even experienced a few panic attacks. Worse of all, I started experiencing daily migraines—to the point where I was taking antiseizure medication in an attempt to reduce them.

Within four months of starting this position, I decided that a career in academic research was untenable for me. I could not spend the rest of my life being this miserable. Fortunately, as I started to share my plans to leave academia, I was invited to join a different lab and given the opportunity to reevaluate. This lab focused on clinical neuroscience, and one of the PIs (and my new mentor), Dr. Wendy Heller, was the instructor of the mindfulness-based stress reduction (MBSR; Kabat-Zinn, 1994) clinical practicum for the Clinical Psychology Ph.D. program. She invited me to audit this course, and by doing so, she changed my life.

Mindfulness is defined by Jon Kabat-Zinn (2003, p. 145) as, "the awareness that emerges through paying attention on purpose, in the present moment, and nonjudgmentally to the unfolding of experience moment by moment." Research on the effects of mindfulness has its roots in clinical psychology. In this research, patients with various mental and physical health diagnoses have experienced reduced symptoms following MBSR treatments (for reviews and meta-analyses see, Baer, 2003; Bohlmeijer et al., 2010; Grossman et al., 2004; Hofmann et al., 2010).

In this MBSR practicum, we spent the first semester meeting twice a week to discuss the research on the clinical benefits of mindfulness practices, the mechanisms of mindfulness practices, and to practice mindfulness together for 45 minutes at a time. It felt like diving into the deep end. Initially, the practices were torturous for me. I had been going out of my way in life to avoid thinking about a lot of things causing me anxiety, and sitting quietly for 30 seconds, let alone 45 minutes at a time, was not helping me to keep those thoughts at bay.

Soon, however, I found that I could sit with those thoughts with less and less reaction. I started to see a lot of my psychosomatic symptoms of anxiety dissipate. Now, ten years later, I have yet to experience another migraine since that semester. I was fortunate to have a good instructor and a supportive group with which to practice. I responded well and started to feel capable of making decisions for my life again. I continued in the practicum for two more semesters (the last as the instructor of record for the course, as my PI was away on sabbatical). During this time, I worked with the clinical psychology Ph.D. students as they led community groups through the MBSR training.

This was the first time in my training as an academic that I was encouraged to slow down and reflect. Engaging in this reflection helped me to realize that despite my extensive training in research, I was more rewarded by community outreach and teaching. Up to this point, I had been following the academic career path of which I was expected. I was trained in a doctoral research university, I had a postdoctoral fellowship at a top-ten doctoral research university, so I thought I should only want to pursue a career as faculty at a doctoral research university.

By engaging in this reflection, this was the first time I was consciously risking being myself. With more years of postdoctoral funding offered to me, I decided to go on the job market and seek out positions at institutions that emphasized teaching. I wanted to be in positions that emphasized interactions with students and others over spending time in a lab. This decision was still met with criticism from others. They expressed concern that I was throwing my career away.

When I look back at my early years as a trainee now, I realize that this was inherent in my development. I organized an article club, writing group, and a regular happy hour for my graduate program. As a postdoc, my lab had no tradition of training undergraduate research assistants, yet I convinced the PIs to let some in under my mentorship, and I co-founded a postdoctoral writing group with a friend. My need to create community and elevate groups of people through shared experiences and knowledge had been bubbling under the surface all along.

WHEN ACADEMICS PURSUE AUTHENTICITY

When you encounter an academic that has dedicated their research to the mechanisms and effects of mindfulness practices, mine is a common story. My transition from a stress-addled trainee to a calmer, more reflective scholar mirrors what we have learned about how mindfulness practices influence the brain and behavior. By choosing to stay present, especially when stress is running high, we can act with intention and not get wrapped up in negative emotional spirals, as opposed to reacting and becoming overwhelmed with worry, regret and doubt (Brewer, 2021).

For example, I made a mistake my second year as a professor. A student of mine had been awarded a research grant to purchase gift cards to be used as compensation for her senior thesis project. To publish the project, we needed more data collected after my student graduated. I continued running the study and compensating participants with the gift cards the following fall. University policy was to return any unused materials from a student research grant to the office of undergraduate research once the student was done, not the project.

When my mistake came to light, the director of the office of undergraduate research was livid. She was pure reaction. Any of us in academia know that the financial aspects of running a department or program can be wrought with politics. She was concerned that my error would put the financial aspects of her office under scrutiny by administrators and result in possible repercussions for her budget. She responded with stress and fear at the forefront and went as far as to threaten to bring me up on charges of financial fraud in an email that included eight university administrators.

If this had happened to me before I started practicing mindfulness, I would have been thrown right back into my own anxiety spirals. Instead, I asked for a meeting where we could discuss how to correct my error. During the meeting, I admitted my mistake and suggested ways that I could make sure the office was reimbursed for the gift cards I had used as compensation after my student had graduated. I also reminded her of the other students I was mentoring in research and how my goals and the goals of the office of undergraduate research were the same. Though not easy, I was able to stay present throughout this experience, act with intention, and let go of habitual thought patterns of anger and worry.

The meeting ended with the director complimenting me on my professionalism and apologizing for her reaction. More than once after that meeting, I would get an unexpected knock on my office door and find a junior faculty member there in distress. They had been directed to me because of a conflict they were having on campus and were told that I could help them with navigating the situation. We could spend another chapter unpacking a work culture that would rather direct people on how to cope with problems rather than dealing with correcting problems, but I digress. My point here is that I risked being myself, and the skills I developed through training in mindfulness allowed me to be present and authentic in my job and provided a bridge for me to connect with other faculty in meaningful ways.

It is curious though, that to be drawn to the study of mindfulness practices, you often must first develop clinical symptoms of anxiety and/or depression. Couldn't academia be structured in a way where this was not a common, shared experience? Could not creating communities on campuses rather than competitions and conflicts lead to progress in the quality of education, scholarship, and satisfaction with academia among university members?

The positive effects of mindfulness practices on patients have led to a mindfulness movement in K-12 education. Again, when mindfulness programs are incorporated into our primary schools, students and teachers benefit (for meta-analyses see, Carsley et al., 2018; Klingbeil & Renshaw, 2018; Zenner et al., 2014; Zoogman et al., 2014). What we are learning through the study of neuroscience are that these benefits come from increases in grey matter (processing power) and white matter (processing speed) in regions of the brain associated with attention, self-awareness, cognitive control, and memory (e.g., Fox et al., 2014). These changes allow one to better control their thoughts and responses to their experiences, and subsequently better regulate their emotions.

It was only after experiencing these effects firsthand that I spoke to faculty from my graduate program about overcoming my stress. More often than not, they would respond by relating to my story, sharing how they too had struggled or were struggling with stress, anxiety, and/or depression at one time or another due to the pressures of academia. One close mentor told me how she was on anti-anxiety medication throughout graduate school and relied on marriage counseling to keep her relationship together as she struggled with stress. I was shocked to learn this only after completing my Ph.D.—after training with these mentors for five years.

It is hard not to dwell on how different my experiences as a post-doctoral fellow would have been if the faculty of my graduate program had been willing to have these conversations with me when I was under their training. If they had been willing to risk being authentically human with a student, perhaps I could have realized the importance of developing communities of support and resiliency to stress earlier in my career. Why were academics, especially those in psychology, willing to accept getting broken by academia as a standard, normal experience? Why were we contributing to the stigma of having mental health symptoms by not openly talking about our own experiences? Why weren't we being more open and preventative about coping with stress as academics?

As I accepted my first offer for a tenure-track faculty position, I kept these questions in mind. I told myself that I would not be the type of professor to hide my personal experiences from my colleagues and students. I would openly share about my own struggles with anxiety and the importance of finding ways to cope with stress and develop resiliency. I began each of my classes with a brief mindfulness practice. I wanted to see if I could make a dent in the perpetuating cycle of stress in academia. If nothing else, I knew that shared experiences lead to increased feelings of belonging and affiliation (e.g., Enfield, 2008), and exposure to people who had dealt with a mental health diagnosis and recovered helps reduce the stigma around mental health (Carroll, 2018).

During that year, I met a colleague in Teacher Education. She was presenting to new faculty on using reflection in the classroom. Afterward, I asked her if she had ever used a practice like mindfulness as a tool for reflection. She had not but was interested in collaborating on a mindfulness project for her Master of Arts in Teaching courses. I thought, "Why not?" I was not trained to do mindfulness research, but I was passionate about it and wanted to help other graduate students learn to manage their stress before academia broke them. I was also deeply curious about the changes I had experienced as a result of my own mindfulness practice.

The following year, one of her classes came to my lab for neural and cognitive assessments of attentional control at the beginning and at the end of the semester. In between, I came to her class once a week to lead a 30-minute mindfulness practice, and students were asked to practice and reflect daily outside of class. Another class served as a control group. We found that the students who practiced mindfulness as part of their class had improved neural indices of attentional processing and incorporated their understanding of classroom content with their understanding of themselves as teaching professionals better than the control class (Hall & O'Hare, 2016; Hall et al., 2017).

It just so happened that these classes were for the Master of Arts in Teaching program, so all the students I was leading through mindfulness practices were in-service teachers and already teaching in area K-12 schools. For them, the connection to practicing mindfulness as being part of a professional educator became obvious. They shared their practices and experiences with their colleagues, administrators, and students.

Following are some excerpts from these students' reflections on the course and the mindfulness training (some of which are also published in Hall & O'Hare, 2016):

> I would like to focus on using the mindfulness training as a way to bring faculty together after school as a way to increase the sense of community and decrease the feelings of isolation.
>
> By establishing an emotional connection with students, their ability to learn and make appropriate decisions in the real world is increased...it becomes increasingly apparent to me that it is absolutely essential to establish emotional connections with my students through the curriculum. Contemplative practices can serve as an avenue to do so.
>
> I consistently reminded myself to be centered in the present, to breathe and be non-judgmental... This engagement has not only benefited my deep learning, but I hope in time (after years of practice) will improve my students' understanding, comprehension, and cognition. By interacting, becoming more present and aware, I feel as though all individuals will benefit and become more focused in engaging education.
>
> I can say that when a student is talking to me, and my mind starts to drift because I have a million things to do, I do notice myself pulling my

attention right back to the student. I am more focused on what is going on right in front of me and try to give my full attention to it. I guess even being aware that I am sometimes not focused, and changing, is a benefit.

I was unsure about how this practice would fit into my career as a teacher and my life, but as we went through the training, I found the practices to be very valuable. I found myself feeling that I could cope better with the rigors of life and work when I practice regularly. Although mindfulness is difficult for me, I know that these tools will help elevate all aspects of my life.

I feel that the training has improved my perception on dealing with stressors in life, social issues in any relationship and confirmed my belief in the whole child curriculum for our nation's education system (as well as my own classroom).

When it comes to mindfulness, 'just being' is a part of my strategy for dealing with a rough day, a tough conversation with a student, or a tense meeting with an administrator. I sit in my car, let it all go, and just be. I accept it for what it is, accept that it happened and move on with my day and go home to my family…I definitely find that my stress levels are lower, and my mood is more pleasant when I let it go and just be in the moment.

These students' reception of the mindfulness practices inspired us to organize our first of three "Building Community and Mindfulness" events for area K-12 community members. These events created a space to share recent research on evidence-based practices for socioemotional development for all K-12 stakeholders and were each attended by roughly 100 participants. Primary education was hungry for programs that promoted socioemotional well-being for students and teachers. The question remained, could we also tap into this type of development in the higher education arena?

That summer, I was fortunate enough to be able to attend the Mind and Life Institute's Summer Research Institute. This program creates a space for a traditional academic conference, where researchers who study contemplative practices share their work, interleaved with a contemplative retreat, where practitioners in contemplative practices share their trade and knowledge. While there, I met the keynote speaker for the conference, Dr. Judson Brewer, a psychiatrist and neuroscientist who has found innovative ways to use tools of neuroscience to complement the training of mindfulness practices and has developed programs to treat addictive behaviors and anxiety with mindfulness interventions (Brewer, 2017, 2021).

Two things have stuck with me from that meeting. First, Dr. Brewer had walked a path much like mine. He too had been overwhelmed by anxiety and stress during his training as a medical student and found himself in mindfulness practices. Second, he emphasized the importance of faculty being able to pursue research in these areas early in their careers. He was authentic as he listened to my experiences and shared reflections of his own. He praised me for my willingness to take on an area of scholarship that was not well supported by my colleagues or mentors. His support empowered me to dive in all the way.

The Mind and Life Institute is an organization that originated in 1987. It is the collaborative manifestation of His Holiness the 14th Dalai Lama, a neuroscientist, Francisco Varela, and an entrepreneur, Adam Engle. The institute "brings science and contemplative wisdom together to better understand the mind and create positive change in the world" (https://www.mindandlife.org/about/). Discovering the Mind and Life Institute helped me become aware of a community of academics who shared my interests and values. They further supported my career by awarding me a small research grant a few years after the Summer Research Institute and by supporting a biannual research conference for contemplative studies where I have presented my work.

When Academics Create Community

Encouraged by my experiences with the Mind and Life Institute, I applied that summer for a fellowship position in my institute's Office of Faculty Development. My proposal was to lead a year-long workshop for other faculty on how to incorporate contemplative practices into their classrooms. I was awarded the position. Fourteen of my colleagues applied, all but two more senior faculty than me, spanning the Colleges of Arts and Sciences, Nursing, Engineering, Fine Arts, and Law. We spent the fall semester learning about and engaging in different contemplative practices, using Barbezat and Bush's (2014) *Contemplative Practices in Higher Education* as our guide. During the spring semester, each participant conducted a contemplative intervention in one of their classes and compared it to a control class. As is consistently found in research on K-12 education, students in contemplative classes performed better and reported better indices of mental health and well-being compared to the control classes at the end of the semester.

While again, it was fulfilling to see our work has positive impacts on our teaching and students, I personally received a lot of benefit from the community this fellowship created. For the first time in my career, I was regularly meeting with like-minded faculty from all over campus. I was gaining recognition and support and increasing my sense of belonging at my institution. This was instilling a sense of value in my role at my university that was not entangled with my research.

While running the faculty fellowship, I also decided to start a faculty and staff mindfulness group on campus. I reserved a room during lunch hours once a week and sent out a campus-wide announcement inviting others to join me for a midday/midweek practice. Faculty and staff from all over campus showed up. Some attending for one or two sessions, and others becoming steadfast regulars that continued to meet for the next five years.

This small group, consisting of staff from our Center for Women, Gender & Sexuality, Accounting and Finance, and Student Services, and faculty from Teacher Education, Religious Studies, and Psychology, became a core support group for each other. We would share our frustrations and anxieties with each other, engage in mindfulness practices together, and debrief on how the practices were influencing our experiences. Through this group, I was able to make connections with more and more members of my campus community, as whenever the topic of mental health and/or mindfulness came up, my name was included in the conversation.

Soon, these meetings became what I looked forward to during the week. The sense of community and support I received from this group helped me work through feelings of imposter syndrome, stress, and at times, full existential crisis related to my work and our campus. I credit a lot of my early success as an academic to this group despite the fact that our time and activities together were not resulting in peer-reviewed publications or grants. We had simply created a space where our current selves were enough, which is not a message that is common in the "publish-or-perish" culture of academia.

I also continued to develop a line of research around the cognitive and emotional impacts of mindfulness practices and their applications in the higher education classroom. Incorporating mindfulness practices into classrooms was consistently showing improved attention, decreased distraction, and reduced anxiety, stress, and negative affect in students. Not surprisingly, there was also evidence for increased academic performance in these students. What still continues to drive me to teach mindfulness to my students, regardless of if it is contributing to my research, is the reflections on their experiences with the practices that they will share.

For example, during one class where I introduced the practice of staying present with the breath, I noticed an outstanding honors student in tears. I checked in with her after class to make sure that everything was okay. Her response was, "It just felt so good to have permission to sit still." As her professor and a person in a position of authority for her, it had to me that modeled these behaviors and validated them in science, theory, and practice in order for her to feel comfortable doing them as part of her experience as a student.

As my reputation for working in mindfulness grew, so did my connectivity with others on campus and the surrounding community. Resident assistants for the student dorms were required to organize guest speakers and programs for their residents throughout the academic year. I became a frequent guest at the dorms, speaking on the importance of developing stress coping and resiliency skills, the value of sleep, and the need for connectivity to others and feelings of belonging on campus. These programs would always incorporate an introduction to mindfulness practices as one avenue for supporting these skills. Students were open and receptive to the programs and even started their own mindfulness group.

My campus' center for unity and diversity hosted an event to recognize the International Day of Peace each year. This event featured speakers from all of the different diversity groups on campus who spoke on their group's need for community and recognition from others. I was invited to lead a practice on loving-kindness or metta meditation, a specific type of mindfulness practice where you stay present with thoughts of compassion toward yourself, others, and/or all beings.

I was asked to present my research to a group of K-12 school counselors that were on campus for a training day. I was invited to give a campus-wide presentation on my work. I would join other faculty's classes to guest lecture and lead mindfulness practices throughout the year. I was the keynote speaker for "Greenlight for Girls"—a science and math camp for K-12 girls hosted by my campus.

As my interaction with others around mindfulness expanded, I was contacted by a local cardiologist, Dr. Michael Rocha. Dr. Rocha is one-in-a-million when it comes to physicians. He frequently prescribes his patients yoga and mindfulness practices and has his floor take yoga breaks during their busy shifts. He founded a local, free, community-based wellness program to support physical and mental well-being in the community, and he plays a mean trombone in a brass band also of his founding.

Dr. Rocha and I saw eye-to-eye when it came to the need for wellness education in our community and the feeling that sharing our knowledge and time toward such efforts as being inherent to our professional lives. The community wellness program offered free fitness and wellness classes every Sunday at the Boys and Girls Club community center. I became one of several mindfulness instructors who would cycle through leading classes and eventually sat on the board of directors for the program.

The exposure through teaching mindfulness in the community led to several more invitations. I spoke to school parent-teacher associations (PTA), met with school district administrators, spoke at a local unity conference and started to create a broad network of friends and other practitioners in the yoga community. I took their classes and learned from them, and they learned from me.

My students at the university also started to develop a keen interest in the applications of mindfulness in education. Two students from my research lab conducted senior thesis projects at two private middle schools. I trained these students in mindfulness practices, and they went to the schools twice a week for the duration of a school term to teach mindfulness to fifth-to-eighth grade students. In both projects, we again found that students who practiced mindfulness as part of their school education reported lower levels of negative affect.

During this time, I also applied for a teaching position in the Emory-Tibet Science Initiative (https://tibet.emory.edu/). This program was a collaboration between Emory University and the Dalai Lama Institute to teach modern science to Buddhist monastic scholars living in the Tibet settlement camps in India. I was accepted into the program and spent three summers traveling to southwestern India to teach affective neuroscience to Tibetan Buddhist monks.

While I was connecting and building a community around mindfulness both on my campus and off, I was downgraded by my dean for my scholarship (the same dean who invited me to give the campus-wide presentation). My publications on mindfulness and education were deemed not rigorous enough. The grant I was awarded was a small foundation grant that garnered no indirect costs; therefore, the university did not financially gain from the grant or my research. Despite being perceived as interesting and applicable across all levels of engagement on campus, it was still not valued by the academy's standards.

When Academics Humanize Work Environments

Social support and the quality of relationships are found to be the strongest predictors of mental health and overall life satisfaction (Harandi et al., 2008; Waldinger et al., 2014). Not surprisingly, research in primary school teachers has also found supportive relationships with colleagues to positively influence feelings of belonging at one's school and job satisfaction and predict decreases in emotional exhaustion and motivation to leave (Skaalvik & Skaalvik, 2011, 2019). Yet, there is no systematic research examining these effects in higher education.

One study that examined job satisfaction among science faculty at intensive research universities found the respect of colleagues to positivity affect job satisfaction (Bozeman & Gaughan, 2011). Interestingly, hypotheses of hours teaching undergraduates having a negative effect and hours conducting research and number of collaborations having a positive effect on job satisfaction were not supported. This suggests that the feelings of respect from colleagues were coming from non-research interactions and creating communities through one's research alone is not enough to increase positive feelings about work.

Faculty report spending on average 54–61 hours per week on work (Jacobs & Winslow, 2004; Link et al., 2008; Ziker et al., 2014). As such, we are likely to spend more of our waking hours during the week with our colleagues than with our own families. With research supporting that quality, non-research focused relationships with colleagues have a positive impact on an individual's well-being and job satisfaction, it makes sense for institutions of higher education to create ways for individuals to create communities on their campuses.

During my first faculty position, my colleagues and I took a grassroots approach to creating communities on and off our campus. We were successful but often felt embattled and at odds with administrative groups on campus. I am now at a new institution and have discovered that there is an institutionalized way of creating spaces for communities on campuses. Eight years into my professional career, I first heard the term "community of practice." A community of practice is a "mutual engagement in a joint enterprise with a shared repertoire" (Arthur, 2016, p. 231). My new institution promotes these communities, and I have joined one around the concept of positive pedagogy.

Without my knowing, both the faculty fellowship I had led and the weekly mindfulness group I had created were communities of practice. They created spaces for like-minded individuals to gather and learn about a common interest through our shared experiences. They cultivated feelings of belonging and tapped our intrinsic motivation to continue our career paths. They had no explicit goals of producing any sort of scholarly output, but rather, they just held the space for us to be humans, as well as academics, while at work.

While a newer concept to me, communities of practice are not new to academia (Arthur, 2016). However, they are rarely supported at the institutional level, despite frequent calls for interdisciplinary courses and research on campuses. Theoretically, they could be used to not only meet these goals on the institutional level, but also contribute to the well-being of staff and faculty at these institutions (Jakovljevic et al., 2013; Lea, 2005).

Through the positive pedagogy community of practice, I have been invited to join other groups focused on well-being and campus community at my new institution. These include a committee dedicated to faculty and staff wellness, where I serve as my college's "wellness ambassador," and a committee dedicated to embedding practices of positive psychology across all levels of campus to increase student wellness and reduce suicides.

Concerns about feelings of isolation and levels of stress experienced by all members of university campuses have increased over the last year during the global COVID-19 pandemic. Further, these effects have been stronger on already disadvantaged academics, such as young mothers (Krukowski et al., 2021). I cannot imagine what the last year was like for new faculty starting their careers in virtual university environments. They have missed out on the traditional meet-and-greets that introduce them to campus (Buckley, 2021). Through one of my handfuls of days on campus during the pandemic, I met a new professor in engineering. After talking for a bit, he mentioned that I was one of five people outside of his department that he had met eight months into his first year.

One of the committees on which I serve was asked to suggest ways to help people stay connected and manage social isolation during the pandemic. Not surprisingly, I offered to lead a virtual mindfulness group for faculty and staff. My vice provost loved the idea and ran it up the flagpole with our human resources department. Imagine my amazement when their response was to hire two individuals to offer virtual mindfulness groups for campus twice a week. My new institution not only is proactive about supporting faculty and staff well-being, but they act on new ideas!

I feel fortunate that early in my career as an academic I found avenues for expressing my individualism and creating communities of support on my campus. When I reflect on the journey I have been on, I am grateful for the challenges and opportunities for growth I have experienced. I do, however, think that feeling like I was always having to cut a new pathway for myself was at times stressful and exhausting. My hope is that academia can move beyond having "pioneer" faculty who break the norms and prioritize work environments that support mental health to having this be the norm and be the guidance and advice that is given to junior faculty.

Further, the deindividuating environments in academia may counter the broader goals of these institutions. Promoting well-being and communities of practice among faculty can engender faculty who can do better work. When faculty do not feel supported in expressing their passions and creating relationships with colleagues outside of their silos, they experience more stress and burnout. They are more likely to withdraw from the campus community in an act of self-preservation.

These effects can be strongest in junior faculty who are told to not speak up, keep their heads down, and be productive until tenure. These isolating mentalities can interfere with feelings of belonging and job satisfaction for years. Rather than suppressing the identities of young faculty, universities should be encouraging them to pursue work and relationships that are intrinsically motivating to them. This will increase their productivity, creativity, and retention.

As such, faculty will no longer have to "risk" being themselves... they can just be accepted as themselves. When this happens, our impact on our academic and surrounding communities expands and strengthens, as can be seen in the course evaluation comments from students who were not part of my research projects:

Not to be dramatic, but I think you should know that the mindfulness skills you taught us in class have LITERALLY saved my life... and I can never thank you enough for that. Thank you, THANK YOU.

I think mindfulness helped me focus, sleep, and be less anxious, all of which have contributed to my learning.

I feel like I am able to concentrate longer on things like lectures and articles...

I noticed being much less stressed out than in previous semesters. But my workload has increased!

I have always been skeptical of meditation but practicing and learning about the neurological changes associated with mindfulness has changed my perception of it. I have also become more accepting of challenges in my life.

I feel that learning and practicing mindfulness has helped me with learning this semester. At times, practice has reduced my feelings of stress, allowing me to focus on assignments.

References

Arthur, L. (2016). Communities of practice in higher education: Professional learning in an academic career. *International Journal for Academic Development, 21*(3), 230–241. https://doi.org/10.1080/1360144X.2015.1127813

Baer, R. A. (2003). Mindfulness training as a clinical intervention: A conceptual and empirical review. *Clinical Psychology: Science and Practice, 10,* 125–143. https://doi.org/10.1093/clipsy.bpg015

Bohlmeijer, E., Prenger, R., Taal, E., & Cuijpers, P. (2010). Meta-analysis on the effectiveness of mindfulness-based stress reduction therapy on mental health of adults with a chronic disease: What should the reader not make of it? *Journal of Psychosomatic Research, 69,* 539–544. https://doi.org/10.1016/j.jpsychores.2009.10.005

Bozeman, B., & Gaughan, M. (2011). Job satisfaction among university faculty: Individual, work, and institutional determinants. *The Journal of Higher Education, 82*(2), 154–186. https://doi.org/10.1080/00221546.2011.11779090

Barbezat, D. P., & Bush, M. (2014). *Contemplative practices in higher education: Powerful methods to transform teaching and learning.* Jossey-Bass.

Brewer, J. (2017). *The craving mind: From cigarettes to smart-phones to love—Why we get hooked & how we can break bad habits.* Yale University Press.

Brewer, J. (2021). *Unwinding anxiety: New science shows how to break the cycles of worry and fear to heal your mind.* Avery, Penguin Random House LLC.

Buckley, H. (2021). Faculty development in the COVID-19 pandemic: So close—Yet so far. *Medical Education Adaptations,* 1189–1190. https://doi.org/10.111/medu.14250

Carroll, S. M. (2018). Destigmatizing mental illness: An innovative evidence-based undergraduate curriculum. *Journal of Psychosocial Nursing, 56*(5), 50–55. https://doi.org/10.3928/02793695-20180108-04.

Carsley, D., Khoury, B., & Heath, N. L. (2018). Effectiveness of mindfulness interventions for mental health in schools: A comprehensive meta-analysis. *Mindfulness, 9*, 693–707. https://doi.org/10.1007/s12671-017-0839-2

Cerasoli, C. P., Nicklin, J. M., & Ford, M. T. (2014). Intrinsic motivation and extrinsic incentives jointly predict performance: A 40-year meta-analysis. *Psychological Bulletin., 140*(4), 980–1008. https://doi.org/10.1037/a00 35661

Dinh, H., Strazdins, L., & Welsh, J. (2017). Hour-glass ceilings: Work-hour thresholds, gendered health inequities. *Social Science & Medicine, 176*, 42–51. https://doi.org/10.1016/j.socscimed.2017.01.024

Enfield, N. J. (2008). Common ground as a resource for social affiliation. In I. Kecskes & J. Mey (Eds.), *Intention, common ground and the egocentric speaker-hearer* (pp. 223–254). Walter de Gruyter GmbH & Co. KG.

Fox, K. C., Nijeboer, S., Dixon, M. L., Floman, J. L., Ellamil, M., Rumak, S. P., Sedlmeier, P., & Christoff, K. (2014). Is meditation associated with altered brain structure? A systematic review and meta-analysis of morphometric neuroimaging in meditation practitioners. *Neuroscience and Biobehavioral Reviews, 43*, 48–73. https://doi.org/10.1016/j.neubiorev.2014.03.016

Gormley, D. K. (2003). Factors affecting job satisfaction in nurse faculty: A meta-analysis. *Journal of Nursing Education, 42*(4), 174–178. https://doi.org/10. 3928/0148-4834-20030401-08

Grossman, P., Niemann, L., Schmidt, S., & Walach, H. (2004). Mindfulness-based stress reduction and health benefits: A meta-analysis. *Journal of Psychosomatic Research, 57*, 35–43. https://doi.org/10.1016/s0022-3999(03)005 73-7

Hall, M. P., Falk Jones, L., & O'Hare, A. J. (2017). Internal ways of knowing: A case for contemplative practices in pre-service teacher education. In K. Byrnes, J. Dalton, & E. Dorman (Eds.), *Contemplative practices in pre-service teacher education* (pp. 8–24). Rowman & Littlefield .

Hall, M. P., & O'Hare, A. J. (2016). Wide-Awakeness in the classroom: The power of mindfulness attention training for in-service teachers in a graduate educational research course. In R. Collister, J. Buley, & D. Buley (Eds.), *Art of noticing deeply: Commentaries on teaching, learning, and mindfulness* (pp. 7–18). Cambridge Scholars Publishing.

Harandi, T. F., Taghinasab, M. M., & Nayeri, T. D. (2008). The correlation of social support with mental health: a meta-analysis. *Electronic Physician, 9*(9), 5212–5222. https://doi.org/10.19082%2F5212

Hofmann, S. G., Sawyer, A. T., Win, A. A., & Oh, D. (2010). The effect of mindfulness-based therapy on anxiety and depression: A meta-analytic review.

Journal of Consulting and Clinical Psychology, 78, 169–183. https://doi.org/10.1037%2Fa0018555

Jacobs, J. A., & Winslow, S. E. (2004). Overworked faculty: Job stresses and family demands. *The Annals of the American Academy of Political and Social Science, 596,* 104–129. https://doi.org/10.1177%2F0002716204268185

Jakovljevic, M., Buckley, S., & Bushney, M. (2013). Forming communities of practice in higher education: A theoretical perspective. *Paper presented at the Management, Knowledge, and Learning International Conference,* Zadar, Croatia.

Kabat-Zinn, J. (1994). *Wherever you go, there you are: Mindfulness meditation in everyday life.* Hyperion.

Kabat-Zinn, J. (2003). Mindfulness-based interventions in context: Past, present, and future. *Clinical Psychology: Science and Practice, 10*(2), 144–156. https://doi.org/10.1093/clipsy.bpg016

Kabat-Zinn, J. (2013). *Full catastrophe living (revised edition): Using the wisdom of your body and mind to face stress, pain, and illness.* Bantam Books.

Kinman, G. (2001). Pressure points: A review of research on stressors and strains in UK academics. *Educational Psychology, 21*(4), 473–492. https://doi.org/10.1080/01443410120090849

Klingbeil, D. A., & Renshaw, T. L. (2018). Mindfulness-based interventions for teachers: A meta-analysis of the emerging evidence base. *School Psychology Quarterly, 33*(4), 501–511. https://doi.org/10.1037/spq0000291

Krukowski, R. A., Jagsi, R., & Cardel, M. I. (2021). Academic productivity differences by gender and child age in science, technology, engineering, mathematics, and medicine faculty during the COVID-19 pandemic. *Journal of Women's Health, 30*(3), 341–347. https://doi.org/10.1089/jwh.2020.8710

Lashuel, H. A. (2020). Mental health in academia: What about faculty? *eLIFE, 9,* 1–3. https://doi.org/10.7554/eLife.54551

Lea, M. R. (2005). 'Communities of practice' in higher education: Useful heuristic or educational model? In D. Barton & K. Tusting (Eds.), *Beyond communities of practice: Language, power and social context* (pp. 180–197). Cambridge University Press.

Link, A. N., Swann, C. A., & Bozeman, B. (2008). A time allocation study of university faculty. *Economics of Education Review, 27*(4), 363–374. https://doi.org/10.1016/j.econedurev.2007.04.002

Palmer, P. J. (2002). Foreword. In W. M. McDonald (Ed.), *Creating campus community: In search of Ernest Boyer's legacy* (pp. ix–xvi). Wiley.

Pega, F., Náfrádi, B., Momen, N. C., Ujita, Y., Streicher, K. N., Prüss-Üstün, A. M., Technical Advisory Group, Descatha, A., Driscoll, T., Fischer, F. M., Godderis, L., Kiiver, H. M., Li, J., Magnusson Hanson, L. L., Rugulies, R., Sørensen, K., & Woodruff, T. J. (2021). Global, regional, and national burdens of ischemic heart disease and stroke attributable to exposure to long working hours for 194 countries, 2000-2016: A systematic analysis from the WHO/ILO joint estimates of the work-related burden of disease and injury. *Environment International*, 016595. https://doi.org/10.1016/j.env int.2021.106595.

Skaalvik, E. M., & Skaalvik, S. (2011). Teacher job satisfaction and motivation to leave the teaching profession: Relations with school context, feeling of belonging, and emotional exhaustion. *Teaching and Teacher Education, 27*, 1029–1038. https://doi.org/10.1016/j.tate.2011.04.001

Skaalvik, E. M., & Skaalvik, S. (2019). Teacher self-efficacy and collective teacher efficacy: Relations with perceived job resources and job demands, feeling of belonging, and teacher engagement. *Creative Education, 10*, 1400–1424. https://doi.org/10.4236/ce.2019.107104, https://tibet.emory.edu/

Waldinger, R. J., Cohen, S., Schulz, M. S., & Crowell, J. A. (2014). Security of attachment to spouses in late life: concurrent and prospective links with cognitive and emotional wellbeing. *Clinical Psychological Science, 3*(4), 516–529. https://doi.org/10.1177/2F2167702614541261

Zenner, C., Herrnleben-Kurz, S., & Walach, H. (2014). Mindfulness-based interventions in schools—A systematic review and meta-analysis. *Frontiers in Psychology, 5*, 1–20. https://doi.org/10.3389/fpsyg.2014.00603

Ziker, J. P., Wintermote, A., Nolin, D., Demps, K., Genuchi, M., & Mein-hardt, K., (2014, April 21). *Time distribution of faculty workload at Boise State University.* Poster presented at the 2014 Undergraduate Research and Scholarship Conference at Boise State University, Boise, ID. http://schola rworks.boisestate.edu/cgi/viewcontent.cgi?article=1022&context-sspa_14

Zoogman, S., Goldberg, S. B., Hoyt, W. T., & Miller, L. (2014). Mindfulness intervention with youth: A meta-analysis, *Mindfulness, 6*, 290–302. https://doi.org/10.1007/s12671-013-0260-4

CHAPTER 3

Living Divided No More: Cultivating My Own Forest Biome in Academia

Maureen P. Hall

You are never so strong that you don't need help.
— Cesar Chavez

INTRODUCTION

Academics often suffer the pain of dismemberment. On the surface, this is the pain of people who thought they were joining a community of scholars but find themselves in distant, competitive, and uncaring relationships with colleagues and students. Deeper down, this pain is more spiritual than sociological: it comes from being disconnected from our own truth, from the passions that took us into teaching, from the heart that is the source of all good work. (Palmer, 2017, p. 21)

M. P. Hall (✉)
University of Massachusetts Dartmouth, North Dartmouth, MA, USA
e-mail: mhall@umassd.edu

M. P. Hall and A. K. Brault (eds.), *Academia from the Inside*,
https://doi.org/10.1007/978-3-030-83895-9_3

Scholars, including myself, have many unrealistic notions of what it will be like to be part of the academy. In line with Palmer's quote above, I too believed that in joining the academy I would become a part of a community of scholars, a group of intellectuals focused on the greater good. Yet, the lived reality is more complicated, at least it can be at times. Palmer (2017) asks this question: "How, and why, does academic culture discourage us from living connected lives?" (p. 36). In response, he points to the surface issues that cause disconnection, for example: the competition that makes faculty and students wary of each other, the grading systems, the fragmented fields of knowledge, and other sticky layers of academic bureaucracy. Nevertheless, he argues that those things are minor in comparison to the inner fear pervasive in academic culture.

My goal for this chapter is to give an "insider's view" of my experiences in negotiating the academy and how my journey has shaped and continues to shape me. As I document my experiences, I draw upon my extended metaphor of the *academic forest biome* and map it onto Parker Palmer's notions about academia to tell my lived reality in higher education. I invite readers, tenured or tenure-track faculty, graduate students, and others—to listen to Palmer's voice in concert with mine to see inside this *academic forest biome*. I illustrate some of the "pollution" that threatens one's health and well-being in the academy, and I also recount how the *academic forest biome* acts as a "carbon sink" fostering routes to health and healing in academia. Palmer views good teaching as a conscious and repetitive act of vulnerability. In this case, I make myself vulnerable by sharing my experiences. Finally, I share specific examples of how I have followed Palmer's Alternative Educational Reform model, inhabiting it and finding my own way. My hope is that, as a good teacher, I can provide readers with a birds-eye view inside of the academy and arm them with new knowledge and awareness as they enter higher education. Ultimately, this chapter provides an analysis, and a pathway forward for coping with difficulties encountered in the academy. While all careers are marked by challenges, there are productive ways to face these challenges.

My Academic Journey

In recounting and making meaning of my academic journey, here I provide some context and a road map for navigation. I am a woman, now in my late-fifties; I am a person who has been involved in education for my whole life. I earned tenure and associate level in 2009 and full professor in 2016. I tell my students, "I have been either a student or a teacher since I was five years old." At this point, I have both gratitude and angst for the academy.

From my writing desk, overlooking the shimmering silvery waters of Seymour Lake in far northern Vermont, it is the height of the global pandemic, and I am living through it. For context, Seymour Lake, in the northeastern highlands of Vermont, is aptly referred to as the Northeast Kingdom of Vermont (NEK). Since March of 2020, I have been teaching my classes on Zoom from this small red cabin we purchased in 2015. What's more, we were able to winterize and transform our little northern home into a creative retreat and place of refuge during this pandemic.

While living here, I've become aware that the NEK is part of the world's few boreal forests. A boreal forest is one kind of a biome, mainly characterized by coniferous forests where spruce, pine, fir, and larch trees flourish. A boreal forest is also known as a "snow forest," and that rings true for me. As I finish writing this chapter, it is the first day of May 2021, in the second year of the global pause created by the pandemic, and it is snowing! While I am a resident of Massachusetts, due to the pandemic, I am now a resident of this "snow forest." Other boreal forests are found in Scandinavia, Russia, Canada, and a few other places around the world. Here in the NEK, I am located on the southern edge of the boreal forest that begins in Canada. Being here in northern Vermont, immersed in this boreal forest, I have been reflecting on my academic journey. My gaze on the lake is almost constant, and, while the diamonds of light sparkle on Seymour Lake, I bring this light inside me.

As Paulo Freire (1998) asserts, "there is no teaching without learning, meaning that teachers are learners and learners are teachers" (p. 29). That said, I am a teacher and a learner, and I have learned that environmental biomes are places that heal ecosystems by storing carbon, purifying the air and water, and regulating the climate. A biome itself is a "large community of vegetation and wildlife adapted to a specific climate" (National Geographic Society, 2021, Biomes, par. 1). Through reflection on my academic journey, *I came to realize that I am cultivating my own 'academic biome' within the larger ecosystem of academia; I am not made of spruce and fir—but of heart and soul.* Although there are resources available to me as a member of the academy, I am not always offered the nourishment that I need. With that said, to explicate my journey, I utilized the metaphor of the *academic forest biome*. This metaphor helps to describe the interrelated and interdependent organization(s) inside the academic environment. It also provides a useful way of describing how the complex systems of people, policies, and technologies develop, use, and sustain the academic social milieu as an ecosystem. I found this analytic lens to be the best way for me to unpack and understand academia's complex settings and its inherent oppressions.

Similar to what nature does with her biomes, I apply my metaphorical argument to academia and link it to Parker Palmer's model for Alternative Education Reform as a route for navigating and adapting to the ecosystem of higher education. As a result, this model has helped to guide in standing strong and overcoming some of the toxic elements inside the academy. In other words, this model has helped me to not only survive in academia—but thrive.

The stages of Palmer's Alternative Educational Reform model consist of:

> Stage 1: Isolated individuals make an inward decision to live "*divided no more*," finding a center for their lives outside of institutions.
> Stage 2: These individuals begin to discover one another and form *communities of congruence* that offer mutual support and opportunities to develop a shared vision.
> Stage 3: These communities start *going public*, learning to convert their private concerns into the public issues they are and receiving vital critiques in the process.
> Stage 4: A system of *alternative rewards* emerges to sustain the movement's vision and to put pressure for change on the standard institutional reward systems (2017, pp. 172–173).

Keeping with my academic biome metaphor, in many ways, I attribute my successes in part by my adherence to Palmer's roadmap for reform. Instead of storing carbon and purifying air and water as nature's biomes do, I continue to navigate, pivot, and adapt to find symbiosis in the academy. Over my eighteen-year career in academia, I have accomplished much in terms of my scholarship, my teaching, and service to the university and the community. These accomplishments include collaborative scholarship in areas including English Education, Mindfulness in Education, and Teacher Leadership. Over 2010–2011, I spent seven months in India as a Fulbright Scholar. While there, I began a positive and symbiotic collaboration with Dr. Chinmay Pandya and his university in India,

Dev Sanskriti Vishwavidyalaya (DSVV). During my work in India, I developed a deep interest in mindfulness and education, and that interest led me to a collaborative partnership with Dr. Aminda O'Hare, who was a neuroscientist at my home institution.

I have written two books, and this will be my third. My first book was about literacy and its ability to change lives; I co-authored that work with lead author and English Professor, Dr. Robert Waxler. My second book was a collection of chapters about *lectio divina*, and was co-edited with two professors from other institutions, Jane Dalton and Catherine Hoyser, whose expertise was Art Education and English, respectively. I have published these two books as well as numerous articles and chapters in peer-reviewed venues. This body of work documents my success in the areas of scholarship.

My effectiveness as a professor, though perhaps harder to quantify, can be measured in a few different ways, including being an important part of the success of our Masters of Art in Teaching (MAT) programs, my positive student evaluations and comments, and the many generative relationships I cultivate with my students. Two examples below illustrate these relationships I have created with my students.

The first example illustrating my success in my teaching pertains to my ongoing relationship with Danielle Johansen. I was her University Supervisor for her student-teaching experience in the fall of 2012 and previously had her in one other graduate education course. At the celebratory dinner for all student teachers who finished in December 2012, Danielle said something like this to me: "I would like to go to India and teach there." I wrote to Dr. Chinmay Pandya that same night to see if there would be a possibility for Danielle to teach at Dev Sanskriti Vishwavidyalaya (DSVV). He responded, "Absolute Confirmation" by email the next day. Over a few months in the spring of 2013, I was able to guide her in getting ready for her trip to India and arrange for her to teach at DSVV. Going forward to the present, this collaboration builds on my existing relationship with Danielle, in that we have co-written Chapter 13 in this book, where we characterize our experiences at DSVV in order to illuminate the uniqueness of DSVV's educational approach and Dr. Chinmay Pandya's guiding philosophy. It is so gratifying to now write with a former graduate student, and, in this case, to document our experiences at DSVV and the Embodied Education theoretical framework outlined in the introduction to this book. Danielle is part of my *academic forest biome*, and more than that—she is a lifelong friend with whom I now collaborate.

The second example pertains to my role as a doctoral dissertation committee member for a Nursing student, Terri Legare. Although I am in Education, I was invited to be part of Terri's committee in nursing because her study focused on the importance of reflection. Terri Legare's study investigated the role of reflection and reflective practice for nurses in transition to become nurse educators. I supported Terri and gave her feedback on her dissertation throughout the whole process. I was part of Terri Legare's *academic forest biome*, and she was part of mine. I am happy to report that she was successful in her dissertation defense in April 2021. In June, she went through the doctoral hooding ceremony and proudly earned the Ph.D. distinction. A week after her dissertation defense, Terri sent me a package, one that included a lovely card, a gorgeous multicolored scarf, and a beautiful sterling silver tree on a silver chain. I couldn't believe she gave me a tree and wrote this in the card: "*Trees symbolize many things in different cultures. Wear this in knowing you have helped me grow as trees represent spiritual nourishment and transformation.*" She had no idea that I was writing about my own *academic forest biome*, and that makes the gifts she gave me—especially this silver tree—all the more serendipitous. I was overjoyed to uncover this connection to my *academic forest biome* and how it extends to and from my students. Students are a very important part of my ecosystem in academia, and I have a deep gratitude for my relationships with them.

However, my experiences in academia have not always been nurturing and generative. I have also had painful and "dis-membering" experiences in my academic journey as Palmer talks about. I am grateful for Parker Palmer; I have benefited in many ways from his wisdom about academic life. In fact, it is through following the stages of his Alternative Educational Reform model and using it as a map in academia that has helped me to thrive and also to heal from some of the toxic elements in the specific climate of academia.

Following the map that Palmer provides is what I am calling my *academic forest biome*. Parker Palmer's words about academia at the beginning of this chapter claim that pain in academic life is "more spiritual than sociological." I am now understanding this pain is also "ecological." From my boreal forest outlook on Seymour Lake in Vermont, I now see academia as an ecosystem. Paradoxically, the environment where we flourish as thinkers and creators of knowledge is the same one that can cause pain and dismemberment. However, our connection to ourselves can keep our ecosystem healthy. Through embracing my own work and my collaborative work with others, and through my ongoing experiences in India, I have created a safe place within the larger ecosystem of academia. I have created my own biome within the larger biome—I refer to this as my *academic forest biome*. Nature has inspired me in such a way that I can be healed and find ways to navigate academic environments in healthy and generative ways.

Dismembering and Re-membering

Palmer's quote at the beginning of this chapter talks about the *dismembering* that can happen in academia. My work is about "re-membering" to take good care of myself and to find ways to be in a community with my teaching self. These actions are important in part because I want to be healthy as an individual, as a member of the academy, and as a role model for my students. Palmer (2000) also reminds us that "our deepest calling is to grow into our authentic self, whether or not it conforms to some image of who we ought to be" and that "true vocation joins self and service" (p. 16). My truth is that I have, at times, felt that the academy had "dismembered" me, and as I reflect on this I'm brought to a moment in another chapter of this book. In Chapter 10, Agnes Curry reminds us how Rumi saw the "wound" as the place where the light enters. Since coming across this perspective, I've wanted to reframe my experiences and push forward in this way. By "re-membering" who I am at heart and focusing on healing in the light, I have been re-emerging as a stronger person and growing into my authentic self, and will continue to do so.

However, by cultivating community with my teaching self, and, by finding others who are like-minded, I have recently been finding success and happiness in my career. A healthy boreal forest requires each individual tree to maintain a strong identity. Deciduous trees are found in the boreal forest, and they lose their leaves each year. Similarly, I may have lost my leaves or gone through difficult times. Despite the fact that there have been contexts that didn't always suit me, that I felt unwelcome in, and/or unappreciated, I have retained my authenticity and personhood. Like Deciduous trees in the spring, my leaves have grown back. The boreal forest as a biome has helped me to flourish and sprout new green leaves. In academia, that represents new growth as a professor and person. As a single tree in this *academic forest biome,* I have also found other like-minded trees to populate this forest. One tree by itself cannot do the work of cleaning the air and water, or stabilizing the climate. My *academic forest biome* has grown by finding community with others in the academy—both inside and outside my institution.

Pursuing authenticity, creating creative community, and humanizing education are themes in my work as a teacher and teacher educator. When combined, they paint a picture of what it means for me to "*live divided no more.*" For those readers not familiar with Parker Palmer's work, this will require more unpacking on my part. For Palmer, this living divided no more represents the starting point of a movement. Think Gandhi—living divided no more means "being the change you want to see in the world." More specific to a life in the academy, Palmer explains that this decision happens when "isolated individuals who suffer from a situation that needs changing decide to live 'divided no more'" (p. 173). Further, he adds that individuals in the academy can get pushed to a point where they must decide whether to keep their integrity or allow their selfhood to perish. As a tree in my *academic forest biome*, I have weathered the gale-force winds of academic storms. My branches have bent in the wind, but I have remained upright and strong. Academia, like other professions, is not free from stressors and tensions. But, because teaching is soul-work and calls for engaging the heart—this decision to "*live divided no more*" is critical for keeping it real and keeping my authentic self and voice alive.

Early Life

I come from a family full to the brim with teachers. My mother and father were both in the profession, along with several uncles, aunts, and cousins on both sides of my family. Even Pearl O'Leary, my maternal grandmother, was a teacher. Beginning her career in the 1930s in northern New Hampshire, in a one-room schoolhouse on Gore Road in Lancaster, Pearl embraced both keeping the woodstove going during the cold winter months and kindling a fire of learning in her students. Now, I am located only forty or so miles west of where my grandmother Pearl started her career in teaching. This pandemic, with all of its challenges, has provided me with time for deep reflection.

I think back to my younger days when I had no idea as to what vocation or path called my name or any clear vision for what I wanted to do in this life. I understood one thing very clearly at that time: I was not ever going to become a teacher. Every family gathering had a charged discussion about education, and, almost every night at dinner with my parents there was some educational issue ingested with the meal. There wasn't just one thing that dissuaded me; there were multiple. In part because I majored in English as an undergraduate, my family members assumed I would naturally become an English teacher. When I envisioned a job beyond college, I dreamed of becoming a food critic or a ski patroller. Although I loved reading, writing, and discussing good literature, I couldn't see past the family educational quagmire to actually even consider entering the teaching profession.

I remember one incident when I was in college and nearing graduation. I planned to extricate myself from answering the expected barrage of questions from my aunts and uncles, including "What are you planning to do with your life?" followed by, "You are planning to be an English teacher, correct?" My escape plan from these questions was simple—I would distract them. The day before the family gathering, I got my long hair cut short. Usually a haircut is an end in itself, but I had a hidden agenda for this particular haircut. Did my plan work? Only somewhat. At the gathering, Aunt Sally, my mother's sister and one of the teachers, complimented my shorter hairstyle and then moved to the inevitable question about my plans after graduation. I can't remember exactly how I answered her question. But when I think back on my complete hesitancy about becoming a teacher, it wasn't just the sheer number of relatives who taught or the non-stop "teacher-talk" in my family. It also had to do with my view on women becoming teachers was limiting and traditional. I looked on becoming a teacher as becoming a "schoolmarm," a move that would break no new ground. For these reasons and others, my overall view of the teaching profession at that time was quite dim.

In 1988, more than thirty years ago now, I started my first teaching job in Lancaster, New Hampshire—the same town where my grandmother had taught and where my mother had grown up. I taught seventh and eighth-grade English and Eastern Hemisphere Geography for five years. In 1993, I was hired as an English and U.S. History teacher in Keene, New Hampshire, and I also taught there for five years. In 1998, I decided to go back to graduate school, this time at the University of Virginia. I finished my dissertation in 2003 and was lucky enough to be hired on a tenure track. I earned tenure in 2009, and achieved the rank of full professor in 2016.

My Dear Uncle Tad was my biggest supporter. Since I was a little girl, he and my Aunt Lorrie provided unconditional love and support. Uncle Tad, who left his body during this pandemic, used to have a few sayings that I now carry with me. One was, "Everything will work out—just not always the way you think it will." I now understand what he meant. Fast forward in my journey: I became a teacher and then a professor, which was the only career path that I was sure I would not take. And so, some of Uncle Tad's wisdom continues to resonate through me.

THREATS TO THE ACADEMIC FOREST BIOME

In the academic ecosystem, students and faculty alike have a range of fears: fear of not being good enough, fear of failing, fear of being ignorant, fear of not measuring-up, and many others. These fears are embedded and structural; they are built into higher education. In 2013, in my own *academic forest biome*, I began to collaborate with a psychology professor on some mindfulness in education research. The written strategic plan of the university promoted interdisciplinary work, and we considered our work to be a way to build new knowledge. In this case, our research could build on existing work in psychology and also help pre-service and in-service teachers. In spite of this, my psychology colleague was told during an administrative review that she should not be spending time working on this research with me in Teacher Education unless the work appeared in peer-viewed venues that had impact factors. Here is where fear took hold. I was tenured at that point, but my psychology colleague was pre-tenure. Mindfulness in education was not brand new, but research on it at that time rarely appeared in peer-reviewed venues with quantitative impact factors. Now, not quite ten years later, many research studies on mindfulness in education appear in peer-reviewed venues with impact factors. One would think that an institute of higher education should be a place where fields of knowledge can interact and create new knowledge. While the idea of collaboration between faculty across departments and fields of knowledge should be encouraged and supported, our experience and work was discouraged and seemingly penalized.

In my *academic forest biome*, the upper administration caused fear in my colleague and cast shade on me as a "sick tree," creating unhealthy growth conditions in our forest. However, by standing strong alongside each other, we two trees persisted, successfully harvesting interdisciplinary research and publishing several articles and chapters together. Here, Palmer's ideas offer hope and a way through; he writes, "By understanding our fear, we could overcome the structures of disconnection with the power of self-knowledge" (p. 37). If we avoid what he calls "live encounters," hiding behind our specialties or even avoiding live encounters with ourselves, we learn "the art of self-alienation, of living a divided life" (p. 38). I am happy to report my partner earned tenure, and none of these threats to my boreal forest caused lasting damage. Part of these fears grew from structural issues in academia. The administration viewed our work as somehow not good enough to be valued in the academy. Here is where the "silos" of higher education keep departments and professors from collaborating, in part because of a narrow vision of the possibilities and the ways in which professors' work is evaluated. It takes time to have these experiences in academia, reflect on them, and find another way. For my partner and I, the *academic boreal forest* provided sustenance and fortitude. Separately and together, we remained true to ourselves and to our work. We trudged on amid the negativity of bureaucracy, and the *academic forest biome* grew, evolved, and became healthier than before!

Healing Power of the Academic Forest Biome

Before further extending my metaphor of the *academic forest biome*, I would like to share a few additional facts about biomes as ecological communities. Biomes are found in different locations around our earth and can be distinguished by their climate, flora, and fauna. A range of imbalances can damage biomes, including changes in the climate and the introduction of new plants and animals. Come back with me to Seymour Lake, the place where I "weathered" the pandemic and innovated the *academic forest biome*, and allow me to provide additional details about boreal forest biomes. It is an elevated woodland plateau where, "Temperatures in boreal forests are, on average, below freezing. Conifers, spruce, fir, and pine trees are the predominant needle-leaf plant species in boreal forests" (National Geographic Society, 2021, Forest Biomes, par. 1). As mentioned earlier, the boreal forest biome plays an important role in removing carbon dioxide from the atmosphere as a "carbon sink."

In 2013, when I was an Associate Professor with tenure, my institution made the decision to merge my Teaching and Learning Department with the STEM Education Department. From the view of the administration, this was a fiscal measure. This cost-cutting measure may have been considered practical, but as a structural change, it caused many cultural clashes between the two departments.

Although both departments shared some general views on education, each had strikingly different approaches to what they actually did with and in education. The Teaching and Learning Department focused on teacher preparation with programs where pre-service and in-service teachers could earn their Master of Arts (MAT) degree. The STEM Education Department was a doctoral program where students could earn their Ph.D. While the STEM Education faculty focused mainly on educational research, the Teaching and Learning Department focused on teacher preparation.

From the view of the inhabitants of each department, it was as if an invasive species had infiltrated the other, or that the soil was all wrong, or both. Looking through the lens of the *academic forest biome*, there were significant challenges to the combined ecosystems. When departments are merged in higher education, it is similar to combining species in a biome. Combining species that lack biological synergy can destroy a biome—or at least severely damage its health and well-being.

The new department was re-named "STEM Education and Teacher Development." There were fewer faculty in the former Teaching and Learning Department than in the STEM Education Department. On any voting issues, the STEM side always came out on top. My Ph.D. is in English Education, and if someone had foretold my future that I would soon be part of a department focused on STEM—I would have had a hard time believing them. My thinking on this was that Democracy is the least-worst form of government, and also part of what they mean when they say real life is stranger than fiction.

Soon there was a new threat to my *academic forest biome*. I started to be bullied by the department chair. For example, I wanted to make sure that Ph.D. students who were given roles in the MAT program had the background and professional skills needed. I was told by the department chair in front of the whole department that I could not talk about this concern. This pattern of intimidation and restricting free and open discourse in the same public manner continued with junior faculty. As the department member with the most seniority, I felt the need to protect myself, and well as those who were pre-tenure. Academia was created as a place where free and open communication and the sharing of ideas should be encouraged not stifled. These basic human rights were being denied, and I knew that this kind of treatment was unjust and inappropriate. I finally decided to make a formal complaint that my chair (now a former chair) had been bullying me.

The most profound bullying incident involved a meeting with my chair to discuss my bid for full professor. I knew that I met and exceeded the requirements for scholarship, teaching, and service, and I had reviewed my body of work with other colleagues who had achieved the rank of full professor. I was nervous about this meeting because I didn't feel supported by my chair. In academia, without the support of one's chair, moving forward is almost impossible. I was also aware of national statistics about how few women, as opposed to men, ever achieved the rank of full professor. At this meeting, the chair disparaged my academic work and shared two (mis)perceptions: (1) that I was not current in my content area, and (2) that I had not articulated my area of specialization. I tried to stay calm, and responded in this way: "I am trying to take what you are saying in a positive way, but I am having a hard time. I asked the chair, "Have you read any of my work?" The chair answered, "No, I have not read your work."

This was a gut punch. It made me feel sick. How could someone, especially the department chair, make a broad judgment about the "worthiness" of my work without ever having read any part of it? Although I stayed calm on the outside, I felt raw and hollow inside. Right then, I had the lived experience of what Palmer termed the "pain of dismemberment" in the academy. I felt devalued as a tree in this particular biome of academia. It was as if the soil had dried up and I wasn't getting the nutrients I needed or an ice storm had taken some of my limbs and kept me from flourishing.

One more contentious department meeting later, when I was again told that I couldn't talk about something critical to our department, I decided to share my concerns with the Equal Employment Office (EEO). A mediation session was suggested and tried; it did not help. At that point, I made a formal bullying complaint and documented details of multiple incidences that had occurred. Here's where it gets even worse. A few days after I made my formal complaint, I found out the leader of the EEO office not only did not investigate my complaint but also informed the chair that I had made the formal bullying complaint. I "called out" this EEO Officer for revealing this confidential information to my bully. But this officer only attempted to normalize something unethical, describing it instead as standard practice. The pulse of the "pain of dismemberment" struck again—but now it came from an institutional office on campus—the very one I'd gone to for help.

To be frank, I was hesitant in writing about these experiences in academia. When I shared my hesitation with a colleague friend, she wrote: "Remember why we share our stories...the hope that our vulnerability would touch others' lives and empower them too" (Bifuh-Ambe, personal correspondence, December 31, 2020). My colleague's sage advice for me as the lead editor of this book, one that delves into the interior of academia, gave me energy and courage to tell this story of being bullied and the academy's (my institution's) disregard for my mistreatment. Telling this story brings in my own voice and truth—grounding Palmer's precepts in my lived experience. My colleague's voice joins with Palmer's in showing how vulnerability is important in teaching and learning. Palmer explains that good teachers have the ability to be vulnerable. However, this vulnerability can become overwhelming and can cause teachers to disconnect from themselves, their subject, and their students. As a result, vulnerable teachers are more likely to become so distraught that they decide to leave the teaching profession.

The hierarchical nature of the academy fragments and distorts the practice of mutual respect, and Palmer considers respect an antidote to fear, a way to re-connect to others. He believes that academic life can be transformed by practicing simple respect. He writes:

> I don't think there are many places where people feel less respect than they do on university campuses. The university is a place where we grant respect only to a few things—to the text, to the expert, to those who win in competition. But we do not grant respect to students, to stumbling and failing. (p. 18)

Respect, far too often overlooked, should be an essential component to all relations in the academic culture. This extends from teacher to student, teacher to teacher, teacher to administrator, and all other possible relations in educational settings.

As Palmer aptly points out, "In company with others who are on the same path, these people are helped to understand that 'normal' behavior can be crazy but that seeking integrity is always sane" (Palmer, 2017, p. 179). Palmer describes how academics can often "suffer the pain of dismemberment," and adds that this pain really comes from being disconnected from their own truths. If I chose to let this experience in the academy define me, I would be dismembered. But Palmer shows us another way of being.

Gratitude for These Experiences: Pushing Me to Live Divided No More

Ironically and unexpectedly, I have some gratitude for these negative experiences as they became tipping points for me to find another way of inhabiting higher education. Other experiences had shown me that my institution did not respect faculty concerns. However, this experience took the cake. Palmer (2017) makes clear that we are drawn to higher education institutions because they "harbor opportunities that we value," but goes on to point out that the claims these institutions make on us become "pathological when the heart becomes a wholly owned subsidiary of the organization, when we internalize organizational logic and allow it to overwhelm the logic of our own lives" (p. 174). When the EEO did not investigate my claim and informed my chair that I had made a bullying report, I realized that my values, freedom, and liberty were not only disrespected but also disregarded. Further, the dean at the time hired a mediator for the department. But, because anonymity could not be assured, no one in my department shared anything with the mediator. The university had likely spent thousands of dollars on this mediator, and this person had to work for their pay. This mediator just sat in our department meetings to observe—as no one would agree to any mediation or talk about any situation in the department.

This whole situation was a turning point for me. As mentioned earlier, I hadn't realized I was unwittingly following Palmer's steps or stages in his vision for Alternative Educational Reform. My inner decision was to live my own truth and not internalize the values of the institution. This did not mean that I would alter my teaching or scholarship; instead, I began to inhabit the first stage of Palmer's Alternative Educational Reform. In Palmer's words, this first stage is described as "an inward decision to live 'divided no more,' finding a center for their lives outside of institutions" (p. 172).

Healthy news to report in terms of my current departmental biome— we now have a new leader in our department, one who has been able to bring together members from two vastly different biomes. Is it the 'ph' in the soil that this person has helped to change? Is it the valuing of very different trees and finding ways for them to respectfully co-exist? Whatever the change in the biome, there seems to be more commonality than divergence.

My View on the Academic Forest at Mid-Career

I had mixed feelings about beginning this chapter with Palmer's quote about academia. At first glance, it paints a somewhat grim view in a book about the inside of academia. Palmer warns about how academics may feel this "pain of dismemberment," but that the deeper problem is disconnection from "our own truth." Palmer discloses to us in the *Courage to Teach* who he is; he writes: "I am a teacher at heart, and there are moments in the classroom when I can hardly hold the joy" (p. 1). He goes on to celebrate the learning adventures of engaging the life of the mind in dialogic community with his students. But he follows up with a caveat: that other moments in the classroom can be "so lifeless or painful or confused..." that "his claim to be a teacher seems a transparent shame" (p. 2).

THE REWARDS OF TEACHING AS "SOUL-WORK"

Palmer talks about the teacher within. He makes plain that mentors can guide us and help us to know ourselves, but that this "call to teach does not come from external encounters alone." Palmer explains further, "No outward teacher or teaching will have much effect until my soul assents" (2017, p. 30). Teaching is soul-work. Part of my soul-work in teaching has been to explore more deeply what being a teacher means to me. As Palmer reminds us, community cannot "take root in a divided life" (p. 92). The inner work we do is deeply connected to our outer work in the academy. The inner work of the mind and heart must be prioritized—especially in our society that seems only focused on what happens outside of us. Valuing one's self, connecting to our truths, embracing our passions, and all the while keeping our hearts open is what "Living Divided No More" means in "Palmer-speak."

Teaching is a vocation that has both great risks and great rewards! I am happy to report that teaching is still my heart's passion. I continue to feel fortunate to have this rewarding career in helping people improve their own lives and the lives of others. I can't imagine myself in any other role. Palmer's work emphasized a much overlooked element of educational reform; that is, the development and self of the individual teacher. Teachers are the facilitators of the ecosystem and teaching and learning space. They can foster relationships with individual students and link students with other students into an ecosystem of trust and a safe space for learning. Palmer underlines that there must be a valuing of and emphasis on developing the individual self of the teacher, or educational reform efforts remain incomplete.

SERENDIPITY FOR THE BIOME: A PANDEMIC BOOK GROUP ON PARKER PALMER'S (2017) THE COURAGE TO TEACH

In August 2020, during the height of the pandemic, I received an email. It was an invitation to join a book group on Parker Palmer's, *The Courage to Teach*. I quickly responded that I was interested in joining. A few days later, I received the notice that I was accepted. I couldn't believe that the Office of Faculty Development (OFD) at my institution had chosen this book for the group. Almost two decades earlier, I had started my journey with Parker Palmer with *The Courage to Teach* as the focus of my dissertation. Since my very first day in academia, I have chosen to "live and breathe" Parker Palmer's work.

The small group consisted of approximately ten professors who committed to read the book and meet five times over the semester to discuss this seminal work. I viewed this book group invitation as a timely gift to what Palmer would refer to as my "inner teacher." Palmer makes clear: "The teacher within stands guard at the gate of selfhood, warding off whatever insults our integrity and welcoming whatever affirms it. The voice of the inward teacher reminds me of my truth as I negotiate the force field of my life" (2017, p. 32). My decision to join this book group was an affirmation to my teacher within. I was interested to see how my current colleagues today would respond to Palmer's work—more than twenty years after the book's publication. What's more is that during this same semester, I had my graduate students read Palmer's stand-alone piece, "The Heart of a Teacher," which gave rise to deep discussions within my own courses and connected to the book group. Overall, this book group was a chance to see a contemporary community of truth in action and be part of it; it was pure pandemic serendipity.

Conversations within the book group centered on issues of power in higher education and the vocation of teaching itself. In my embodied experiences as a university professor over the last eighteen years, I have realized there is both privilege and toxicity in higher education.

After the final meeting of this book group, in a private conversation with one of the facilitators, I shared this: "Two things have saved me in higher education: Parker Palmer and India." For me, this is a deep truth. I have gratitude for Parker Palmer's influence in my teaching and life, and I have gratitude for the times I have spent in India. As mentioned previously, I first went to India in 2010 when I was a Fulbright Scholar. Over 2010–2011, I spent seven months in India, and it has become my "second home." Since then, I have been back to India nine more times. It has been very hard to be away from India during this global pandemic. However, I will continue to visit my second home throughout the rest of my life.

India Has Become My Second Home

Enter Dr. Chinmay Pandya. In October 2010, when I arrived at Dev Sanskriti Vishwavidyalaya (DSVV), I met Dr. Chinmay Panday. I didn't know it then, but DSVV was to become my "second home." Connections abound between and among Parker Palmer, Dr. Chinmay Pandya, and India. For example, there are routes to self-knowledge that come from ancient Indian practices. As mentioned previously, see Chapter 12, written with former student Danielle Johansen, for more about DSVV and connections to India. Using information from interviews with Dr. Chinmay Pandya, as well as our lived experiences at DSVV, as well those of others, we delineate embodied education, which is the theoretical framework for this book.

The revelation that I had after being a participant in this book group was two-fold. One part is related to India and the other to Parker Palmer. Starting with my Fulbright in India in 2010.

I have spent considerable time at DSVV over the past decade. After lecturing and interacting with hundreds of students and teachers in different parts of India over my first seven-month trip there, my heart resonated with the ideas and practices that connected head and heart. My good friend (and father figure) Agamveer Singh always reminds me of what I said at his institution in my first lecture there. After traveling for many months to Kerala, Tamil Nadu, Delhi, and other places, I came back to DSVV, where Agamveer works as a student welfare officer. Agamveer recounts that I talked about the differences I perceived between teachers in India and teachers in the United States. I shared this: "American teachers teach from the head, and Indian teachers teach from the heart." This is not to say that all American teachers only teach from the head. But this was my experience with Indian teachers and students. I realized that I had been living the stages of Palmer's Alternative Education Reform for the last several years in academia. Why did I need something to save me in higher education? I realized that India, as my "second home," provides a refuge and safe place for my heart.

PALMER'S VISION FOR ALTERNATIVE EDUCATIONAL REFORM

In addition to fully articulating the contours of community and community-creation, Palmer also offered an Alternative Model for Educational Reform, which I shared in the opening of this chapter. When writing my dissertation, I was focused on the concept of community. Almost two decades later, with a beginner's mind, I have been constantly revisiting and realizing just how important Palmer's model for educational reform is to me now. Note that these stages of Palmer's model are also in the Introduction to this book; we point out that as a Community of Practice (CoP)—our book project is a living example of the workings of Palmer's Alternative Model for Educational Reform. They are meaningful to our collective journey as contributors to this book, but in this chapter explore their personal meaning. I realized that I have been working on embodying each stage of his reform; I have been living through Palmer's stages as a professor in academia.

As I revisit the stages set forth by Parker Palmer, I can't help but map these stages onto my own life, and the collaborative communities I helped to create within my own *academic forest biome*. As I began to "map" my experience as an academic to Parker Palmer's stages of educational reform; I see myself and my experiences with collaborative colleagues when I "walk" through these stages. I see this "mapping" as a kind of deep reading and deep identification with each of Palmer's stages.

Stage 1: I have to consciously work at living "divided no more" by first finding my interior center, outside of my institution. This "Living Divided No More" involves precarious balancing acts—something quite similar to eating healthy foods and exercising regularly. Sometimes I go a day or two without some restorative physical exercise, or I cheat and eat some fast food. Then I re-balance and get back on track. As these healthful life habits are part of self-care—staying out of the politics in my department or my institution is important. I do admit that this conscious and embodied effort to *"live divided no more"* is something that I have gotten better at over the past couple of years. Some might say that I have achieved the rank of full professor, and now I don't have to worry so much about my job security. As I write this, I do realize how privileged I am to have this job security that many others do not have. While it is true that I don't have to worry so much about my job security, it is a far different thing to thrive in academia than to just survive.

I am entering my nineteenth year at my institution, and, over this span of time, I have had 11 different department chairs. There's a whole and separate narrative to explore right there, one that has lacked leadership and stability in and of itself. However, as I mentioned in the opening, I have more than survived. I have actually flourished in many ways amid situations that have been toxic and lacking a sense of community.

Stage 2: When I got hired at my institution, the woman who hired me gave me some advice. She said with emphasis, "Make friends both inside and outside of the department." And I have followed that advice. In fact, I have been fortunate to write and do projects with many colleagues at my institution, and the majority of these partnerships have been with individuals in other departments. My partnerships with colleagues at my institution then morphed into collaborations with professors from other institutions—both near and far. As Palmer outlines, individuals begin to find one another, and create *communities of congruence* that lend mutual support and opportunities to develop a shared vision.

The genesis of my *communities of congruence,* which I refer to as *collaborative communities,* grew in and through the burgeoning relationships I have fostered with other academics. Usually, I would meet someone, sense our commonalities or like-minded natures, and then find some opportunity to write together, present together, or work on some project where shared goals are palpable.

For example, in Provincetown, Massachusetts in the summer of 2014, I first met Catherine Hoyser, a person who became an important member of my *collaborative community*. We met by chance, as we had both signed up for a poetry class at the Fine Arts Work Center (FAWC). The class we took was called, "One week, I Wrote a Ton of Poetry." Our teacher was the glorious poet Gabrielle Calvo-Coressi. In one class session, Catherine and I started to chat, and I asked her if she might like to join me at the beach after our class that afternoon. She was happy to join me, and we had a wonderful afternoon at a Truro beach with lots of sun and waves. Our conversation, as many conversations are on the beach, was expansive and continuous. Although she was a professor of English, and I was an education professor, we found that we had much in common. The following day in class, Catherine and I paired up for a "storytelling-to-poem" exercise that Gabrielle outlined for us. We were each to tell the other a story from our lives. No notes could be taken—we were instructed just to listen deeply. The literacy task after listening to the other's story was to write a poem about the story we heard, or to craft a poem that combined elements of both stories.

We didn't know it then, but this one exercise led us to write a scholarly article about this work, and to present our work at both national and international conferences. Catherine and I had created community with each other. In each other, we found a like-minded friend and colleague. We could have never imagined when we met in that poetry class that we would go on to publish articles together and co-edit a book in collaboration with Jane Dalton, entitled, *The Whole Person: Embodying Teaching and Learning through Lectio and Visio Divina* (2019). Meeting Catherine serves as one example of finding like-minded colleagues and creating *"communities of congruence."*

Stage 3: The writing of this book has been a collaborative process, and a way to go public with our work. The three Zoom calls, as outlined in the Introduction to this book, centered on our common concerns across academia. Through other communication efforts, including the emails and drafts we sent to one another, we continued to uncover the connections and interconnections between ourselves as writers and ourselves as academics. In one of our first Zoom meetings, we leveraged our initial connections to each other and started to build community, and the contributors to this book began to transform into a *community of congruence*. These interactions are also chronicled in the Introduction to this book. As a group of academics, we have woven ourselves into a tapestry where the threads of self and subject join together. As a community going public, we are bringing both concerns and joys of academia to light so that others can provide critiques and join this ongoing conversation. We look forward to having our book as part of the ongoing dialogues about life and work in academia.

Stage 4: In terms of Palmer's fourth stage, I have experienced alternative rewards through my lived experiences of this reform model. For example, I do feel supported by the members of my *communities of congruence*. Some members are from my own institution, others are from different parts of the U.S., and many are from foreign countries. What I am less sure about in Stage 4 is that our work puts pressure on higher education to make changes. One thing that has been overtaking the academy is its transition into a business model, one that relies heavily on full-time and part-time faculty who lack any security or power in the system. I am part of a dying breed in academia; I am a tenured and full professor at my institution. Perhaps making change in the actual institution is less important than not allowing the institution to change you. As Palmer points out in Stage 1, we cannot let the values of the institution overtake our own values. This is especially true if the institutional values and environment try to morph us into vehicles for profit and power. By remaining true to our intended purpose, we can thrive in an environment that may not be ecologically symbiotic. One of the alternative rewards of deepening one's self-knowledge is that it provides a way to stay strong. My hope is that this book will generate dialogue and discussion about lived realities in higher education and perhaps will increase pressure for change for educational reform.

Palmer's Views on the Teaching Self: Identity and Integrity

Palmer distinguishes between authority and power. He argues that power works from the outside in, while authority is something that comes from the inside and works outwardly. Therefore, a teacher must work to develop such authority by developing his or her own identity and integrity, then use it to shape classroom learning. By exercising authority as opposed to power, a teacher can more effectively interrogate and enact his or her own pedagogical practices.

While other approaches to improving teaching practices attempt to give new answers to the *what* and the *how* of teaching, Palmer's approach involves answering: "*who* is the *self* that teaches?" Undergirding this approach is his assertion that "good teaching cannot be reduced to technique; good teaching comes from the identity and integrity of the teacher" (Palmer, 2017, p. 10).

According to Palmer, effectiveness with one's students and one's subject depends greatly on the degree to which one attains this self-knowledge. He goes even further, asserting that if a teacher does not know his or herself, then it is almost impossible for that teacher to know his or her students. He considers a cognizance of one's self as a prerequisite for knowing any subject. Further, he considers one's integrity as an essential piece of that self-knowledge and articulates it this way:

> By integrity I mean whatever wholeness I am able to find within that nexus as it vectors form and re-form the pattern of my life. Integrity requires that I discern what is integral to my selfhood, what fits and what does not and

that I choose life-giving ways of relating to the forces that converge within me. (p. 13)

There are choices involved in both identity and integrity; learning about one's self is intentional work. Additionally, Palmer explains that identity and integrity can never be fully named or understood by anyone. He claims that they are a part of a "familiar strangeness" that people carry throughout our lives; it is not something that is necessarily apparent to anyone other than the individual. Integrity is derived from the grounding of one's being and is premised on self-knowledge.

Just as teachers need to find ways to know themselves, they also need to create and facilitate their students' own self-knowledge: the teacher needs to find ways to connect the students to the learning through the students' own experiences. Meaning does not exist in isolation; rather, it exists as a person makes meaning through connection(s). If, as Palmer asserts, teachers need self-knowledge, then how does one attend to that self and find out about it? Palmer makes various suggestions for what a teacher might try: walking in the woods, finding a friend who will listen, writing in a journal, and meditative reading. Through such reflective activities, teachers can develop the necessary authority to guide students.

When a teacher operates through his or her authentic self, students respond in kind and the educational space becomes humanized. Here is an example of attention to humanizing the space of the classroom from teachers in one of my graduate education courses. One group of students was preparing for their interactive Facilitated Discussion assignment. They read many articles on Social Emotional Learning (SEL) and Teacher Well-Being, and they all attended a Contemplative Practice Conference this past semester. I received this email inquiry from the leader of one group in planning for their discussion, and this was part of it:

Hi Everyone!
My team and I will be presenting our Facilitated Discussion to the class this upcoming Thursday. We were hoping everyone would do a small act of kindness we can include in our presentation! In order for this to work, we would need each person to compliment, use a quote, encouraging words, or recognize how great of an educator/person they are.

Each person from our class will be assigned/asked to create this small note for another classmate. If this is something you are willing and interested in doing please send a reply to this email. Also please indicate if you would like your response to be kept anonymous or not.

P.S if you would like to compliment/share kind words to additional people within our class you may, but please be sure if you are willing to include the person below! (Personal communication with Sarah Campbell, April 8, 2021)

I was so pleased to receive this email from the leader of this one group, and I see this as an example of a positive action for kindness and gratitude in the learning space. As bell hooks points out about the class-room, "There must be an ongoing recognition that everyone influences the classroom dynamic, that everyone contributes. These contributions are resources...excitement is generated through collective effort" (2014, p. 8). By calling on all class participants to value each other, the learning space is enhanced in so many ways. How gratifying it is for me to see my students knitting together the classroom community, valuing each other, humanizing the space, and finding new ways to engage with their own students in their own classrooms. This is one of the joys to be found on the inside of the academy.

Self-Knowledge and Community: How They Are Connected

Self-knowledge is the first step to cultivating authenticity, but then we all need community with others. Palmer reminds us, "Community cannot take root in a divided life...only as we are in community with ourselves can we find community with others" (2017, p. 92). Palmer (2003) explains that "although higher education can stock people's minds with facts and theories, and train them in skillful means, it cannot help them grow larger hearts and souls" (p. 378). He goes on to say that, "A teacher has the power to compel students to spend many hours living in the light, or the shadow, of the teacher's inner life. Are we doing enough to help teachers-in-training understand their inner terrain in ways that will minimize the shadow and maximize the light?" (p. 378). This is especially important in teacher preparation. Teacher educators must stay healthy in body, mind, and spirit so that the teachers they instruct (and their students) will live in and through their respective teachers' inner light and soul, not their shadows.

Palmer asks, "What does it take to build relational trust?" He answers his own question by explaining that relational trust requires people "who are explorers of their own inner lives. It takes people who know something about how to get beyond their own egos; how to withdraw the shadow projections that constantly involve us in making 'enemies' out of others; how to forgive and seek forgiveness; how to rejoin soul and role" (Palmer, 2003, p. 385). Again, Palmer's wisdom comes through and speaks directly to the spiritual domains of teaching and learning.

A Call to Action, Deciding to Live Divided No More, Be Your Own Academic Forest Biome

In conclusion, this chapter is a "call to action" to readers to live in their own truths, to be authentic, and to bring their hearts into dialogue with their minds. Using the language of nature, I have mapped out my own journey. I urge my readers to create their own *academic forest biomes*. This does not mean isolation; it means living in your own truth, investing time for self-knowledge, and finding other like-minded individuals with whom you can create community. To those already in higher education, as well as those who are contemplating a life in academia, I give you one of my favorite sayings, "Revelations are for those who are having them." And, yes—it has been a revelation. The revelation itself is that, over the past several years, I have been going through a shift. This shift involves a process of transition and transformation in realizing I have created my own *academic forest biome*. The shift represents a blossoming and deepening of how Palmer has affected my life in academia. This "blossoming" for me has been in finding ways to *"live divided no more"* and to follow Palmer's articulated route for educational reform. By revisiting Palmer's work over time, I have realized that I had been following Palmer's educational reform without being fully aware of it. That is the revelation.

This chapter captured episodes of my academic journey from doctoral student to Assistant Professor, to earning tenure and Associate, and to Full Professor. As mentioned previously, I have found ways to survive—and even to thrive in academia. Some of my experiences of adapting to the *academic forest biome* have been full of joy and others have been soul-wrenching. I have gratitude for all of my experiences—as I learn so much from reflecting on them.

Living divided no more has kept my teaching-heart safe and my soul intact. Echoing Cesar Chavez' words at the beginning of this chapter— yes, we all need help—even if we are strong human beings. We need to stand strong as individuals, listen to our inner teachers, and cultivate self-knowledge. We also need to be in community with others, and, through this community—we can accomplish much and make a difference for ourselves, our colleagues, our students, and the academy itself.

References

Campbell, S. (2021, April 8). *Personal communication via email.*

Dalton, J. E., Hall. M. P., & Hoyser, C.E. (Eds.). (2019). *The whole person: Embodying teaching and learning through lectio and visio divina.* Rowman & Littlefield.

Dalton, J. E., Hall, M. P., Hoyser, C. E., & Jones, L. F. (2019). An ancient monastic practice. *The whole person: Embodying teaching and learning through lectio and visio divina* (pp. 1–10). Rowman & Littlefield.

Freire, P. (1998). *Pedagogy of freedom: Ethics, democracy, and civic courage.* Rowman & Littlefield.

Freire, P., Macedo, D., Koike, D., Oliveira, A., & Freire, A. M. A. (2018). *Teachers as cultural workers: Letters to those who dare teach.* Routledge.

Hall, M. P. (2019). Embodying deep reading: Mapping life experiences through lectio divina. In J. E. Dalton, M. P. Hall, & C. E. Hoyser (Eds.), *The whole person: Embodying teaching and learning through lectio and visio divina* (pp. 11–21). Rowman & Littlefield.

hooks, b. (2014). *Teaching to transgress: Education as the practice of freedom.* Routledge.

National Geographic Society. (2021, June 8). *Forest Biome.* https://www.nationalgeographic.org/encyclopedia/forest-biome/

National Geographic Society. (2021, May 31). *Biome.* https://www.nationalgeographic.org/encyclopedia/biome/

Palmer, P. (2000). *Let your life speak: Listening for the voice of vocation.* Jossey-Bass.

Palmer, P. J. (2003). Teaching with heart and soul: Reflections on spirituality in teacher education. *Journal of Teacher Education, 54*(5), 376–385.

Palmer, P. J. (2017). *The courage to teach: Exploring the inner landscape of a teacher's life.* Wiley.

CHAPTER 4

A '*World in Between*': A Reflection on Teaching and Learning

Aubrie K. Brault

If we want to grow as teachers -- we must do something alien to academic culture: we must talk to each other about our inner lives -- risky stuff in a profession that fears the personal and seeks safety in the technical, the distant, the abstract. (Palmer, 2017, p. 48)

INTRODUCTION

My chest was tight. I was short of breath. My eyes wanted to stain my taupe satin shirt with drops of salt water but they wouldn't come. I was holding on too tight, my body was too tense for even that simple release. It also felt like I didn't have time to cry. I was due to teach my class in about 50 minutes, and here I was hiding away on the other side of campus. It was an early afternoon in October of 2015. I sat in my 2000 Nissan Sentra, which, at that point, felt more put together than I was even with a blown up stereo, right-side windows not working, and an

A. K. Brault (✉)
University of Massachusetts Dartmouth, North Dartmouth, MA, USA

M. P. Hall and A. K. Brault (eds.), *Academia from the Inside*, https://doi.org/10.1007/978-3-030-83895-9_4

industrial tarp that my dad had taped down for me where a moonroof used to be.

I understood that stress was in my body. What I didn't understand was how I could move forward in this new role as the leader I knew myself to be. It was the third week of my very first teaching experience and my anxiety had finally caught up with me. The first few weeks I was able to maintain a facade, or step into my "representative" as author Glennon Doyle would call it (Doyle, 2017, p. 19). I had absolutely no prior teaching experience, and I believed I needed a facade because I didn't know who I really was as a teacher.

It is now 2021, and I am an Instructional Designer. I have lived through the pandemic. During this time, I, as a co-editor for *Academia from the Inside,* have spent considerable time excavating what I experienced inside academia during my graduate career from 2015 to 2017. While I can immediately draw connections to the ways in which my Master's in Professional Writing degree has helped me ascertain my professional goals and current standing, the writing of this chapter has allowed me to unearth the deeper meaning behind my time in the academy. Perhaps one example speaks this truth best, and serves as the basis for my chapter. In 2015, I believed that my journey in the academy began the day I entered orientation for a teaching fellowship I had earned. After writing this chapter, I see that it really began in the car that one October afternoon, when, for the first time, I asked myself, "who am I as a teacher?".

As I reflected on my journey of asking this question all throughout my time in the academy, I heard educator Parker Palmer's words. I believe these words embody the very challenge I faced in the academy, and the one I explore in this chapter. With his seminal work *The Courage to Teach,* Palmer dedicates chapters to one "simple premise" and that is that "good teaching cannot be reduced to technique; good teaching comes from the identity and integrity of the teacher" (2017, p. 10).

THE MOUNTAIN

My graduate journey began in Fall of 2015, the same year that I earned my bachelor's degree. I had just entered the Masters in Professional Writing Program at my same institution. As a graduate student in this program, I was awarded a teaching fellowship while also earning my degree. This meant that while I would take my own graduate classes at night, I would also teach two sections of an undergraduate English course, *Business Communications*. In terms of responsibilities, the teaching fellow role can be thought of as a part-time lecturer, making my graduate a dual experience. In the summer leading up to it, I spent a number of my days at the beach, but not in the water much or with friends. Instead, I was ten toes deep in the sand, pouring over the textbook I would base my syllabus on.

As someone who has been working since the age of fourteen, I have had experiences in various business settings. I thought this would be enough to give me context for some of the forms of communication I was about to instruct on in the course. In addition to the typical application writing such as resume and cover letters, I'd written customer communications such as information pamphlets and email marketing campaigns for my Father's waterproofing business growing up; throughout my sophomore and junior collegiate years, I'd written editorial articles that were published in the University's official magazine as well as for a national non-profit wellness publication. Then, in the summer between my junior and senior years, I held a marketing internship position at a local performing arts center. In that role, my main responsibilities included market research and drafting campaign materials. These were just a handful of experiences and there were many areas I didn't have experience in. As fear would have it, I focused on those gaps more than I did the experiences that added to and refined my capabilities.

To cope with that fear in my first semester of teaching, I relied heavily, and, explicitly on the textbook's material. I stuck as close to it as I could and as far away from my own experiences (voice and self) as possible, thinking that this would keep students further from imagining that I was an imposter. Class time followed over-intellectualized lesson plans to the minute. Lesson plans began with five minutes to recall what our last class covered and then how the current day's agenda connected to it. This would then be followed by a thinking, pairing, and sharing activity. I would pose a question to the students that was connected to their homework. They would then have several minutes to work on it individually before sharing their thoughts in small groups, and then once more as the class came together as a whole. Ultimately, I utilized this teaching method in an effort to spur creative ideas and eclectic conversation.

Ideally, points emerging from the think, pair, share activity would connect to the lecture that was intended for that day's class. This transition didn't always happen as smoothly as I would have hoped but it usually offered a jumping point. A PowerPoint lecture from anywhere from fifteen to thirty minutes would follow. The amount of time would vary depending on whether or not I included an additional activity to reinforce some of the lecture's key takeaways. I also included additional activities frequently in that first semester because I hadn't yet gotten comfortable introducing other supplemental sources. I would also apply the text quite literally. Lectures and instruction focused more on how to write within certain business genres than it did why and when to. This rigid class time was constructed intentionally to leave as little time as possible for students to have open dialogue with me, fearing they would ask me questions I wouldn't have answers for.

As much as fifty minutes could drag, it did. Feeling ridden with anxious agony, my breaking everything down into these small minute segments and activities helped carry me to the the end of class. In my mind I thought it was a win–win,—a way in which students were kept in close, hands-on contact with the material, freeing me to hide behind its rules, schemas, and infrastructure. Unfortunately, I was exposed more than ever, and saw that for students, hands-on contact with material by no means meant engaged. Around the 3-week mark, I overheard several students discussing how homework and in-class exercises just felt like busy work and then a student flat-out told me this to my face. This was in front of the whole class.

As someone who loved learning and felt like she was trying so hard, this criticism crushed me. I wanted to do right by the department, the students, even the curriculum, and of course, myself. I felt like a failure and I'd only just started. In this moment, I knew something had to change. Changes needed to occur in my teaching and I didn't know what that would look like or how to accept it.

THE FIRST PLATEAU: LOT EIGHT

On the day of my next class that change ended up being in parking lot eight. A misfit plot of land the university didn't quite know what to do with, half-full of maintenance trucks, campus transportation vehicles and admission faculty's cars who worked in the basement offices. As random as it sounds, and as bizarre a place as any to be one of personal growth, this was where I would begin my first self-care practice. I sat there, in that same taupe, satin shirt, with the car in park (still running) and one leg bent and up on the seat with me. My shoes were off, hair ruffled but makeup done just right, and as I was staring out at the lamp post in front of me the anxious stress in my body started to slow.

At first, I was just ruminating, steeped deep in a pity party of self-degradation. I hated the way I was feeling. My skin buzzed with nervous, prickly-like energy, and I hated how that intensity made my mental state-of-mind tight and snarly. Feeling like I was watching myself moment to moment in the classroom, trying to tuck every piece of my quirky self away so none of my own doubt would slip out and be recognized by others. I hated not being comfortable enough to be myself. I wanted to try and step out of the immediate hole that was paralyzing fear and, at the very least, build a bridge to navigating the classroom.

Finally, my mind, that had just felt so synonymous to a Jackson Pollock painting, began to slow, and a thought emerged. I recalled another teaching fellow, (Leslie, we'll call her for privacy's sake), who introduced me to guided meditation. Leslie was a yoga teacher and this meditation was one she often practiced herself. It was a guided meditation to cultivate gratitude, and while gratitude didn't feel like the exact area I was lacking in, or that might directly address where this fear was coming from, I intuitively knew that it didn't matter right then. I just knew I needed to shift my energy, create some space. So, I connected my phone to the Bluetooth speaker that had become my shotgun companion (since, recall my little 2000 Nissan Sentra's stereo had blown up), and played the guided meditation on gratitude. I had time; it was just over seven minutes.

In the guided meditation, I was asked to visualize different loved ones and embody why I was grateful for them. Feelings, thoughts, and memories unfurled for about seven people that came to my mind. Some were of mentors I had learned from, others were of friends I had cried with, and others were of some I had learned and laughed with. The memories elicited a deeper reflection of how I saw those people and what qualities they embodied that made it such a joy to be around them. At the height of the exercise, I was asked to envision hugging them each. I finally cried. In their embrace, I felt a release. I was reminded that I was part of an incredible, supporting, and loving community. The authenticity I had cultivated in that circle gave me strength and it was through consciously connecting to them in such a way that I felt reinvigorated. At the sound of a crystal clear bell, I opened my eyes.

While a part of me was hoping I'd meditated my way through a great class, and was recounting this story with my best friend at our favorite local coffee shop, I finally felt a sense of calmness. There was the beginning of an acceptance in those moments of gratitude, an acceptance of my stage in teaching development. I recognized that while, sure, I didn't have much of any *specific* teaching experience to pull from, I had people who believed in me. Further, I realized I was pressuring myself to display a greater level of experience than the Teaching Fellow Program demanded. This helped me decide that I was just going to have to be okay with where I was at and remain determined to keep growing. Once I held this acceptance and made this decision, I felt myself invite my own creativity back to the table. I was going to have to observe myself, react more honestly in the classroom, and be okay with coming up with new ideas, solutions, and connections in the moment. I was going to have to lean less on the how-to instruction of the book and more on the meaning-making I was capable of helping students generate and navigate...

I'm not going to lie and say I walked into the classroom that day with my head held high, firing on all cylinders with an engaging lesson plan. Paradoxically, it *was* the first time I didn't *pretend* to. I hadn't magically softened into a more comfortable way of moving throughout the classroom, but it was the first time I noticed more about the space, how the desks were lined up and how I stood behind my desk more often than not. I felt moved to make some small changes. I didn't take a whole minute to write the agenda on the white board and I was glad I wasn't wearing a dress. I wanted to more casually lean against the front of my desk and start to maintain a more conversational position in the classroom. It wasn't effortless but now for the first time I wasn't walking on glass.

The Power of Meditation

The effect of that one meditation had held enough impact that I felt compelled to make it a practice before every class that semester. I still poured over lesson plans in the hours or nights before a class; with the material in front of me, there were specifics I could obsess over and re-puzzle continuously. I just couldn't help myself. But when I carved out that time to meditate in my car, I intentionally didn't bring any of my class notes, computer, or even expectations. It was a space to listen to myself, quiet myself, and let go—to just be.

Gradually, I dedicated more time to this practice. By the third session, my meditation's purpose shifted from needing immediate relief and calmness to seeking understanding, as other feelings began to surface and name themselves. It was time to unpack some other, previous life experiences through which I questioned and developed my sense of identity. Up to that point in my life, I felt like I had been running a race, moving from one growing pain and social expectation to the next. Like many young adults growing up, my energy had primarily focused on how to be a good kid and student. I had been busy navigating cultural norms, social expectations, a changing body, evolving dreams, and practical milestones like graduating high school. For the ways in which this position challenged me, I hadn't thought of myself yet.

For the first time, I wasn't on the move, on to the next main milestone, concerned mainly with how it was adorned in promise and easily-identifiable opportunities, nor was I just a student sitting in a systematic structure that first and foremost asked me to wear the hat of—listen and participate. Now, I had agreed to spend time in a specific role wherein I was taking charge on the learning objectives and how to engage students. Rather than just gauging my own capacities and interests, I was involved with pushing the boundaries of learning for others, and to help students build bridges to their own ideas in connection to the material. In order to create a space for their exploratory participation, help them make those connections, and be present myself, I had to be more than intellectually available. I also needed to be emotionally available.

Realizing some immediate house-cleaning was in order for myself, I started leaving for parking lot eight earlier. The fifteen minutes it took me to decompress and walk through the guided meditation began collecting layers. Now, I wanted more time before the meditation to check in with myself on what I was feeling that very day, trying to see if it connected again to things that had already come up for me. My intention was to identify themes—and process what came from them—to trace back to deeper sources. It felt less about finding solutions, though that would have been nice, and more about unearthing connections, feelings, thoughts, experiences, and the like. I saw and felt that the more I dug, and sat in this all, the more I was cultivating some peace in my life. So, the 30 minutes I'd originally carved out for myself to get to the parking lot and meditate, quickly morphed into an hour. I began researching and integrating other guided meditations along with bringing a personal notebook for thoughts and reflections after.

Expanding My Sense of "Teacher"

Clearly, there was more to me as a teacher than the simple notion of it I had created for myself; I didn't realize that my experiences from other areas and times in my life would inform parts of my communication style, or problem solving, in the classroom. Of course, part of my confusion and frustration at the time came from not being able to see this connection fully. It has been in writing for this chapter that I am just now able to apply the deeper self-awareness I've cultivated from my years since graduate school to those experiences. And so, as I reflectively write about the assumptions I made then on what it meant to be a teacher, it seems naive to me, ludicrous even, that I had ever compartmentalized the teaching title and role in that way. If *I* was the one stepping into the classroom, how would my life experiences *not* be coming with me? Especially when those were the very things I was able to pull from to be selected for this teaching position during the interview process. On one hand, now that I know more about what it means to fully show up in circumstances, and that I'm the one who has to bring her authentic self to the moment (because most of the time no one else is going to ask me to and why should I rely on them to do that anyway), I'm stunned I didn't make this connection when hitting this mental, emotional block as a teacher. On the other hand, I look back over the years since and see how many life experiences, and my reflections on them, have brought me closer to this understanding. It's taken time, deep reflection, self-accountability, others holding me accountable, and blunt, hard honesty with myself. And I think in order to enact each of these,   it also required a renewed and deeper relationship to self-love.

But this is why parking lot eight was so critical. It was my beginning down that path. In those moments, I was tending to those things, those areas in between my other feelings, life experiences, ideas. Abstractly soothing and bringing them together to show up with me in my hours of teaching. While the larger revelations would take years as I mentioned, one immediate and major benefit I felt from developing this practice was a rejuvenated sense of creativity. I had resigned myself to a stereotype of what it meant to be a teacher. I had resigned myself to staying in the lanes of the syllabus I had been assigned, and I had resigned myself to thinking only in terms of that syllabus and class text. Prescription. Prescription. Prescription. Now that I had gotten that feedback from both my students verbally and my own body physiologically, I had new information that this level of prescription wasn't working. It gave me the permission I needed to think more outside of the box and for myself. In asking myself to pause and pivot, I was finally going back to a way of being present and trusting my capabilities in any given moment, whereas before I had allowed the intense and sole focus on the curriculum to demand this be a mutually exclusive exchange. In other words, I was done trading in technique for soul. I was craving to apply technique *with* soul.

Looking back on it now, I imagine some of those initial meditations also included moments of self-forgiveness. Now, I feel more self-aware than critical of myself but back then I was enormously, incredulously, unnecessarily critical of myself. At that time, it was hard for me to accept—I hadn't started off being as impactful as I'd imagined. I had to have that small ego-death in order to move forward, Ultimately, I used it as information to educate me on how I could reach the real potential I wanted. Unsurprisingly, this level of acceptance also helped me create a deeper sense of community around myself. I then felt more comfortable talking about the challenges I was internalizing. I wanted more than my journal to reflect on and comb through my thoughts. This was when I started opening up to my friends and family.

ESCAPING THE "MONKEY TRAP"

At times, my family and friends were sounding boards, listening to me as I ranted off my realizations and lamented my frustrations. Other times, I went to them with questions and felt the role of a student perhaps more than ever, as I internalized their life experiences, wisdom, and opinions. Many times it was a mixture of all of the above. However, there was one conversation that stands above almost all others. One afternoon in that first semester, my Stepfather introduced me to the metaphor of the South Indian Monkey Trap. Whether this was a method for trapping monkeys remains debated by historians. In this context, it was a metaphor put forth by Robert Pirsig in his book *Zen and the Art of Motorcycle Maintenance.* In his book, he explores the impact of how we assign value to our beliefs and decisions, using an illustration of a monkey. The monkey believes his best chance of food (and survival) is a mound of sweet rice at the center of a coconut, which was placed within and made accessible via a man-made hole in the coconut. This hole is just big enough to allow the monkey access to the rice when entering with an open hand. But it is not big enough that he can redact his hand with the fist full of rice. The only way to get his hand back out, would be to let go of his prized food. The coconut is also chained and staked to the ground, so he cannot leave with it either. But out of fear of losing this newfound food, the monkey is afraid to let go... How long does he stay here, stuck? To paraphrase Educator Keri Zurlini et al. (2015), Pirsig's metaphor demonstrates human nature's "value rigidity", a situation in which a person has prescribed a high level of value to a specific item, outcome, or idea. The danger in prescribing this high value is that a person is then prone to manipulation as the mind idolizes that item, outcome etc., as it was first envisioned or encountered. Such a fixation can keep a person within a short-sighted mindset—even when the very item may be harming them in some way. If their grip remains tight, this also distorts possibilities for recognizing alternative resolutions, keeping the individual in a perpetual state of disconnectedness and ultimately, failure. An individual may have the very thing they always thought they wanted but it comes at a cost that takes more away from the person than it provides, it is not life-sustaining.

With this metaphor, my Stepfather was illustrating where I was fixated like the monkey—where I held on to my ideal version of what I thought my experience should look like in that semester. I was so set on the idea of teaching I'd created beforehand (which was also compounded and reinforced by my insecurities) that I had carved out my own coconut hole and refused to let go of the rice (Keynes, 2002). Then, when I was faced with the unexpected feedback from both my students and my own body, I panicked. The feedback was disproving the construct I had created for myself. I felt unable to let go of it at first because, without it, where would my sense of stability come from? I sat in this fear until my stepfather simply but sternly stated, "you're holding on too tight". I don't know why that simple statement was what it took but when he said this, it clicked. Why my creativity had disappeared. Why I felt like I was walking on glass. Why I felt stuck. I was. Stuck.

I realized my construct of teaching, my ideal, was born out of my limited experience. Up to that point in my academic life, I had maintained the role of student, and I had mastered it. My aptitude and skills for navigating the art of study were both reinforced verbally to me and reflected back to me in my grades. And I had been proud since that wasn't always the case; for most of my elementary and middle school experiences, I struggled academically. Even with the most supportive parents, it was hard for me to focus in those early years, making for fairly mediocre grades across the board. What's more is that I wasn't interested in reading yet and math was my worst subject by a long mile.

Alongside my student career, I only had the limited perspective of what it meant to be a teacher through the instructors I had access to and was assigned growing up. They were my method models; over the years, I observed various methods for time management, communication, activity building, and more. Some I enjoyed, others I didn't. That aside, what I didn't understand when initially internalizing these observations, and then trying to call on them for teaching, was that teaching couldn't be reduced to technique.

Teaching proved to be more multi-dimensional than learning as a student. It brought an entirely new layer to the academic experience for me; whereas a student I would receive information on a process, framework, or algorithm and oftentimes apply them, those graded tests of application would happen on a smaller scale, and essentially, in a vacuum. Projects and outcomes, the applications of my knowledge, weren't being applied to real-life situations and allowed to play over time. Of course, I shared my ideas in class and with other students but I knew they rippled out with less bravado, less impact, because others' ideas affected me that way. From what I recall, I generally didn't listen to other students in quite the same way I attended to the teacher during lectures or individual work. It was never personal but practical. I wasn't being graded by my peers. So, if I was emotionally and cognitively available to pick up on their shared content in class, great, but otherwise it wasn't much neither here nor there. I grew out of this small degree of isolation and complacency the further I went in my schooling, especially college. But the one area of my student career that always qualified this early disposition, was when called to work with group projects since grades and learning are so interconnected.

As a first-time teacher, I was embodying a new sense of agency—I had to drive the direction of the classroom; I was now working with others who had a different kind of vested interest in what I brought forth. It was the first time my words, questions, lesson plans, class structure ideas, and more were being practiced in real time and accounted for by not one, but two parties. Of course, the department was evaluating my methods, measuring how well I helped students meet the articulated learning objectives of the course. Simultaneously, students were evaluating my ability to clearly introduce and deconstruct ideas so that they in return could make meaningful projects out of them, or at the very least make satisfactory grades. Now, my academic experience extended beyond that of just my own expectations, criteria, and motivations, it included all of theirs as well. What's more, is that unlike the student experience, wherein one's relationship to course material remained within the boundaries of that one class, I was now responsible for this course over a period of time. There was a new longevity to it, and for the first time I had room to take feedback I'd gotten in the classroom and apply it to other iterations of that class.

With Reflection, Space, and Community, New Teaching Practices Emerged

That first semester broke me open. Under the surface, behind the mask, my body and subconscious had been itching to be freed. With my younger emotional maturity and confidence, I didn't see that it was me who could offer that permission. So, I unknowingly waited to receive that validation from an external source—my students. Their feedback was the catalyst to the personal journey I've described throughout this chapter. In the months that followed, I incorporated critical changes such as investing more personally into my teaching. I invested more into our Teaching Fellowship Program's pedagogy class and restructured my days to maximize my personal working style.

Upon first hearing about the required pedagogy class, it seemed mostly a smart and practical decision made by the department. Many of the Teaching Fellows coming into the program had no prior teaching experience. I saw this class as helping to add to that critical area of inexperience, a little like a crutch. But as the first few weeks unfurled in parallel to my very real exposure in the classroom, the value I put on this class increased. By design, the course integrated reflective and project-based learning with pedagogical practices. Elements of the course included bi-weekly reflections on published articles, stemming from various areas of expertise and perspectives in education. We also had to apply frameworks from different pedagogical practices to our own lesson plans and present them to the larger group for discussion. Personally, this was an ideal outlet for me. I was both encouraged and incentivized to creatively approach curriculum design and had ample opportunity to get feedback on it. What's more is that this was happening in a protected, small space. Teaching fellow numbers averaged about 15 between the 2-year cohorts, and this class was required of us all on a bi-weekly basis. I took more and more time to prepare for this class. Looking back on this element of my graduate experience, I think it was an incredibly well-designed, impactful prototyping experience.

A second key experience was the designated teaching fellow space, termed "The Balcony". I developed a love-hate relationship with this space, mainly given to the fact that it would become a space that would hold just as much stress for me as it did joy and pride. Ironic now that I remember it as one of my fondest places on campus... Physically, it was an odd little space. Sometime in the 30 years prior to my getting there, it was converted into an office space, supporting both staff and faculty. By the time I got there in 2015, it was specifically for teaching fellows. In tandem with the unique, obtuse, and all-cement-style that our campus was designed in, this little piece of real estate could best be described as a jetty, hanging out and over one of the three main atriums in the Liberal Arts building on the third floor. It was the first door/office space welcoming students to the administrative realm of the English Department. (I always felt this location was metaphorically representative of how we as teaching fellows were both a hybrid position as well as a conduit for other students. To some degree, we could relate to both worlds simultaneously.)

"The Balcony" was a shared space for teaching fellows, pushing an interesting mix of corporate style desks and circular lunch tables together. Depending on who taught at what time, and how much work they wanted to do here, teaching fellows would find a space to hunker down and prepare for their day. In this space, I prepared lesson plans, printed materials, and held office hours. But I would also grade here, eat lunch here, and do my own graduate research here. Others did as well. Within less than a month of our first semester this became an established watering hole for my first-year cohort (there were two cohorts of teaching fellows at a given time). For whatever reason, the cohort I belonged to seemed particularly close. I might now attribute this to sharing similar values of education, politics, and work ethic but for whatever the reasons, I found myself working alongside them in this space most days, and it was influential to my identity as a teacher.

Unlike the required pedagogy class, "The Balcony" served as an unstructured, familiar space. This is where I felt I truly got to know the others in my cohort as people, not just "the other teaching fellows". In casual conversations, I eventually learned varying aspects of their other interests, family members, hobbies, and lessons learned. As I cultivated friendships in this space, I naturally felt more comfortable and inclined to discuss work with them as well. As teaching fellows and first-time teachers, we faced many of the same challenges, considered many of the same things. At "The Balcony", I had the opportunity to explore these at length and with some opportunity to do so in more light-hearted ways when appropriate for the situation, simply given the more casual context of the space. I distinctly recall enlightening conversations around grade norming, learning objectives, and homework assignments. But most influential to my teaching identity, and my favorites, were the discussions around classroom lecture style and approaches, new, supplemental resources, and new lesson plan ideas. Ideas and resources from these conversations started flooding "The Balcony" for shared content, as well as my head. Before or after these conversations, it's likely you would have found me scribbling away in one of my little black notebooks, drawing connections to previous ideas on other pages and beginning new ones.

The little black notebooks were part of a personal system I created for classroom reflection and curriculum creativity. In part, this practice was inspired by my car meditations, which had gotten me more into a practice of thinking out loud with myself on paper. I bought this same style of notebook every time I needed another—all black covers with clean, simple, unlined white pages. I naturally veered toward an outlet for myself with no lines. Growing up I felt that lines, not even metaphorically limited me, but literally constrained my thinking. I've always engaged better with ideas, and connected them to each other, in non-linear ways. Blank space allowed me to mind map, brainstorm, and illustrate concepts to myself freely. In lesson planning, I also found planning lessons through the computer both confounding and annoying. While I know of course, I'm not the first to make this seemingly simple shift, it had a profound impact on me. I found it simpler to organize and reiterate my approach for the day's lesson plan when using a pencil and being away from the screen. (It felt more natural and also offered a more easily accessible place to add contextual notes for observations made in class wherein I had a moment to myself. Granted, I would learn a balance for this practice as well...).

One day, on seeing several pages of what could have possibly been mistaken for a Pollock-sketch, I realized I was overcomplicating a lesson. I had revised the same lesson three times over. Some could only be so well thought out beforehand, and others would be just what they needed to be if I allowed them to rest and come to life on their own. I had enough structure and methods for approaching a day's lecture, it was more a matter of from what angle I preferred to execute it. It was at that point, I had another pivotal moment of self-awareness—I would be best prepared to teach in the mornings... when I had no time to make further changes, and (what felt like) my biggest social-emotional exercise would be done for the day. I call out the latter because there were still some nerves I experienced in the classroom, and believe that these are what fostered most of the fuel for those of my excessive efforts. Fortunately, the department had an 8 a.m. slot that I could take on in the next semester. I did, and it worked beautifully. Evidently, a reasonable enough bedtime (when I could manage it) the night before was the kind of book-end motivation I needed to close one of my little black notebooks and let what I had already prepared be enough.

A third area of influence, filling various corners and margins of my notebooks, was my own student experience. Within hours of teaching my class sections, I transitioned back to my graduate studies where I observed tenured professionals maintain what felt like a balance of both a hands-off approach as well as an incredibly involved one. Looking back on it, I would attribute this to ideas of presence and authenticity. They appeared personally interested in their areas of expertise and allowed this to naturally show both in classroom and office hours.

I interpreted their time in the classroom as present, trusting, and flexible. A degree of full presence in that they seemed focused on the day's objectives—and yet generally—also socially-emotionally and cognitively available to meet their students at the moment. I felt they cultivated a sense of trust-worthiness through their actions. Over time, I saw many of them openly invite me to take a stance, or offer a perspective, opposing their own. They showed me that I could have a measure of free reign in the classroom. It was, in part, my territory to explore and landmark ideas. I can't recall ever being interrupted mid-point. Instead, I recall being allowed to explore tangents and have revelations in the moment. This created a more comfortable space for me to ask questions of them as well as other students. I internalized this observation, making note that I would like to create a similar atmosphere in my classroom as well.

In addition to observing their disposition and communication styles that created this dynamic learning space for me, I also observed the ways in which they worked with their course content. Rather than spending a notable amount of time introducing exercises and examples, and examining it in it of themselves, my professors used them as touchpoints. They weren't a primary focus. Instead, they were vehicles to present us with rhetorical strategies, so that we could ask better questions of them. I recall that shift in critical thinking, and how it was reinforced, and yet more how it pushed me as a student to take the examples further still. In doing so, I developed more practice and tools to stretch from the micro to the macro and back again. In other words, they helped me access underlying theories in more tangible ways. As a result, I returned to the explicit examples and project-based outcomes with more specifics, tools, and context, more mastery of execution. I see this as an incredibly marketable skill for teachers and benefit for students as such examples and project-based outcomes evolve into real project deliverables and business outcomes after graduation.

In taking at least two graduate courses at any given time, I could also more easily draw on the proof that there were different ways to accomplish the principle-based, dialogical style of teaching my professors exemplified. Short of knowing the life experiences that shaped them to that point, the only variable I could identify that made these approaches work for them—was their personalities. It was their embodiment of this authenticity that in part gave me permission to do the same. And so I did.

CONTINUED CHANGE, TRANSFORMATIVE FEEDBACK

The reflection, space, and community created through the resources explored in the section above culminated into continued change for me as a teacher. Over the weeks in my own teaching, I revisited curriculum design. I looked to where I could recenter lectures on the rhetorical strategies driving them, and use more thoughtful exercises as homework assignments rather than blocks of time in the short 50 minutes we had. As I integrated these notions in, pivoting constantly along the way, I became more comfortable walking among students and returning to the white board to illustrate varying points of our conversation. More supplemental resources were accompanying homework exercises in my now flipped classroom, with examples from them holding more screen time in class; lecture slides throughout the different cornerstones of my class lessened in words and became stronger in concept. This of course allowed for more direct engagement with the students... something a revered professor of mine noticed when observing me in my last semester...

About three months before I graduated with my Master's, I was observed by a faculty member. Their evaluation of my classroom strategy was one of the final requirements of the Teaching Fellowship Program. It just so happened to be one of the program's leading coordinators and a professor I revered greatly. Albeit nervous, I pushed on with my intended objectives for the day in the rhythm that I had found and established for myself that semester. At the end of class, I felt confident in how the class had gone and was excited to hear any feedback. A few students still gathered their belongings as my professor and I shuffled out of the classroom. My professor made a general remark of how it went well and that they would review specifics with me in our meeting later that day.

When I later met the professor in their office, they shared with me how they experienced the flow of my classroom. They specifically called out the transitions from one activity to the next, as being well scaffolded and supporting of the intended objectives. They paused for a moment, then summarized how I also used different modes and mediums of communication to support those different learning moments—moving from sitting with students in their groups, to the white boards at different ends of the room, and back again to some lecture material. What my professor shared with me next, I simply never would have imagined. With a heartfelt tone and kindred eyes they looked at me and said, "I wish I could teach like you."

To this day, I am moved by that admission. I revered this Professor because I felt they did exactly that! I felt they embodied a sense of self in the classroom that allowed them to move through the content, academic expectations, student responses, and classroom dynamics alike with many of the isms that just made them, them! For example, this professor would openly admit in our class when they didn't know something well, share some of their life experiences that related to discussion points, and made it clear when they were choosing not to answer something in the classroom as an attempt to push us further in reaching a conclusion. What's more, is they didn't adhere to an overly professional, almost corporate-like stature or garb in the classroom. Still maintaining professionalism, it was clear where they made small choices that were simply more comfortable for them and somewhat reflective of their personality. Again, it gave me some permission to essentially think in a little less sterile and perfunctory manner, and be more creative.

Reflecting on this evaluation led me to also consider other experiences indicative that some growth as a teacher, and person, had occurred. In my last two semesters teaching Business Communications, several key student experiences stick out, each profound to me in their own way.

In the Fall semester, I was working with a student who didn't feel particularly motivated for one of the course projects. The assignment was to research and apply for an internship in their field of interest. Some of this student's effort in class, and on homework, suggested to me they felt it was a "why bother" or an "it's over before it even started" type of situation. So, in homework and in class time, I took extra effort to align their work with the rhetorical strategies I sensed that they felt were so far away from them. I wanted to show them they weren't—that they were accessible, just like my professors were showing me.

Over several weeks, I slowly witnessed more classroom engagement. To my surprise one day, this student enthusiastically asked for some of my time after class. At that time, they shared with me that they had gotten an interview and were excited about it. Thrilled for the student, I congratulated them and let them know that I'd be happy to be a sounding board for ideas they wanted to talk through for the interview or anything related. Months down the road, I would find out they got the internship. I know, that had this student been in my first year's class, I would have nervously brought them to the book and drowned them in genre-writing and document design techniques. Whereas now, instead, I was asking the bigger questions and helping them to create a foundation of reasoning. The motivation this student needed was in understanding "a why" beyond techniques, and the book wasn't going to do that without me bringing my own sense of identity to the situation. I know that it was my ability to draw on other life experiences that helped me help the student. Tapping into my own experiences allowed me to consider and apply frameworks that I saw would best answer the situation's context. Perhaps most clearly and succinctly, I drew on how I could relate; I could relate as a young adult trying to navigate social norms and my own personal expectations as well as a student frustrated at times by how little I felt empowered to shape my own educational experience.

There was a second, meaningful event wherein another business major student decided that they wanted to minor in English Writing, Rhetoric, and Communication. It was two months into that same Fall Semester of the previous anecdote, when this second student stepped away from a group activity to share with me that this class inspired them to make such a choice. To paraphrase, they said the course had made them consider other areas of opportunity and skills they felt they weren't getting in their major but that would be beneficial for them in how they envisioned their career. Being the whole-hearted English nerd I was (double-major undergrad) this simply made my heart jump with joy. I knew this student was about to go on a journey of asking more questions and having illuminating theoretical conversations. What sunk in later that night as I wrapped up homework grading for the day on "The Balcony" was how our class discussions and focus on rhetorical strategies had inspired her. As this chapter has illustrated, I didn't allow those to be a part of my first year's lesson plans in the way that it was now. I immediately felt a lightness and a grounding at the same time. I was starting to see more and more just how valuable those parking-lot-eight moments were.

Conclusions: Recycle, Upcycle

Writing this chapter has been a deeply reflective experience and practice in and of itself. It has impacted me in ways that I continue to see unfold, even now in my corporate job as an instructional designer. Educators, such as Palmer and Freire, were some of the first thought-leaders to provide me with language and concepts to unpack the sense of identity I developed during my time in the academy. With their works, others', and time to make meaning of my own experiences, I have developed a much deeper relationship with, not only the past version of myself who experienced these events, but also my definition of identity in the academy in general.

As I reflect further on the impact this reflection has had on me, I can't help but think of my own metaphor. In 2019, I had the privilege to take a trip through parts of Europe. On my first day visiting the city of Amsterdam, I came across a small store that upcycled materials people would normally throw out. Here artists took soda bottle caps, melted them down, and cut them into jewelry. They also had some of the most unusual and yet equally enticing bracelets transformed from bicycle tire rubber. Those aside, my favorite purchases came from years' worth of work—generations that had been hidden. Multi-colored and also oddly shaped, I bought two pairs of earrings that portrayed the unique colors they did because they had been scratched off from the furthest back wall of the store. There, for decades, almost every business that newly rented the space would paint over the brick wall. Creating layers upon layers. The latest store owners and artists, that I was now buying from, discovered these layers of paint when coming into the space and wishing to restore the wall to its original brick.

I now see my teaching identity (and my identity overall) as one of the earrings from that wall. Over the years, it, like me, collected new colors, and when having the opportunity to change yet again, was transformed and made into something more wholesome—from its collective experience—something even more beautiful than the individual colors that it was previously asked to hold one at a time.

References

Carpenter, S. R., & Brock, W. A. (2008). Adaptive capacity and traps. *Ecology and Society, 13*(2). https://doi.org/10.5751/es-02716-130240

Doyle, G. (2017). *Love warrior* (Reprint ed.). Flatiron Books.

Freire, A. M. A., Macedo, D. P., Koike, D. A., & Oliveira, A. (2005). *Teachers as cultural workers*. Routledge.

Keynes, J. M. (2002). *The general theory of employment, interest and money by John Maynard Keynes*. Marxists Internet Archive. https://www.marxists.org/reference/subject/economics/keynes/general-theory/preface.htm

Palmer, P. J. (2017). *The courage to teach: Exploring the inner landscape of a teacher's life*. Wiley.

Pirsig, R. M. (1999). *Zen and the art of motorcycle maintenance: An inquiry into values*. Random House.

Zurlini, G., Petrosillo, I., Bozsik, A., Cloud, J., Aretano, R., & Lincoln, N. K. (2015). Sustainable landscape development and value rigidity: The Pirsig's monkey trap. *Landscape Online, 40*, 1–19. https://doi.org/10.3097/lo.201540

CHAPTER 5

Embracing Otherness in the Self that Teaches

Elizabeth Bifuh-Ambe

Tired, but not defeated; knocked down, but not knocked out
Much distance to cover; so, we stand, and again we walk!

The story of a first-generation Black woman who came from Africa and
entered U.S. academia may seem straightforward, but my story is not.
In this chapter, I examine the differences and similarities in both educational settings, the challenges encountered, and successes achieved; but
most importantly, the courage that helped me transcend the difficulties
inherent within these settings, and find the grace not only to belong, but
thrive in academia. Where one starts a story matters. If a story starts from
the beginning, it may very well have a different plot than one that starts
from the middle, then twists and turns, and flashes backward to loop
with earlier occurrences; then skips forward again, in an attempt to weave
all the threads of the plot together into one whole tapestry. Although

E. Bifuh-Ambe (✉)
University of Massachusetts Lowell, Lowell, MA, USA
e-mail: elizabeth_ambe@uml.edu

the plot may not be clearly defined, the emotions associated with each event are always crystal clear. Usually, when I look back at my life in U.S. academia, I recognize a series of tumbling events and a cascading mixture of emotions associated with each. The emotions seem to vie for primacy, often leaving me wondering if the feelings associated with the events determine the significance of each event; or serve to remind me of a chronology: such as the beginning, the middle, or somewhere near the end of this road that I still walk. One feeling that has mostly been present though, is the feeling of Otherness. I have always had to remind myself that despite what appears on the surface as Otherness, we as educators can each fit into the intricately crafted mosaic of the U.S. educational landscape. If we dig deep into our souls we will find within, a common humanity and oneness with our students and our colleagues.

Edmund Husserl, the founder of phenomenology, describes Otherness as the identification of the other human being, in their differences from the Self. The Self constitutes the cumulation of factors in the self-image of a person, which amounts to the person's acknowledgment of being real. These factors could be age, gender, socioeconomic status, or other markers that contribute to a person's self-worth. In my case, race, national origin, my outfits, and even my bubbly personality, appeared to set me apart as different from my colleagues. Many in the academia are taciturn, and clearly, there is a preference for an austere demeanor. Otherness is a term that serves to identify the "Who?" and "What?" of the Other, as distinct and separate from the symbolic order of things that constitute the Self. The Other is therefore, that which is different from, and opposite to the Self. In group settings, Self is synonymous with "Us" and "the Same," and Otherness, with "Them." Us and Them, constitute oppositional, but correlative relationships which are defined by essential, yet superficial characteristics. Otherness is often viewed as different from the Real (the authentic) in social norms and social identity, and therefore out of the Standard. According to *The New Fontana Dictionary of Modern Thought*:

> The condition of Otherness is a person's non-conformity to and with the social norms of society; and Otherness is the condition of disenfranchisement (political exclusion), effected either by the State or by the social institutions (e.g., the professions) invested with the corresponding sociopolitical power. Therefore, the imposition of Otherness alienates the person

labelled as "the Other" from the center of society, and places him or her at the margins of society, for being the Other. (p. 620)

In every space there exist degrees of difference also referred to as diversity. These differences can simply be to small degrees of preference or entirely different ways of thinking, being, and doing. When diversity or difference in social, professional, or political spaces are viewed as inferior, the practice of Othering that sets in can lead to exclusion and displacement of the subaltern from the social group, to the margins. Academia is no exception. Whether this is admitted or not, Othering exists in academia. While important strides have been made to acknowledge, accommodate, and even profess to celebrate diversity, it is an understatement to maintain that much work remains to be done in valuing and validating diverse ways of thinking, doing, and being, in academia. Having been an educator in this system now for almost 20 years, I know this well, first-hand.

Entering U.S. Academia

I was born in Cameroon, West Africa. I first came to the U.S. in 1998 when I was in my mid-thirties. Although I already had a Post Graduate Diploma in Education, I came to the U.S. to pursue a Master's Degree in Education (M.Ed.) in order to hone my professional skills. I was teaching English to middle and high school students at the American School of Niamey, Niger, serving as a UNICEF consultant, and writing grants to improve the literacy rate, especially for girls in parts of Africa. This American university, where I was taking my M.Ed. courses was located in the southern part of the US. They offered a summer program in graduate education, which afforded me the opportunity to commute between Africa and the U.S. during the summer months. For two consecutive summers, I would teach during the school year, and then travel to the U.S. and take 12 credit hours of education courses. While back in Africa, I would take classes online to complete the 30-credits Master's Degree requirement.

Online learning was just starting to become an option in the U.S., and my cohort of graduate students in the summer program were unaware participants in the experiment for the virtual learning model that was being adopted by many universities within the U.S.A. I became a "lab rat" par excellence for testing online learning from another continent, at a time when 5G high-speed Internet had not yet been invented. Home

Internet was not a commonplace amenity and most handheld devices did not have Internet Operating Systems (IOS). While some nations in the Western hemisphere had already advanced in these technologies, Africa had not yet adopted these technologies and approaches. The time zone difference was also a challenging factor with learning online from another continent. Niger is 6 hours ahead of U.S. standard time; so, taking online classes meant that when a graduate class was scheduled for 5:00 p.m. U.S. standard time, it was 11:00 p.m. Niger time. The only computer that was hooked up to the Internet was in my husband's office, and we had to drive across town to get there. It was always a hazardous drive, since we had to cross the main bridge over the River Niger, which runs through the town of Niamey, separating the commercial section of the city from the other side of town that hosted the main campus of the University of Niamey, Niger. The students and faculty of this university have historically been involved in protests demanding socio-political change in the country, and violent strikes were commonplace.

On one such night, after we had crossed the bridge to the other side, university students staged a sit-in strike, burning car tires to block off the bridge to any incoming or outgoing traffic, as they demanded better housing conditions. We could not get back home after my classes ended at about 2:30 a.m., and had to wait huddled up in the car, shivering in the cold harmattan temperatures, terrified for our lives. It wasn't until mid-morning that the police dispersed the student protesters and cleared the bridge so that townspeople trapped on either side of the bridge could cross over. I had put in at least 12 hours just to attend one online graduate class session! But I was determined, and I did not complain. The lack of consideration by those offering online courses of the possible lack of technology in certain communities, and how this could potentially exclude those communities from acquiring an education, crossed my mind occasionally, but I would quickly shut down that thought. After all, this was something I'd chosen to do, and I was not going to blame anybody for not accommodating me. Looking back, I believe that those difficult experiences as a graduate student prepared me for the challenges that I would face when I joined the U.S. academia as a full-time faculty. Being a Black woman from Africa, with a non-American accent, embodying speech patterns that were different (and often referred to by colleagues as having a voice that carried, a euphemism of being too loud), wearing clothes that were different, teaching courses in Language Arts and Literacy in Colleges of Education that were predominantly White, in both student and faculty demographics, in the U.S. where 84% of full-time college professors are White, spelled Otherness, in many ways than one!

I completed the M.Ed. in the expected year and a half (two summer semesters, with online and independent study courses completed in fall and spring semesters between the summers), and applied to the doctoral program at the same institution and was accepted. My plan was to continue commuting between Africa and the U.S., but the Dean of the College called me into her office and told me that this would not be feasible. She said if I did that, it would take almost forever to complete the program. Whether I decided to persist in commuting or not, she wanted me to know that part of the doctoral program required a year's uninterrupted residency, without which I would not be conferred the degree. I was undecided how to proceed, but the Dean, who saw something in me that she admired, came up with a solution. She offered me a teaching assistantship. I accepted her offer and subsequently moved to the U.S. with my family to pursue a Ph.D. in Education. I continued to take 12 doctoral credit hours, while teaching three undergraduate courses (9 credit hours) as part of my assistantship. It was a heavy workload, and the schedule was grueling, but I'm a hard worker—so I threw myself into the work with determination. But twenty-four hours in a day was not enough to accomplish the responsibilities of doctoral student, undergraduate instructor, and mother. So, I did the only logical thing I could think of to gain more time for my many commitments. I started sleeping less and less hours, and continued cutting back on my hours of sleep, until I reached an average of two hours of sleep per night. For the next three years, while I completed my Ph.D., I slept no more than two hours per day! It was a huge sacrifice. I had no social life. All I did was work. I spent most of my waking hours either in classrooms, in the library, or in my office. When I look back, I don't really know how I did it. Most of the time I was tired, but I could not allow myself to "feel" the tiredness. I kept pushing myself because I knew I didn't have the "luxury" of sleeping longer hours.

DOCTORAL PROGRAM STRESSES AND THE NEED FOR SELF-CARE

Usually some of my peers and I would go to the cafeteria to eat, and I would always be the last to finish my meal. I just didn't have the energy to eat fast enough, and frankly, eating fast is not a cultural thing with which Africans are familiar. In Africa, mealtimes are a time of communion, and people savor their food and linger as long as they wish. In fact, the French colonial system which Cameroon had inherited had a break in the middle of the day. Workers came home at noon, ate lunch, and some would even wash it down with a glass of wine if they were so inclined, then take a nap, and return to work at 2:30 p.m. So, I struggled with 'wolfing' down my food as my colleagues seemed to do, and after a while they got tired of waiting around for me to finish. They would eat their food quickly and head back to the department without me, while making benign remarks like "Liz is just a slow eater." I didn't mind. I knew we were all very busy, and nobody had time to waste sitting around in the cafeteria. On a certain day however, one of my peers watched me a little more closely and asked me if I was alright. I said "yes," but I was just tired. She asked me if I had taken my vitamins that day, and I asked her what vitamins were? Her eyes grew large with disbelief. She said something like "Do you mean you are doing these rigorous programs with no vitamin supplements?" I told her I didn't even know what she was talking about. When I was done eating, she told me to follow her. We went directly from the cafeteria to her dorm room, where she gave me one tablet of Vitamin C (I don't recall how many milligrams), and one tablet of Vitamin E, and a glass of water. I swallowed them, and that whole day I felt a surge of energy coursing through me. So, I approached her the following day and asked her where I could purchase some of the vitamins she'd given me. She wrote the names down on a piece of paper and directed me to the Walgreens Pharmacy that was just around the corner of the street, across from the university. I still tell people today that vitamins and other food supplements gave me the sustenance I needed and saved me from dropping dead at some point in my doctoral program, and that is no lie! While I did everything within my powers to uphold my professional career, my kids and spouse had learned to do most of the house chores by themselves. The last of my four sons, who was only 9 when we moved to the U.S., learned how to slot quarters into machines to do his own laundry at the laundromat that served the students in the student housing units. Before we moved to the U.S., my kids had not done any serious housework. Their parents, being expatriate workers in international organizations in Niger, had benefit packages that included paid house help, drivers, gardeners, etc. It was a difficult adjustment for the whole family. My two teenage sons were forced to grow up very fast;

do their homework and help their junior siblings in their schoolwork too. The oldest learned how to drive at 16 and became a lifesaver because he could shuttle his siblings to after-school activities, while doing his own activities such as playing soccer in the junior varsity team. My second son used the time that I was not attentive to his needs to hang out with the wrong crowds. In pursuing a Ph.D., I had set unrealistic expectations for my teenage sons.

REFLECTIONS ON MY EXPERIENCES IN U.S. ACADEMIA

My experiences within academia are filled with a range of emotions. There are moments of deep sadness, like when I was denied tenure and promotion from Assistant to Associate Professor at a Predominantly White Institution (PWI) in the Northeastern part of the U.S. I had done everything a tenure-track faculty needed to do to get promoted. In fact, I had exceeded the standards, when compared to the two White men and one White female who had just been promoted to Associate Professors in the years leading up to my application. I know because I had borrowed two of their binders to see how items were organized. I had published nine scholarly articles (eight as solo or first author) in national peer reviewed journals. One of my publications "Inviting Reluctant Adolescent Readers into the Literacy Club: Some Comprehension strategies to Tutor Individual or Small Groups of Reluctant Readers," published in the *Journal of Adolescent and Adult Literacy*, *50(8)*, 632–639, had been selected by the International Reading Association (IRA) as one of its first 10 podcasts, when the organization decided to start producing academic podcasts. They had selected my article, due to its impact on the field, and the goal for going digital was "to reach a new, wider and possibly younger audience," (IRA, personal communication to author, October, 2007). I had published a monograph, completed eighteen (18) presentations at international, national, and regional peer-reviewed conferences, and participated in over twenty-six (26) professional meetings at international, national, local, and departmental levels. In grant writing at the institution where I was applying for tenure, I had participated in securing eight grants: five as the Primary Investigator (PI), two as the Co-PI and one as Partner, with an interdisciplinary group of colleagues from other departments across the university. Four of the grants were internal grants awarded by the university, one small grant funded by State Farm, and one, funded by the Massachusetts Department of Secondary

Education (DESE). Among the grants that I had acquired as Co-PI was a $1,631,722.00 (One million, six hundred and thirty-one thousand, seven hundred and twenty-two dollars) Professional Development Grant awarded by the U.S. Department of Education. We submitted under the title: *Preparing Excellent Teachers for All (English) Language Learners (PETALLS)*. It was the largest grant ever acquired in the Graduate School of Education where I worked, and I was the expert on English Language Learners, with many publications on this demographic of students, and experience teaching them in my previous professional engagements. One of the primary requirements for being PI or Co-PI on this grant was to have a diverse faculty member. Between the Pi and (Co-PI), I was that diverse faculty member, and the only one equipped with the experiential and scholarly background to implement the grant in the targeted demographics for students. It is safe to say that the grant was awarded because one of us met all the requirements set by the Federal Government. One year after we got the grant, (the year that I was going up for tenure), the PI and Dean of the College conspired with other unknown personalities at the University, and wrote a letter informing me that my services would no longer be needed on the grant. They had no right to do that! It was a U.S Government Federally funded grant! But they did it anyway. How that incident evolved and was resolved would be a chapter for another book! I was very active in seeking grants, and one big grant that I'd applied for as PI that was not funded but is worth mentioning, was a planning grant submitted to the United States Agency for International Development-Higher Education for Development initiative (USAID-HED), with the goal of promoting bilateral education initiative between U.S. universities and universities abroad. I was also very active in service, both to the university, and in the community. At the time I was denied tenure, I was serving as a reviewer to six (6) scholarly journals as well as acting as a reviewer for the American Educational Research Association (AERA) annual conference. I was also serving as a consultant/workshop facilitator and a member of the hiring committee for administrators in local public school districts. I had served as a keynote speaker for events in the Northeastern region in the years leading up to my application for tenure, including: The American Association of University Women (AAUW) annual conference, and events in neighboring towns to the university, where I spoke eloquently on the topics like: *Challenges in a New Land*. My teaching evaluations in all my courses were excellent, and significantly above university average in some courses, although there would be some outliers with very negative comments from isolated students.

I had been producing and exceeding expectations for promotion and tenure, based on the job performance standards set by the White men in this institution. So, when I received the email stating that I, the only woman of color among the fourteen candidates who had applied for tenure and promotion that year, had been denied, I felt something beyond shock and sadness. There were eight members (mostly Full Professors representing the various colleges) of the Rank and Tenure Committee that year. When I later researched their backgrounds, it turned out that seven members were White, and one member was a Full Professor of color. The votes denying me tenure reflected the demographics of those sitting at the Rank and Tenure Committee: seven "No" votes, and one "Yes" vote! Coincidence? I doubt it! Because I have been constantly reminded of my Otherness in this institution, it is fair to assume that the White people who created these standards did not have me in mind when they designed them. Although most of those who looked like them, who had gone before me, fell short of their own standards when compared to my accomplishments, it would not be surprising that those judging my work at Rank and Tenure, must have found it difficult to use those standards to judge a Black woman from Africa fairly, because those standards were not designed with Others, like myself in mind.

Sadness engulfed me, filling me with a despondency that comes with the knowledge that I was faced with a problem whose solutions lay completely out of my hands, and resided within the realms of some powers that did not think I belonged. The guidelines for obtaining tenure and promotion are listed in every faculty handbook in academia as consisting of excellence in three areas: Research, Teaching, and Service. The measurements of the degree of these accomplishments are often vague, qualitative in nature, and often left to the interpretations of whoever sits on the Department, College Personnel or the Rank and Tenure Committees. These blurred lines give room for capricious behavior of those that have the power to validate one's work and make one's professional life fulfilling, or reject Others' accomplishments, and reduce them to misery. In fact, less than two weeks after the decision was made to deny me tenure and promotion, an email was sent to the Human Resource department by the Provost carbon copying me. The email, followed by a formerly signed letter, directed HR to discontinue my salary at the end of the month of August. Traditionally, at this institution, when a faculty member is denied tenure, s/he is usually given a year to tidy up before leaving campus: (for example, apply for other jobs, or do whatever is needed to be done to transition to another place in a humanely reasonable time span). Yet, the email I got was asking me to pack up and leave the campus immediately. Someone must really be offended at my presence in this institution, I thought! This establishment, where I'd given 6 years of my hard work and services, had just vomited me out without bothering to give me sound reasons why! My grief and confusion were profound, confounded by the series of unexplained actions.

When two weeks later, the decision to deny me tenure was reversed after an appeal to the Chancellor and the Provost of the university (the same Provost who had presided over the Rank and Tenure Committee that initially denied my application), what I felt was not the gratitude that comes with an unexpected "victory," but rather, incomprehension about another illogical behavior of the powers within academia. As I prepared for my appeal, I had been warned by one sympathizer that university Rank and Tenure decisions were rarely reversed; so, I should not get my hopes up. Any feeling of joy that may have lightened my heart at the reversal, was tainted with not knowing the answer to the questions that plagued me most: "Why? Why was I denied? Why was the denial reversed? What had changed?" My portfolio was still the same one that had been reviewed a couple of weeks before the rejection decision. I had not added anything new to my accomplishments in just a matter of a few weeks.

It has been 8 years since that traumatic experience, but the "Whys?" are still as present today as they were then. They rise up and gnaw at me whenever I'm faced with an unexplained and illogical event at my institution, and there are many. While I remain mystified, because no tangible reasons for the denial have ever been provided, other experiences within academia have illuminated the pathways through which interpretations of such adverse occurrences may be made. Academia, though known to be an institution founded to spread knowledge based on scientifically empirical facts and ethical values about human society, can be very intolerant of ways that do not conform with the "academic culture" of specific institutions. The tenure process was instituted at universities to safeguard the integrity of research and teaching and guarantee some amount of protection to individual faculty members from being fired based on their informed opinions or scholarship, without due process or cause. That very mechanism of tenure now appears to be under attack by many university administrators and academia at large; it can be misused to control, restrain, or stifle open discussion and the free flow of ideas.

In my state of stupor during the tenure and promotion saga, I had lost ten pounds in two weeks! Ten pounds is a measurement of weight, a number on a scale. If ten pounds of fat were extracted and placed in front of me, I could touch it and feel it, and point to the parts of my body that had shrunk because I lost ten pounds. This could be considered a healthy change, but not in my case. And I did not feel excited about this change in my body weight. I had not conjured up a will to not eat; neither had I dedicated myself to any workout regime during those two weeks. No. These ten pounds seemed to have evaporated mainly due to the stress that I was undergoing. My body felt light like a feather floating in space, as I moved around my house, prepared food for my family, encouraged my children to do their homework, then went to campus to teach my classes, and made small talk with colleagues. Most of them avoided looking me in the eye, and only one of them in a college with more than eighteen full-time faculty members wrote a card to me to say he was sorry to hear that I'd been denied tenure. His card ended with an enigmatic phrase, "...so is academia!" Did this unwelcome lightness in my body result from the physical weight I'd lost? Or was it the trauma within my soul? Was the complete lack of comprehension about the series of events that were coming at me rather quickly one on top of the other, taking away my ability to process events? All of this was hard to tell. What I do know is that, unlike the pounds I'd lost, my emotions from that time have not entirely evaporated. They still haunt me, and every now and then, when in a pensive mood, or when triggered by an event that appears similar, I find myself going down that path again, searching for reasons. Words cannot accurately describe the state of the soul that occupied my human frame during those weeks and for the years that have followed. The state of that soul is elusive at times, but it has been ever present, wounded, and taking its time to heal. Yet, that soul has also resolved that it will not allow the capricious standards and decisions of straight White men, be the yardstick by which I measure my worth. They created those standards for themselves, to measure their own success; and when some of them do not meet those standards, they change the standards to accommodate themselves. When they do, it is never considered "lowering" the standards. The term "lowering" is only reserved for those who are not straight White men! I know that there was nothing I could have done differently, to enable the Rank and Tenure Committee in a Predominantly White Institution to fairly judge my work as equal to, or better than theirs!

Otherness Without, Oneness Within

Although I've felt like the Other, my heart has always felt one with teaching. No matter its state of being: sad or happy, serious or comic, soaring or plummeting, my soul has always searched for the equilibrium that would enable me give the best of myself to my students and at the same time, retain my authentic and undivided self. I do the job of teaching with the belief that it is a calling, and I've nurtured my authenticity with trepidation, especially at those moments when it has risked getting lost, as I sometimes struggled to fit in within academia. It is in this continuous quest for my authentic self in a place that highlights Otherness and demands conformity, that I have managed to live an undivided life that embraces all of me: a Black woman from Africa, a student, a wife, a mother, a teacher, a scholar and so much more. I must remember who I am!

In the *The Courage to Teach*, Palmer (2017) writes:

> Remembering ourselves and our power can lead to revolution, but it requires more than recalling a few facts. *Re-membering* involves putting ourselves back together, recovering identity and integrity, reclaiming the wholeness of our lives. When we forget who we are, we do not merely drop some data. We *dis-member* ourselves, with unhappy consequences for our politics, our work, our hearts.
>
> Academics often suffer the pain of dismemberment. On the surface, this is the pain of people who thought they were joining a community of scholars, but find themselves in distant, competitive and uncaring relationships with colleagues and students. Deeper down, this pain is more spiritual than sociological: it comes from being disconnected from our own truth; from the passions that took us into teaching, from the heart that is the source of all good work. (pp. 20–21)

Parker Palmer has established that all humans, including academics, have a soul. Personal narratives enable us to liberate that soul and nurture it; without which it may shrivel up and die, leaving an inauthentic self that teaches using only techniques and without heart. No matter the challenges, I've maintained a spirit of curiosity and inquiry, and sought to learn and grow, as I interact with my students and colleagues in the community of learners. Some of the lessons have been jolting, but the insights they have provided me have helped me become a strong and tenacious professional who has come to understand that the work that we do as educators transcends classroom walls, and therefore must be done with integrity. I respond to the challenges of the profession with a mindset that recognizes that our teaching is not limited by the here and now but would potentially impact even unborn lives. I do not compromise my stance when pushing back on the injustices inherent within this system. Take for instance the time when I was told "You are not a minority!" and the journey and profound lessons, that my quest to comprehend and not ignore that simple phrase initiated.

You Are Not a Minority!

Those are the words that brought "Otherness" to me in a manner that I would always reflect upon. At times I have attempted to minimize my Otherness, and at other times I have embraced it whole-heartedly. Ultimately, and with my own grace, I have come to see being the Other and having others, as a gift to academia. Sometimes academia has received my gift and given me its own gifts in return; but mostly academia has held up a mirror that reflects Otherness lucidly and in a manner that says: "*Never forget that you are different! You are not one of us!*" The words, "*You are not a minority*," did that to me. "You Are Not a Minority", was the response that a peer gave me, when I took her to task for attacking Affirmative Action in one of my doctoral courses. The course was titled: *Doctoral Seminar on Curriculum Theory*, and the main instructional approach was students' presentations on current issues in education, followed by whole class discussions. The class was made up of eight Caucasian women, one African American lady who was also the Associate Dean at a Historically Black University in the South, and myself, a new immigrant woman from West Africa. It was a mixed group in terms of specializations ranging from Curriculum and Instruction, Higher Education Administration, Special Education, and Language and Literacy practitioners. On this day, the discussion was on falling standards in schools, watered down curriculum, and what we as future educators and administrators could do to reverse the trends.

I have noticed that often, in academic environments when free speech and honest discussions are encouraged, it is hardly ever to heal the wounds of the marginalized in these settings. In Colleges of Education where my experiences reside, what generally emerges as free speech is what has also been referred to in the literature as "blaming the victim," https://dictionary.apa.org/blaming-the-victim. Faculty members express their frustrations about the low academic standards of the handful of minority students in predominantly white institutions, but never seem to examine how they can modify instruction to meet the specific needs of those students. This higher education course that prepared future educators of educators, was no different. The all-female doctoral students in this course, most of whom were also practicing teachers in school districts around the university would use the discussion sessions to talk about Black students in very condescending terms. They would characterize students from diverse backgrounds as, "*coming to school so unschooled that the teacher did not know where to start teaching them.*" Snide comments like, "*the apple doesn't fall far from the tree,*" were not uncommon in this class. I often felt confused about this apparent scapegoating and blaming of the parents of minority students for perceived educational shortcomings; but at each class session, I sat quietly, intent to learn as much as I could about the American educational system. After all, wasn't that why I had traveled thousands of miles from West Africa to the U.S.A.?

A new scapegoat seemed to emerge at each class session; and on this day, Affirmative Action was under siege. One of my peers, emboldened by the instructor's encouragement to speak freely and honestly about burning issues, launched a virulent attack on Affirmative Action. She claimed that Affirmative Action was responsible for falling standards in universities. According to her, because of Affirmative Action, African American students who could not perform at expected levels in high school were being admitted into universities, putting college professors in positions where they had no choice but to pass the students along,... you know, in order to maintain numbers. When she finished her tirade, there was silence. One could hear a pin drop. The class stared at her. The embarrassment of all present was evident. I looked over at the African American lady, and her head was bowed down as she scribbled away at something. The speaker, suddenly realizing the awkwardness of the moment, fidgeted uncomfortably. I kept looking at the African American lady, willing her to speak; but she said nothing. Her head remained bowed, and her scribbling became more animated. So, I spoke. I had not prepared an appropriate response, and honestly, under the circumstances, I don't know what an appropriate response would have been. Even if there was an appropriate response, surely, it would not be from me, a newcomer into the U.S.! What would I know? I was here to learn, and although I fully participated in academic discussions that had to do with the readings, discussions that segued into socio-political realities often left me wanting in prior knowledge. So, I preferred to listen more. But this day was different. I knew that something was wrong, not only with the words that were spoken, but the attitudes and beliefs that informed those words. So, I said what was on my mind, and it came out as follows: "*You know what? I find your views rather interesting. You seem to be the one person in this class who has a knack for saying things that I often sense others agreeing with, but unwilling to say out loud; and I don't know whether to call your behavior courageous or tactless.*" I continued, "*Correct me if I am wrong, but I thought Affirmative Action was...*" She didn't let me finish. She immediately went on the defensive: "*That's not what I meant. It came out the wrong way.*" I waited for her to explain what she had meant, but she didn't; so, I prodded: "*Could you please tell us what exactly you meant, because I'm not sure how to conceptualize Affirmative Action at this moment, based on what you said.*" The instructor (a White male, who had been hired after retiring as Superintendent of Schools in the school district where the university was located), felt the mounting tension in the room and asked us to take a five-minute break. All the White ladies rushed to various bathrooms in different parts of the building. Interestingly, no one chose the one on the first floor where we all hung out and chit-chatted during our five-minute break time.

Being in a pensive mood, I did not quickly tidy up my stuff to step out of the classroom. Frankly, I was getting mad, and could feel the anger welling up inside of me, forcing its way to break through to the surface. I had to swallow that lump of anger down, but it stayed just beneath the surface, making me madder on the inside. I was mad at everybody. Mad at the rest of the class for seeming to agree with the speaker's point of view. Mad at the African American lady for always bowing her head in the face of these insults; and above all, mad at the instructor for giving these ladies an outlet to cast aspersions on minority students and families, in the name of free speech; and not requiring that they back their claims with empirical research evidence, as we had been taught to do in doctoral courses. I was especially mad that he had not given us the opportunity to stay in class to explore the topic further, right there and then. It wasn't yet time for a break! Why had he asked us to take five? Finally, I stood up and slowly followed the African American lady to the bathroom she'd chosen to go to, upstairs (not at the same floor where the incident had occurred, although there were plenty of empty stalls down there). She too had hung back in class while others rushed out, taking her time to put together her books. When I caught up with her, I whispered fiercely, *"Why do you just sit there and let these people, insult us like this?"*

She looked at me dolefully, and with resignation, responded, *"What is the purpose of beating a dead horse?"*

"What do you mean?" I retorted.

She shrugged her shoulders and said, *"Maybe I should have told you that these people value us less than their dogs!"*

I opened my mouth to say something, but no words came out. So, I veered off to the door that would ultimately take me outside of the building. I sat on a bench and took deep breaths. I did not use the lady's room. I did not drink water from any fountain in the building, because although my lips were dry, I didn't think water would quench the kind of thirst I was feeling. I was just angry, and I needed an explanation for the insults directed at certain demographics of students and their parents. So, I let my anger roll around in my belly like a ball of fire whose fumes were looking for an outlet; but I had clamped that outlet shut by pressing my lips tight.

When I returned to class, everything seemed to have gone back to normal, but I was in no mood to continue this class as if nothing had happened. I wrestled with what action to take. Should I drop the whole thing and pretend like everybody else that it had not happened, or should I ask the whole class to return to the topic? Before I could decide what to do, the period was over and the instructor dashed out of class and literally ran into his office, leaving us to pack up our stuff in silence and walk out separately. No call for "any questions?" No conclusion to the previous discussion. No directives as to what to expect in the next class. Nothing. He just bounded out, and the students scampered out after him. I quickly picked up my books and stepped out of the classroom and waited by the door for the "anti-affirmative action-speaker." When she stepped out alone, I hissed at her: *"How dare you insult minorities in their faces like that!"* She was shocked at my words and quite taken aback. I could see her confusion when she responded, *"What people are you talking about? You are not a minority!"*

I was stunned. *"What do you mean, I'm not a minority?"*

She chuckled, *"Oh No! I don't consider you a minority. You are a strong, Black, intelligent African woman, and I have a lot of respect for you!"* Then she flashed me a bright smile and before I could find the right words to respond, she walked away.

I stood there perplexed. Several questions were racing through my mind: "What am I then if I am not a minority? How can I be Black, and yet not belong with the Blacks in the U.S.? Who exactly am I?" My search for an identity in the American patchwork of cultures and identities had started before this day. I had often felt a certain unease about the excessive praise for my work in class; the almost fawning attitude of Caucasian instructors that bordered on disbelief that I could do certain kinds of academic work. The loud and exaggerated admiration for my African outfits that I wore with pride. The comments from my peers and instructors about how impeccable my English was, (completely ignoring the fact that I had been a High School English teacher before coming to America). The admiration for my strongly accented, but non-American accent, (Southern Cameroons being a former British colony) often seemed false to me, when I noticed how these same individuals frowned upon African American/Black English, also known as Ebonics. I was uncomfortable about the big "A's" scrawled across my papers with "flattering" comments that sometimes made me blush, and the over enthusiastic cheers from classmates whenever I did a presentation with chants of, "Liz, we want to hear more!" when the presentation was over. All this praise did not impress me. I was a hard worker and believed I earned my successes. The more praise my work received, the more distant the only other Black lady in class with whom I identified racially, became. I could sense the tension between us, and I didn't like it; so on one occasion, I asked her why she was acting so distant toward me. She coldly responded that I was "clueless." When I prodded, she said that the professors were "dividing" us on purpose. I asked her what she meant, and she told me she believed that they were giving me high grades, and deliberately giving her low grades to mask their discrimination. I told her we could work together on some projects, but she did not seem interested in the idea, and continued to maintain a polite distance from me. On this affirmative action discussion day, I felt a growing sense of being neither here nor there. Navigating identity in a society structured along racial lines was a treacherous journey for me. Yet, I was determined to find my place and thrive in the U.S. mosaic of races, ethnicities, and yes, opportunities; even if I didn't quite fully grasp where I belonged in the minority/majority dichotomy. It has been several years, and I am still searching. Other incidents have occurred, but those have not taken me any closer to an identification of my place in the "normal," versus the "Other" divide, that seems to characterize not only higher education, but almost all educational settings in the U.S. that I've worked in.

OTHERING IN K-12 SETTINGS

In the K-12 settings, accountability measures like No-Child Left Behind (NCLB) and the Common Core States Standards (CCSS) have created a "Them" versus "Us" divide as well. Blame games among stakeholders cannot be avoided when these mandates place inordinate amounts of pressure on teachers to improve students' academic performance, and unreasonable consequences for lack of student success. While accountability measures for effective teaching are laudable, it is worth noting that teachers are not often consulted about their abilities to implement some of the policies that are enacted into laws to measure teaching and learning. Among other factors, teaching environments are not assessed, in order to adequately make available resources that teachers need to enact such policies. When this happens, the most vulnerable students who are predominantly minorities, and often perform poorly, receive the most blame from their teachers. Instead of working with families to ensure that all students rise to their highest potential, it is not uncommon to hear teachers complain: *"There is nothing we can do; it is the parents' fault!"*

I have learned to play dumb when these statements are made and ask, "What have the parents done?"

"Oh nothing, they don't do anything, and that's the problem. If only they would do something!"

"What would you like them to do?"

"Well, stay involved. Show up!"

"Show up for what exactly?" Wouldn't you find it distracting if they showed up in the middle of the school day while you were teaching a class?"

"Of course, I would. You know what I mean....?"

No, I don't. I didn't know as a doctoral student and teaching assistant supervising undergraduates during practicum, and I don't know now, as a full-time university Associate Professor. What I do know is that teachers have the ultimate responsibility for doing the best within their abilities to make sure that every child learns. They have a responsibility to understand the diverse cultures, aptitudes, and identities that students bring into the classroom. They have a duty to value these differences, and incorporate them into learning engagements that would enable all children to succeed in inclusive school environments.

In other parts of the world, parents send their kids to school and trust that teachers have the expertise and are well equipped with the strategies and resources to meet their children's academic needs. In Finland for example, where more than 97% of schools are municipal schools, the municipalities make decisions from curriculum, to class size, to students' needs; and provide resources to all schools equitably. Parents participate in their children's education and support the children at the home front, to achieve their educational goals. Parents do not prescribe methods and teaching approaches to teachers. When teachers need the parents' involvement or intervention in specific areas, they let the parents know, and the parents go to school mainly to discuss specific issues with school personnel. There is no risk of either teachers or parents overstepping their boundaries. Parents and teachers are partners in the business of educating children, and there is a mutual appreciation for the role that each plays. The outcome of such mutual respect in partnership is that Finland has routinely scored among the top-ranking countries globally, on the Organization for Economic Co-operation and Development (OECD) Program for International Student Assessment (PISA). There is no banding of systems—i.e., all pupils, regardless of ability, are taught in the same classrooms, and this has accounted for Finland having the smallest recorded academic gap between the weakest and the strongest students, worldwide. Schools assign relatively little homework and have only one mandatory test at age 16!

This is not the case in the U.S. The achievement gap in the U.S. between students of color and that of their White counterparts continues to grow wider. While some studies show that parental involvement leads to higher academic achievement for the student, such expectations are often marked by inequities. While parents of low socio-economic backgrounds may not have the information or the strategies for advocacy, parents of children from higher socio-economic backgrounds can advocate for and get better resources and placements in school programs for their children. Who has not heard of the *"helicopter parents?"* Those who hover around school corridors carrying big binders in leather suitcases that contain all federal laws pertaining to education, and micro-managing every school activity. Often, the higher the socio-economic status of the family, the greater the interference. Since many in our system are accustomed to, and in fact may encourage, this kind of parental "support," those without it, most of the time, students from diverse backgrounds, are deemed unworthy. A lack of parental "involvement" could become an excuse for teachers to allow the child to fail.

The consciousness of being Black, and yet, *not a minority*, has continued to inform how I position myself both as a parent and teacher in the U.S. educational K-20 landscape. Two years after the *affirmative action incident*, I got a job as a tenure-track assistant professor at a public university in North Carolina. One of my sons was about to enroll in twelfth grade in the local public-school district. I remembered all the research studies that I had read as a doctoral student, and the many class discussions that pointed me to the characteristics of good parents. I was determined not only to be a good university instructor to my pre- and in-service teachers, but also an exemplary parent to my sons. This commitment was especially important, since my job description indicated that we would be partnering with some of the local schools for field and practicum experiences. I remembered that I had heard several times from my doctoral peers, some of whom were also beginning their higher education teaching careers after having just received their Ph.Ds., that good parents should at least "show up, and get involved." Because I wanted to be an exemplary parent, I showed up several days before school started, to help my son register for classes. Some may consider this an interesting move on my part since he was beginning twelfth grade and would rather handle this aspect of his academic career by himself.

We walked into the senior counselor's office after waiting several hours in a line that moved painfully, slowly. I was the only person in that line that was over 18! When we finally got into the counselor's office, I offered a bright and cherry *"Hi, my name is 'Mahndi,'* (pseudonym...meaning mother of "Ndi" in Bafut, my mother tongue) *and this here is my son 'Muhndi'"* (pseudonym meaning "Ndi" son of the mother, in Bafut). The counselor had a sour demeanor, and I was beginning to think: *"She doesn't really enjoy this job. Or maybe she is just having a bad day; after all, these lines are terribly long, and the raucous bunch of teenagers in the hallway can actually be aggravating ..."* My son greeted the counselor with equal enthusiasm and pulled out his report card from his former school, indicating that he would like to take some of the AP and honors classes. The counselor said, *"No!"* Our heads jerked up a little higher as we both looked at her. Then she explained that those classes would be too challenging for my son; that there were too many students in AP classes and not enough attention was paid to students in those classes. Mind you, she had not even looked at my son's academic record! I said to the counselor: "*But those are the classes he was taking in his former school, and those are the classes he would like to take!*" She ignored me. After one more interjection from my son, she turned around and said to him, "*Are you sure you can really do this?*" My son hesitated, then turned to look at me doubtfully, as I sat there staring at this woman. It had just dawned on me. With no other piece of information, but the color of my son's skin, this counselor had tracked him into lower-level classes! She had neither asked to see his previous academic records, nor enquired about his career goals. She had simply taken one look at him and determined that his black skin could not handle AP classes!

All of a sudden, Woodson's (1933) words started playing in my head: "If you make a man feel inferior, you do not have to compel him to accept an inferior status, he will seek it himself (p. xiii)." I resisted the urge to ask the counselor to explain her meaning of "are you sure you can do this?" However, I stood by my son's request to enroll in AP and honors classes. As soon as we stepped out of the office, I said to my son, "*Did you hear that lady? She thinks you are not smart enough for AP classes. You've got to prove her wrong!*" Then I immediately regretted it and caught myself thinking: "*No, he doesn't need to prove anything to anybody but himself! Why can't he just take classes that he wants because he has already proven to himself that he can handle those classes? Why does he have to bear the extra burden of proving that yes, indeed, he can do the work, everywhere he goes?*" The joy of being an involved parent, was now tainted with a put-down from a doubtful counselor, and I started second-guessing my desire to be so involved. I didn't want to get insulted again. I never went back to that building, nor interacted with that counselor or any other person in that high school again, for the rest of the school year! My son was doing well in his classes, and I had no need to go back there anyway, until he took the SAT test and the results came out. I could not fully interpret the SAT results, having come from another region of the U.S., where the ACT was the standardized test used for college admissions. So, my son and I took his scores to the same counselor to interpret them and help us with better directives for college selection. I don't think she even remembered us. As soon as we walked into her office and told her why we had come, she urged my son to check out the local community college. She had not bothered to pull up his scores from her computer, nor did she ask to see the copy of the results that my son had in his hand and was extending to her. So, I said, "*I think with his SAT scores, he can have admission to many other colleges, aside from the community college.*" Then, she asked his name and pulled up the scores, (although my son was still extending his mailed results to her); as if she could not trust that any document he would give her would be accurate. She took quite a while reading the results, as if cross-checking that the results she was reading belonged to the same student sitting in front of her; then folding her hands across her chest, she looked incredulously at my son, and said, "*Well, these are not typical scores for an African American male!*"

Although I'd met this lady before and could not imagine that she could possibly do anything that could shock me more than during our first encounter with her, she did. I again felt the sting of her insult directed at an entire race! Images of my doctoral classes flashed in my mind, and the refrain, "*You are not a minority!*" danced around in my head. So, if I'm not a minority, what was the context for this counselor's remark? Or did she make that comment because from my accent she could tell that I was not born in the U.S. and therefore not African American enough? Did she think that by not being "African American" I would not feel the hurt her words caused? Did that give her the permission to cast aspersions on those who "typically" scored lower on the SAT, or was it that this lady was both audacious and callous enough that she just didn't care how we felt? I didn't even try to respond. I was too mortified to speak. I had experienced this before in a different state within the U.S., and I'd spoken up. My speaking up had been met with denial and cynical laughter: denial of my perceptions and feelings about being talked about in a certain manner, and ridicule that I had confused my own identity. Encountering this attitude again made me realize that this might be the "norm." I would always hear and experience these put-downs. I might as well start getting used to them. The image of the African American classmate scribbling away feverishly each time these insults were hurled at the Black race emerged before me. Then, in a resigned manner, I heard myself murmur: "*What is the point in beating a dead horse?*"

Yet, living in a state of resignation is not acceptable. As educators, we have responsibilities. All of us educators; Black, Whites, and all colors in between, have a responsibility to value and uphold each other and our students. The U.S. is a country that uses labels to classify everything, including human beings: people are White or Black, upper or middle class, majority or minority. Macro labels are further broken down into micro-categories. For example, various groups of minorities have descriptors: Asians are the model minorities, Hispanics, the dumb minorities, African

Americans, the criminal minorities, Indigenous people, the lazy, drunk minorities. I have often imagined how nice those who create these labels must think it feels to be told, "*Oh, you are not the dumb one. You are not the criminal one! Or wait a minute, you are not even one of them!*" The problem is that this parsing of human beings creates a "them" versus "us" dichotomy, and that in and of itself, might be the mindset that hinders those in academia from living truthfully and authentically in harmony with each other.

So, at a conscious level I've decided to reject these labels. I spend most of my days figuring out how I can be the best teacher to my students without the labels. I acknowledge their differences, and I celebrate those differences, rather than hold these differences against them. However, many encounters in academia still remind me that despite my rejection of labels, I am labeled, and therefore I often have to think: Who am I? How do I position myself in this situation? *Am I an African American, a minority, who studied in a predominantly White higher-education environment and is currently working in one? How do my African roots inform my teaching? How do those of African ancestry, who came to America on slave ships perceive me? Am I a parent who cares? Am I an educator, who like all other educators, should simply desire one thing: that all students be given fair and equitable opportunities to succeed in school and become fully functional members of society? Who am I, and how best can I fulfill my responsibilities?* These questions (and others) follow me, and I believe other educators in their personal and professional lives. Seeking to answer them truthfully, may help us live undivided professional lives.

THE SACRED ROLE OF UNIVERSITY PROFESSORIATE

University professors, especially those who prepare pre- and in-service teachers that teach K-12 students have a great responsibility. They must position themselves in ways that positively inform and help pre- and in-service teachers provide educational equity for all students. This needs to be done thoroughly, from structural and programmatic areas, to interpersonal attitudes and dispositions. We as professors need to courageously acknowledge that there is a consciousness in the human psyche, one that demands fairness and justice, and all good things. More importantly, we need to admit that based on the way the U.S. society is structured, this consciousness is selective and not often extended toward all groups of people, including some of those that we teach. Many groups fight fiercely for privileges, but often just for their own kind. We demand human rights, but only when ours and that of our own (those that we can relate to) are threatened. This paradox seems to operate at all levels of education, especially in higher education. The politics of higher education often creates "in" and "out" groups based on "loyalties," either to the administration or other not-so-visible forces. This can make it difficult for those who come from cultural or other backgrounds that are not over-whelmingly represented in academia to find their place within this setting. Thus, the answer to the question, "Who am I?" within academia becomes mired in complexity that needs distilling. I can be many things: different, unique, yet valuable, like everyone else, and embracing my Otherness in all its authenticity and undividedness! As educators we need to rise above secretly held "deficit" beliefs about certain people in educational settings, especially those from minority backgrounds. These beliefs are often expressed in veiled, and sometimes not so veiled comments and actions that have negative impacts on already at-risk populations. If we hope to help all students and even professionals succeed in P-20 school settings, we must believe that all are created with the ability to accomplish highly, despite different ethnic, racial, national, or other backgrounds.

More than 85% of teachers in k-20 teaching-related environments are White females (https://nces.ed.gov/). The U.S. census had predicted that in the year 2020, what is now known as the minority will become the majority. Well, 2020 has come and gone! Who will be teaching the new majority of students in U.S. schools? It may be difficult to correct the current imbalance in teacher demographics to match student demographics, but all educators and educational stakeholders must continue working to make sure that all students in U.S. schools, especially minority students and professionals of color are supported to meet their full potential.

The university professoriate, especially in Colleges of Education, must go beyond paying lip service to matters of equity and social justice, and actively work to recruit and retain students of color in the teaching profession, while adequately training the majority White female teacher candidates to develop intense multicultural perspectives in their practices. Extant literature (Banks, 1999; Bifuh-Ambe, 2006; Delpit, 1995; Tatum, 1992) maintain that teachers' beliefs influence and affect their practice. When teaching professionals underestimate minorities' abilities, they limit the chances of people from such demographics from achieving highly. Only through the transformation of belief systems can educators promote educational equity and ascertain successful school experiences for all races (Au, 1993; Bifuh-Ambe, 2006; Nieto, 2003).

A concerted approach is necessary to change the attitudes of the predominantly White college professors who make up 88% of the 35,000 fulltime, regular, instructional faculties in the field of education. These instructors are charged with the duty of preparing the current predominantly White pre-service teacher population for public schools that are vastly diverse (Ladson-Billings & Tate, 1995). For all students to experience academic success, educators at all levels, and especially university professors' attitude, perceptions and instructional patterns that are detrimental to diverse students must be transformed. Until such changes in attitudes and belief systems occur, a good percentage of minority populations that need to be engaged with the teaching profession would continue to be left behind and those that are in the profession will continue feeling excluded from the culture of teaching.

FINAL THOUGHTS

I have narrated some experiences that have left indelible marks on me in academia: for example, being denied tenure and promotion at a Predominantly White Institution, despite exceeding the criteria. I have now been an Associate Professor with tenure for eight years, at the same institution that initially denied me tenure, and I have stopped searching for reasons why these adverse events have happened to me. Rather, I have learned to embrace my Otherness in this educational landscape, and continued my contributions through research, service, and teaching my students with heart. I have found joy in collaborating with colleagues from other universities across the U.S., and the globe, like all of us together who are contributing chapters to this book. It has taken me several years to come to a deep realization and to embrace the fact that there is nothing wrong with being "the Other." Otherness means different. Each of us is different. Our differences make us unique, and each of our unique qualities is a gift that enriches all of humanity. Tenacity, grit, perseverance, and living my truth with a sense of purpose are qualities that have guided me in navigating this landscape. I have channeled these attributes to overcome seemingly insurmountable challenges. I believe that these qualities lie deep within each of our beings, and, if consciously evoked and activated, would help anybody overcome hurdles that are placed in their paths by individuals who seek to deny our common humanity. We are all humans, and it is enough to just be human. We don't all have to look, speak, act or be the same; we just have to be true to ourselves and our purpose, for we already belong to this great construct: humankind!

References

American Psychological Association: Dictionary of Psychology. *Blaming the victim*. https://dictionary.apa.org/blaming-the-victim

Bifuh-Ambe, E. (2006). Fostering multicultural appreciation in pre-service teachers through multicultural curricular transformation. *Teaching and Teacher Education, 22*, 690–699.

Au, H. K. (1993). *Literacy instruction in multicultural settings*. Harcourt Brace Jovanovich.

Banks, J. A. (1999). Series foreword. In *We can't teach what we don't know: White teachers, multicultural schools* (pp. ix–xi). Teachers College Press.

Characteristics of Public School Teachers. (2020, May). https://nces.ed.gov/programs/coe/indicator_clr.asp

Delpit, L. (1995). *Other people's children: Cultural conflict in the classroom*. The New Press.

Ladson-Billings, G., & Tate IV, W. F. (1995). Toward a critical race theory of education [Electronic version]. *Teachers College Record, 97*(1), 47–69.

Nieto, S. (2003). *Affirming diversity: The sociopolitical context of multicultural education* (6th ed.). Pearson.

"Otherness", *The new Fontana dictionary of modern thought*, Third Edition (1999), p. 620.

Palmer, P. J. (2017). *The courage to teach: Exploring the inner landscape of a teacher's life*. Wiley.

Tatum, B. D. (1992). Talking about race, learning about racism: The application of racial identity development theory in the classroom. *Harvard Educational Review, 62* (1).

Woodson, G. C. (1933). *The miseducation of the American Negro*. Seven Treasures Publication.

PART II

Creating Creative Community

'Going Out into the World to Find Wonders': Nature as a Source of Generation, Regeneration, and Community

Libby Falk Jones

Come forth into the light of things,
Let Nature be your teacher.
—William Wordsworth, "The Tables Turned"

Almost 20 years ago, having lived my life variously in the verdant south, leafy northeast, and snowy midwest, I fell in love with saguaros. Really with the austere beauty of the green desert in general—rocks and washes, paloverde and mesquite, a resonant silence broken only by the occasional cactus wren. But during a ten-day retreat on the edge of the Sonoran Desert outside Tucson, Arizona, it was the cacti—and especially saguaros—that captured my heart and mind, my eye and pen.

L. F. Jones (✉)
Berea College, Berea, KY, USA
e-mail: jonesl@berea.edu

It was February, 2004, in the year of my first sabbatical. I had come to Desert House of Prayer, a small retreat center near Saguaro National Park outside Tucson, to pursue several writing projects. We had flown to Tucson from Ann Arbor, where my husband was teaching in the University of Michigan's winter term; I was serving as a visiting scholar at the Center for Research on Learning and Teaching and also auditing a poetry workshop. We came to the desert after almost two months of living in an encompassing white, cold world. We'd begun yearning for a geographical change, and a friend had recommended Desert House. Her description, and what I'd gleaned from the website, suggested that its environment of silence and solitude, its spiritual core, might nourish my growing creative life. And Arizona, in late February, would be blessedly sunny and warm.

Nothing could have prepared me for the clarity and light of the desert, for the endlessness of earth and sky, or for the power of living among these strange tall green beings (Fig. 6.1).

Usually 40 feet tall and living up to 400 years, saguaros command that landscape, with arms that suggest a symphony conductor or a frozen wizard or a pilgrim in prayer. Daily I walked among them, coming to appreciate their individuality—no two alike—and the beauty of the different stages of their lives. My desert walks taught me to breathe, to see. The language of the desert also captured me; my journal is full of lists of names and properties, many garnered from Joseph Wood Krutch's *The Desert Year*. My poems poured forth, and photographs, as my camera became a third eye to explore nuances of colors and shapes. In between walks, I read the journals and poems of Thomas Merton, whose spiritual journey had taken him from France to New York City and then to the Abbey of Gethsemani, in hills and woods of Kentucky not far from my home. That ten-day retreat became a landmark creative time, as I entered into this new and compelling "great, proud, dry and open land" that "flourishes vigorously and lives joyously" (Krutch, p. 6; p. 20).

Returning to Ann Arbor in late February was a shock. A poem I wrote then captures that re-entry:

In the City, Post-Desert

lighted street
sky clogged

stars hide
dawn white

Fig. 6.1 Saguaro National Park, near Desert House of Prayer, Cortaro, Arizona (photo by Libby Falk Jones)

air heavy
  no dove-flurry

cats yowl
  cars throb

dreams whirl
  (thank god)
    desert wild

When I returned to Kentucky in May to my continuing work teaching writing and literature at Berea College, I carried the desert with me. Increasingly, I noticed, I needed to spend silent time alone, in nature, to prepare for my classes and read students' writings, as well as to write and photograph.

As time passed and I began teaching a greater range of writing courses—critical, professional, and creative—I came to see that my students had these same needs. Four years later, during a month-long mini-sabbatical, I returned to spend another week at Desert House, this time to plan a new course I was calling "Contemplative Writing." Thomas Merton, whom I'd continued to read, explores contemplation, which he defines as heightened awareness, deepened experience. In *New Seeds of Contemplation*, Merton describes contemplation as "spiritual wonder... spontaneous awe at the sacredness of life, of being... gratitude for life" (p. 1). My own experience of writing and the needs I saw in my students suggested that such an orientation to the world could lead to the experience of unexpected beauty and meaning, and thus to writing which reflected and probed those experiences. In my teaching, I wanted to create a space—literal and metaphorical—where writers could free themselves from the fragmentation and noise that characterize contemporary and especially academic life, where writers could expand their internal and external awareness. I understood contemplative writing to be not so much a subject but a process of approaching the world and the work with receptivity, openness, curiosity, and freedom—a process that could benefit any writer, at any stage of development. I saw offering such a course as a means of continuing my own journey and inviting student writers to share it.

Developing and Teaching Contemplative Writing

In Berea's 2009 January intensive term, I taught Contemplative Writing for the first time. The twelve students and I worked together for three hours every day, writing together, reading, exchanging and workshopping drafts, and spending time outside in silence. We taught one another; each student had a turn leading the class in a creative exercise or activity, in the classroom, and on retreats.

Twelve days of the course were spent on retreats, possible because this was our only course during the month. Our first retreat, at the end of the first week, was for two days at the Sisters of Loretto Motherhouse in

Nerinx, Kentucky, about two hours from Berea. In addition to exploring the lakes, labyrinth, grounds, and art museum at Loretto, we visited the Abbey of Gethsemani, 15 minutes away. In the second and third weeks of the month, we spent ten days at Redemptorist Renewal Center, across the road from Desert House of Prayer, in Cortaro, Arizona. When we left Berea at 5 a.m. to catch our flight to Phoenix, the temperature was 4°; when we left the airport to drive to Tucson, we walked into 70° sunshine. That physical shift was emblematic of our month-long transformative experience.

In that first course, time in the desert was key, but students also made discoveries on retreats in Kentucky and during the time on campus. Retreats provided the opportunity for genuinely unstructured time; reading, journaling, and writing were required, but students could choose what, where, and when to pursue them. Students were invited to spend their days in silence and in solitude. The only commitments were meals and a gathering each evening to share and to write together. Their journals and the independent writing projects that arose from their interests exhibited a stunning array of substantial, insightful, well-written creative work.

Over the next decade, I taught Contemplative Writing six more times, five at Berea and once at National University of Ireland in Galway. Of the seven classes, four took place in a one-month term, twice in January and twice in May. The other three courses were taught during a full semester, once in the fall and twice in the spring. The courses have enrolled more than 100 undergraduates, second-year through senior, from a variety of backgrounds, majors, and interests. The heterogeneity of each class was an important source of learning.

Regardless of the season, each course invited students to spend extensive time in nature. In Kentucky, locales included Berea, the Abbey of Gethsemani, the Sisters of Loretto Motherhouse, and Furnace Mountain, a Korean Zen Center near Irvine, KY, about an hour from Berea. Beginning with the 2011 course, classes have been able to visit Thomas Merton's hermitage at the Abbey of Gethsemani. There, Brother Paul Quenon, who entered the Abbey when Merton was novice-master, read his poetry and spoke with students about contemplation and writing (Fig. 6.2).

Two courses, the first in January 2009 and the fifth in May 2015, included time in the Sonoran Desert, at Redemptorist Renewal Center, a larger center across the road from Desert House of Prayer.

Fig. 6.2 Brother Paul Quenon leading contemplative writing students across the meadow to Thomas Merton's forest hermitage, Abbey of Gethsemani, Trappist, Kentucky (photo by Libby Falk Jones)

Whether the environment was the desert or the forest, students interacted with nature in many ways. They sat on grass, logs, and rocks; they walked and danced and climbed hills and trees; they read books sitting under saguaros and on patios watching hummingbirds; they wrote, in their journals or on their laptops, on grassy hills and in woodland chapels. Wherever they were, they watched and they listened. Sometimes each was alone; sometimes two or three followed a path or sat outside with their journals; sometimes the whole class walked together, meditatively, in silence. Students' experiences in nature were supported by readings as well as by class visits from a naturalist, who helped us understand better what we were going to see (see Appendix for a list of useful resources).

PROBING LEARNING: A QUALITATIVE APPROACH

Although teaching the first contemplative writing class showed me that this was a unique, powerful experience for students, it was only after teaching the third class, in May 2011, that I realized I wanted to understand students' experiences more fully. I knew a good bit about the outcomes of the course through students' written projects, journals, and reflections, as well as through the College's official course evaluations. Through informal conversations with some students, I knew that they had more to tell me than appeared in these documents—and especially, more to tell me about any long-term effects of the contemplative writing course on their intellectual and emotional growth. In deepening my learning about their learning, I hoped to tease out practices and philosophies I could bring to all my writing classes, regardless of their structure and focus.

In 2012, I began a long term, qualitative research project, conducting face-to-face interviews with students still at the College or living nearby. From the first 2009 class of twelve students, I was able to interview four. In the past nine years, in this IRB-approved study, I've conducted in-depth interviews with almost 60 students—over half the 104 students who have completed the course. The in-person interviews, lasting from 30 to 90 minutes, have been conducted months or even years after the completion of the course. Rather than developing a set interview protocol, I preferred asking students to talk about what they found significant to their growth as well as how they experienced key elements of the course. These key elements included assignments—journals, readings, writing projects (written and often visual components), peer sessions, and reviews—as well as key parts of the course process: silence, solitude, time in nature, time in community. An opening question about what stood out in the course usually led to a fuller discussion of one or more of these elements. Often I asked about their writing experiences prior to taking the class; concluding the interview, I always asked about writing and creative experiences that followed the course.

TIME IN NATURE: OUTCOMES

Of the elements in the course that had a lasting impact, one that stands out is time in nature. In other publications, I've focused on students' experiences in writing, reading, and visual work; here I want to examine and illustrate important effects of students' time outside.[1] This element of the course is easily transferable to other courses, in writing and in a variety of subjects. Understanding the benefits of time spent outdoors can help justify building such experiences into writing and other courses.

My research shows that time in nature, alone and together, contributed to awareness and creativity, as well as to students' comfort and connection to the larger universe. As I explore these outcomes in more detail, I'll draw on my students' voices in the interviews and occasionally, on their writing. Since my journey through these experiences paralleled my students', I'll also illustrate my findings with examples from my own writing and photography.

Awareness: Enhancing Receptivity and Focus

The rare moment is not the moment when there is something worth looking at but the moment when we are capable of seeing.
—Joseph Wood Krutch, *The Desert Year* 48

Awareness—noticing, paying attention—is central to writing and indeed, to living a full life. Spending undirected time outdoors encouraged the noticing of what one student called the "small beauty in things" that are usually overlooked—"kinda mundane things," as another student put it. "It's really nice to get up close and look at the ridges and the veins running through flowers and leaves," she added. "A lot of things caught my attention," another student said. "Little things like butterflies and flowers—those were what spurred on my writing."

Other students found themselves turning inward. "Getting into nature allowed us to get more in touch with ourselves, to quiet our minds and become present," a student said. Students often made small collections of natural objects such as bark, twigs, rocks, dried grass; they photographed or drew these in their journals or sketchbooks. I photographed one student on her knees in the desert, looking closely at small objects on the ground. Being in the natural world led to multiple discoveries, to living in a fresher way.

Students also found that persistent noticing, in nature, led to an unexpected depth of perception. One student wrote a poem about water flowing under ice in a frozen stream. "We see only the surfaces but underneath there are things that I did not pay attention to before," she said.

Awareness is not only visual—it involves the whole body, all the senses. "One of the first things I noticed about the desert was it smelled like the earth," a student said. "There was nature right there," another said. "There was the sun and there was wind." Another recalled instructions from the naturalist who visited the class: "She said get your senses into the wild, and the wet places and the snowy places." Another student, who wrote outside, noted that "it was good to hear the sounds and explore."

In "Broad Desert: In the Sonoran, Tucson, Arizona," an essay for a later writing class, Jesse Wilhite created compelling word-pictures of his time in the desert in 2009, the first contemplative writing class:

> The desert: hardly a place for couch potatoes, but perfect for a group of curious writers enraptured by the thought of a pilgrimage to a place burgeoning with surprise.
>
> We gorged...on the jagged mountain peaks, gray and brown dark shades, at the familiar blue sky and the vast flat shrub-scattered plains unfurling before our sun-struck eyes....
>
> Wading in the soft blue sun-warmed day are foot paths, stretched landscapes, and boulders to mount and nap on....
>
> Earthy colors dash from shrub to cactus like wild jackrabbits. The dry sandy wash winds through the low parts of the desert, tracing out the feet of the mountains. Then the open landscape: streaks of pink, outcroppings of granite caressed by paler yellow tones, orange flooded with light; sun-bleached brushwood dots the flat land....
>
> A windswept hawk shrieks, flapping its feathery wings, weaving across strips of cirrus clouds, reaching, reaching for another current, another horizon. It dallies a moment then pushes past its two companions with one powerful flap. From the beak the sky tilts left to right like a seesaw teetering peacefully....
>
> Days burn like fuel logs lit to keep warm a house full of wintry rooms....
>
> Fingers press the smooth notebook bound with spiraling thoughts of the silent desert and the prayers that swim aloft the Four Winds of the Earth, eager to touch each shred of fabric that ever formed a wandering soul. Prayers carried by beauty that condemns nothing and escapes only by leave of the beholder. Might we have a moment in silence?
>
> Let the darkness enshroud our necks and let the children of the desert turn in their borrowed graves. For in two moons, we rise, on the wings of spring.

Awareness, as Wilhite's writing shows, often arose from the shock of the unfamiliar. "The first day in the desert was like hiking out into the unknown," said one student, echoing my experience in 2004. "In the desert I did not know any of the plants," another said. "It made me wonder if people take nature for granted when they can name it." Another spoke of being able to focus on sounds of birds, crickets, and cicadas not usually noticeable in a city environment. Her focus led to receptivity: "I realized how much the sitting outside was just kind of listening to everything," she said. Being outside was "just me being open and receptive and receiving," another student said.

Such receptivity is an important step in writing, a student in the first Contemplative Writing class noted. In a tip-sheet she prepared on "How to Be a Contemplative Writer," she urged: "Unbecome yourself and become a receptor for what you see." She went on to explain:

> While listening and looking, contemplative writers let themselves dissolve into others—although at first it is hard for them to get out of their own shell of self. They desire to bear witness to things as they are. They are not hesitant to be patient and become part of their attentive objects.

Awareness also offers chances to be surprised, to have aha moments— something humans and especially writers are always hoping for. One student spoke of the power of an unpredicted snowfall during a January retreat in Kentucky. "I like it when nature has its way," he said. "I like days when nature does extremes and forces a thoughtfulness." That a new environment, like the desert, can be dangerous also spurred students into paying attention. "I didn't know what to expect as far as wildlife goes.... That adds a degree of apprehension when you're out hiking, and you also get into the zone," one student said. Years after, some students still recalled rescuing an injured bird and leaping away from a rock around which coiled a rattlesnake.

For me, walking the woods and desert paths with my students helped me re-live my initial natural discoveries. I had the additional joy of introducing students to language and images that had sparked my work. And they in turn helped me to continue to see these worlds afresh, as I had on my first desert retreat:

Anatomy of the Desert

The first day you embrace just colors,
red blur of mountains, green branches
on green stems, purple fuzz of cactus,
a waxy yellow blossom
amid bright white spikes.

Second day, geometries: red rock blocks,
cactus forks and fingers, labyrinthine
branches, barrels with accordion folds,
flat spiny rounds.

The third day you begin to name:
saguaro, cholla, ocotillo;
the fourth, invite them to converse:
gneiss and basalt, mule deer and javelina,
cactus wren and Gambel's quail.

Day five: language of intimacy,
you know the nubbly areoles
from which spring spines and fruits,
ribs beneath saguaro's glossy pulp,
curved bill thrasher's yellow eye,
jeweled scree that slides into the wash.

Day six, you pour out love poems.

Seventh day, dawn, again you stand
wordless: birds chant, saguaros pray,
earth scents finger your skin
while you open to the rain of light.[2]

Creativity: Motivating Writing, Cultivating External and Internal Dialogue

Believe me, you will find more lessons in the woods than in books. Trees and stones will teach you what you cannot learn from masters.

—Bernard of Clairvaux

Students' greater awareness and receptivity led them to become more creative and, in particular, to write more and more eagerly. Being in nature prompted much journal-writing. "I write about what I see," said a student. "You'll see a flower and you'll just have to stop and write about it," another commented. "There were times when I found myself having to just pull over as it were beside a rock and write."

Many students wrote about memories or associations arising from being in nature. "The bulk of my journal was about how nature had changed me as a person, and about how nature triggers a certain memory or aha moment," a student said. Exploring outdoors came to embody freedom: students could discover, rather than hunt for what they thought they should find to fit an assignment. One noted that the class had given her "permission to write and be in nature where it is a weird or antisocial thing to do otherwise." Many found that being in nature created a mental environment conducive to writing. "I was able to write better than in other classes probably because my mind had lots of space to write in," a student said. "Observing the details" of nature, another said, "became a mechanism for generation."

Students were encouraged to explore nature through all of their senses. One student, who created a video with words overlaying natural images, described his process as "immersing myself in plain air and just allowing myself to think about the place instead of thinking about the composition itself." "You are getting input from inanimate objects," said another. A student who said he liked to play with sounds in his writing created pieces emulating the sounds of the creek he had visited. Another recalled, three years later, a poem she had written when another student gave her "a little shriveled-up, dead old cactus arm. I wrote 'soft to young, old to rough, one way we all gotta go.'"

A majority of students' projects focused on or included natural subjects. One student noted the symbolic aspects of nature but said that his goal in his project had been to show nature's actuality. "I wanted to put the thing first, because we do live in a real physical world," he said. "This is what I want to honor and bring forward."

While some students focused on the tangibility of nature, others found that nature sparked their imaginations. One student spoke of connecting intimately to nature, noticing little things and imagining various things, such as how twigs got broken. "You are no longer a foreign creature," he said. "You are part of it. And the little crackings and footsteps around you come alive." Exploring a garden at a retreat center, one student photographed a pile of acorns collected by a squirrel. Viewing the image later prompted her to tell the squirrel's story: "When I sat down with the image, I got to be like there he was and this is what he was thinking here," she said. Another student, after spending time looking at trees, began to wonder if she could hear them breathe and what they might be saying. She described her course project, a chapbook of poems and drawings, as "a collection of interviews of trees and rocks and sand and stars." Another student found nature stimulated his writing not for its beauty but for its interest. Sticks piqued his interest, he said, because they were broken and discarded, no longer part of the tree but still having a place. "There was a story there," he noted.

Nature also provided an emotional connection to writings. One student created an 80-page project of poems and images on and about windows. "That semester, I was really in love with the fall and the process of the changing season," she said. In each of her classes, she said, "I found a beautiful window and I found myself writing down little poetic tidbits about how I felt about the window I was looking at. And throughout the semester I found myself more and more enraptured in the way that the windows portrayed the outside world, how they framed what you were looking at so specifically, so they were a form of containment, a form of control but a form of freedom at the same time." Her passion, seen in her language of "in love" and "enraptured," led her to consider the intellectual as well as the emotional implications of her subject.

Often the emotional connection to nature came through a perception of its beauty. Many students who visited the desert connected with its colors. "Colors have emotional properties, so that is something I am conscious of and think about that when I'm writing because you certainly can use color for that," one student said. "It was a very ecstatic time." Another student spoke of exploring outdoors at a Kentucky retreat center at night. Turning back, she saw water on the ground. "This image was so vivid to me," she recalled, two years later. "It was so beautiful. I wrote one of my favorite pieces ever, about how the sky broke open like a mouth."

While connecting with nature helped students expand their awareness and understanding of the external world, it also stimulated internal awareness. As one student put it, time in nature meant "intentionally setting aside time to turn the lens inward and let yourself think about things." He said he explored his sense of self by connecting "what I was observing and seeing and feeling." Internal awareness often manifested itself in writing. As one student said, "I found myself writing constantly and not always having something to say to somebody, but having something to say back to myself."

My own writings often took a dialogic form:

How to Collect Rocks

Let your eyes do the finding. Look for a
line, a shade, a shape. Look for one
that's like the others, only more. Look
for one that's different. Small's okay,
so is bigger. A flat plane? Round?
See the texture, listen to its music.
How does the pattern move?

Forget sight—just touch one.
Lift it, stroke its surface, turn it round
and round. With your fingers,
know its grain. Feel its heat, its dust.

Forget touch—imagine its center, green
and cool. See its inner sky, those floating
constellations. Think it in your pocket,
then washed and on a railing,
above the darting gophers.

Forget imagination—once you've touched it,
you're hooked. You're I and Thou:
to cast it down, impossible. Slip it
into your pocket, feel it jostle its sisters,
scratch your leg through the thin cloth.

Repeat as desired. Bless your big
pockets. Walk home, your mortality jingling.

Well-Being: Finding Calm, Happiness, Wonder, and Meaning

This life in the woods is IT. It is the only way. It is the way everybody has lost.... It is the life that has chosen itself for me.

—Thomas Merton

Spending time in nature not only fueled students' writing, it also contributed to their emotional health. Many students spoke of experiencing a sense of safety and calm when they were outdoors. "Nature is comforting even in a new and strange place," one student said. "I felt I was in a safe spot," said another. One student noted, a year later, that her main takeaway from the class was "the feeling of peace, quiet, and reflection." "Nature gave me a place to be alone, a chance to be silent," said another. "I'm always overthinking and worrying. When I'm in nature I don't feel like I need to be that way."

One student enrolled in the class as an independent study during a study-abroad term in Japan. Experiencing great isolation and loneliness there, he found comfort in the local mountains that reminded him of his home. "The places that felt familiar were a balm and a refuge," he said. "They were a cup of chamomile tea." Another found that his memories of the nature that he'd encountered during the class helped him later to "conjure up that same feeling of being able to be relaxed and free.... I can think, 'Man, that was a really good day' and go back and relive it." "Being surrounded by so much beauty just contributed to my well-being because it made me feel emotionally happy," another said.

Beauty in nature sometimes took unexpected forms. One student photographed a dead deer. "It wasn't grotesque at all," she said. "It was like I imagined the calm snow before the kill and it was so beautiful and haunting." Another painted a tarantula wasp which she had glimpsed in the desert; in her painting, the wasp is laying its eggs inside a still-living tarantula. "I looked over and saw this very fierce-looking insect," she said. "It was kinda scary. But I also felt like I was watching some kind of nature documentary. So I really enjoyed that experience." Her painting, she said, arose from her thinking about the possibility of new life.

In addition to finding beauty, students also experienced a sense of wonder, a sense of having found themselves a part of greater things. Awe was evident in their voices as they spoke of their experiences. "I wanted to be like wow, look at the trees," one student said. Another noted the sense of abundance she experienced in the desert. "It was almost a spiritual level," she said. Another stressed the importance of approaching the world with a positive expectation rather than as a problem to be solved. "Going out into the world to find wonders was really important," she said. "I took hours at a time to go wander off into the woods in January and it is a time when even I would not have normally wanted to do that."

Experiencing wonder led to a heightened sense of meaning. "It was profound, just to be in the desert," a student said. Students spoke of feeling and thinking more deeply while out-of-doors. "Deliberately putting myself outside things that weren't human-constructed helped me think more about things," a student said. "Being able to open up to nature, being able to go for a day hike in the woods reminds me what really matters," said another.

Many students spoke of the power of feeling a part of a larger universe. "I recall thinking a lot about the connections between everything in nature, between the plants and the insects and the animals and us and just the planet," said one. Another recalled walking a labyrinth at a retreat center, pausing several times to write a short piece. Her writing, she said, "was about why I was put here on this Earth." She often recalled that piece, she said: "I love that piece that I wrote."

Being in the presence of nature led to a perception of human insignificance that, paradoxically, is empowering. One student recalled her experience of the desert: "There were so many things that were tall and looming, like the rock formations and the cacti, and the sky, being able to see so many stars, all those things contributed to me feeling very tiny, not in a bad way, but in a forgiving way," she said. "It just reminded me that I am really small in the grand scheme of the universe so I shouldn't worry as much about myself." To another student, sensing human smallness provided focus. "The desert is so vast, it makes you feel lonely," she said. "It makes you focus on what's now. Realizing it's just you, and what you have to reflect on. It's centering, the desert is (Fig. 6.3)."

Humans' connections with larger things were also reflected in "Creation Speaks," one student's project of poems and watercolors. In one poem, "The Stars," she explored the insight she had gained spending time outdoors at night, that every element of the human body comes from trace amounts of stardust. "This idea of things coalescing into things and coming back as dust and then coming again as new was just a beautiful idea to me," she said. "It was definitely a bizarre project but I felt like I was a better person after doing it."

Students also connected nature to action. Analyzing writings by Thomas Merton, May Sarton, and Annie Dillard led one student to realize that observations of nature could be used "for humanitarian means..., to effect positive social change." (See Resource List in Appendix). Another student found that her experience in nature influenced her design of her senior art project, a series of pieces examining

Fig. 6.3 A contemplative writing students stopping to look closely during a walk in Saguaro National Park, Cortaro, Arizona (photo by Libby Falk Jones)

the wastage and potential reuse of clothing. "I'm hoping to use the experiences [on retreats in Arizona and Kentucky] as a way of helping the environment and creating awareness," she said.

Spending time with my students among Arizona saguaros and Kentucky trees led me to understand the natural environment as a sacred space:

Desert Rising

If an angel is to come to me
I think it would have to happen

in this landscape, where saguaros
beckon, arms crossed in promise,

and flat prickly pear disks witness
the wrap-around dawn. It would have to be

between the three sharp bird trills and
    the rabbit's soundless scurry,

flash of a lizard under mesquite
    and paloverde. Yes, it could happen

among these rocks, knuckles of red gneiss
    edging the dry wash, under my feet

a mosaic of small stones luminous.
    Those could be her fingers, those

streaks of pink and gold, waving
    to wands of ocotillo,

grazing cholla's spines, on my upturned
    face coming to rest.[2]

Every Berea College Contemplative Writing class spent time in the woods of Kentucky. As Suzanne Simard notes, "The forest is wired for wisdom, sentience, and healing" (2020, p. 6).

Recent research into the Japanese practice of *shinrin yoku*, or forest-bathing, suggests that time in the woods provides both emotional and physical benefits. *Shinrin yoku*, drawn from ancient Shinto and Buddhist practices, involves absorbing nature through all five senses. In the past twenty years, Japan has developed miles of Forest Therapy trails and done studies confirming that strolling in the woods lowers blood pressure and heart rate as well as boosting our immune systems (Gilbert, 2019, pp. 1–8, 18–20; Li, 2018, pp. 73–126; Williams, 2017, pp. 19, 23, 27–29). These physiological benefits are joined by emotional boosts. The biophilia hypothesis, rooted in ideas of entomologist E. O. Wilson and psychologist Erich Fromm, suggests that experiencing nature helps us feel mentally sharper and more relaxed, connected, and hopeful (Williams, 2017, p. 22; Gilbert, xiii). My students' and my experience in forests and deserts confirm scientists' arguments for nature's benefits.

Connecting: The Power of Community

Nature, wet or dry, furnishes the most cheerful as well as the most intelligible context for thinking and living and being.
—Joseph Wood Krutch, *The Desert Year* 268

A final benefit of time in nature was its encouragement of community. The contemplative writing class invited students to spend time in solitude and silence, and that experience was necessary to stimulate the deep seeing, writing, and thinking that students engaged in. But also critical to students' growth was being in community to share experiences and ideas.

Companions provided security when students explored unfamiliar environments. For example, women said they felt freer going out at night in groups rather than alone. And students relished the ways nature contributed to their time together. "The natural setting allowed for me to feel comfortable, and not to be constantly worried what everyone was thinking of me," one student said. "You didn't feel like your space was being invaded, everybody got along very well," another said. "We were all in it together and we were all experiencing the same things," another said. "We seemed to play off of each other well."

Students often explored together in silence. "We held to the silence," one student said. "If you just close your mouth a little bit, your brain works a little bit harder." Another commented, "We had a lot of moments when we would go on group excursions at the lake and we'd go out without even speaking."

Experiencing a community of presence and action and not of words was new to many students. "Having other people there who were going through the same experiences, going through the same places but also creative people, it was really nice," a student said. "We were all still together and still sharing energy, in the presence of each other," another said. "Though we weren't conversing, being in each other's presence I think really strengthened my writing and strengthened the bond."

While time together in silence contributed to community, community also arose through sharing and talking about writing. On retreats, classes gathered each evening to share work and to write together. Peer groups met at other times, usually outdoors, to exchange work and give feedback. "Having other contemplative writers, having their presence and their contemplative minds and their writing, was very meaningful for me," a student noted. Another spoke of the gratitude she experienced when others shared their writing. Nature provided space for informal feedback as well. "I got some of my best feedback when I was just walking around [with other students]," one student said.

And being in nature offered students the opportunity to support one another physically and emotionally. Several years later, one student recalled others' responses when she returned from a desert hike on which she'd not taken enough water. "The fact that the others on the trip were worried about my safety in regards to dehydration was really amazing to me," she said. "One of the young women on that trip even sat with me for a while as I cooled off and drank some water, just to be sure I was going to be okay." This experience helped her understand "the capacity humans have for compassion."

My experience of contemplative community with my students led me to write a haiku:

> *We have all the time we need*
> *We have all we need*
> *We have all*
> *We.*[2]

Conclusions: Educating for Wisdom

Enacting contemplative writing, then, became an exercise in deepening learning, in discovering wisdom. The 2016 Contemplative Writing class drew on wisdom gained to suggest some practices for other writers and learners:

- *Submerge yourself in the world around you. The sky, the storms, the hooting owls, and splashing turtles. Explore it, feel it, and connect with it.*
- *Don't be afraid of the unknown. Travel to new places with strangers and soon they'll become your friends.*
- *Take the time to allow—to value—silence. It can be difficult to turn the valve and shut off the connection between flow of thought and the mouth, but not everything must absolutely be shared the moment you've got it in your head. Let the silence fill you like a conversation with the world, the air—and yourself.*

- *Find time each day to stop, literally, and look very closely at something. If possible, touch it, listen to it, sniff it, even touch it to your tongue.*
- *Silence is beautiful, hard, and valuable. Take time to seek it out and cultivate it. It's a practice and takes some effort, but it's so important.*
- *The paths are very different and there are so many. The only mistake in choosing which to follow, is not to choose. Don't forget to enjoy where you are—the journey.*

As humans and as teachers, we can take these pieces of advice to heart. Any writing course—and many courses in other subjects—can draw on nature to stimulate students' awareness and creativity, to enhance their sense of well-being and meaningfulness. Teaching strategies can include:

- Requiring silent time in nature, in solitude and in community.
- Suggesting prompts, but encourage freedom in writing, both in nature and in reflecting on experiences in nature.
- Providing time for students to share writings and to write from one another's prompts.
- Inviting a naturalist to class to speak about the natural environment students are in.
- Offering or requiring readings that explore nature and creativity (see Resource List in Appendix).

Strategies helping students connect with nature have been particularly valuable during the Covid-19 pandemic. Slow time outside, attentive to the unfolding of the seasons, has grounded teachers and students in this past period.

I've found that wisdom has come not only from the process of the course, but also from the process of researching its effects on students. Conducting interviews with my students, resulting in the insights I've explored in this chapter, has also yielded larger understandings about teaching and learning. The process of conducting open-ended interviews has underscored to me that a teacher's primary job is to listen. Often I thought I knew how a student might respond to a question—this course, in particular, afforded me many opportunities to see students in action, to engage with them in dialogue, and to read the extensive thinking and responses that got onto their pages. But often a student surprised me.

Some students who had seemed less engaged during the course turned out to have been processing much in silence and to be articulate in the interview about their learning. The interview process taught me not to make quick assumptions about what's going on inside another.

Another revelation from the interviews concerned the long-term impact of the course. I was often surprised by how specifically students recalled course activities, readings, and their own writings. Often students built on their contemplative writing for projects in later courses, particularly capstone major and general studies courses. The freedom they experienced in contemplative writing to focus their work on subjects and questions important to them led to high investment in the writing. Later courses provided opportunities to pursue their contemplative writing investigations in new ways. Thus the research process itself yielded insights that can inform educational practice within the academy. Might we ask, more often, about students' prior learning and how they might want to extend it? Might we invite them to share important writings or projects from previous classes and to consider ways to develop or re-frame those investigations? Finally, might we in our classes give students the opportunity to reflect on the genesis and development of their work and ways they might build on it in the future? Research can help educators understand the network of learning that occurs across the curriculum as students assume agency for their learning. It can also help teachers see that what you see is not always what you get—each student has her own history and experience, and the better we understand those, the better able we are to design optimal learning experiences.

Through teaching contemplative writing, I've come to learn that optimal learning experiences need to include nature in some form. For me, walking the path of contemplative writing with my students, in nature, has taken many forms. Waiting together in silence by a frozen lake for the sunrise, standing in a desert wash to watch the stars, creating informal altars of natural things like pebbles, leaves, and flowers in our meeting rooms—contemplative writing, for me, is inextricably intertwined with nature. At the conclusion of each class, students and I worked together to create a display of our work: individual and collaborative writings, art, readings, and natural artifacts (Fig. 6.4).

Fig. 6.4 Class-constructed display of writings, art, and artifacts from Contemplative Writing, Berea College, 2013 (photo by Libby Falk Jones)

Today my bookcase shelves are lined with dried gingko leaves, twigs, cholla fingers, vials of sand and stones—tangible reminders of my links to the natural world and to my students. And I treasure a drawing made in 2015 by one of my contemplative writing students and presented to me at our last class, with thank-you notes from each of the students. The drawing shows a gentle teacher-guide, glowing with light, amidst the earth tones of the desert (Fig. 6.5).

I see this drawing as a celebration of teaching as leading out, of teaching grounded in a natural and human world.

Reflecting my and my students' ongoing pilgrimages and our rich connections are two pieces of my writing: a poem and a meditation. I first drafted the poem during an early contemplative writing course, then expanded and revised it during later courses. The poem explores my teaching in all contexts.

Fig. 6.5 Teacher, drawn by a contemplative writing student, presented by the 2015 class to Libby Falk Jones

I Ask My Students

> to stretch
> into silence
>   between   among   within
> (a writer's reach
>   should exceed her grasp)
>
> to listen
> to the world   to words
> music on the page
>   music of the spheres
>
> to write
> write it all, now   hold nothing back
> words yield more words
> a faucet you cannot   will not
> turn off

to be here   go there
essay   sashay
show up   sit down
speak up   speak out

to journey
with me
into language.

And in a meditation written at the conclusion of the 2015 contemplative writing class, I explored the concept of circles in teaching and learning, concepts that inform all my teaching.

Here, near the end of this amazing class, I've been pondering circles. Our campus classroom, where I'm writing now, is a lopsided circle, with square sides. In a circle, there are no sharp turns, just curves. A circle is continuous—you can run circles always feeling you are going forward, never sharply redirecting yourself or turning backwards.

A labyrinth is primarily a circle, but with sharp turns included. In walking the labyrinth in the desert, I felt the expansiveness of the half-circle you are thrust into at one point—you feel like a creature emerging from darkness into light, from fragmentation and twistedness into breath and air.

On the other hand, to "run in circles" is to be lost, not found—to be trapped, stuck, spinning wheels. How to get beyond these feelings of constriction, same-old? Perhaps an ever-enlarging circle—a spiral? Like a circle, a spiral moves in either direction—you can journey in and journey out.

But a spiral never comes to rest; it's always open-ended. A circle is complete. A circle can have a third dimension, as well: depth, like a tunnel. Like the womb one passes through at birth. An enzo, in Japanese brush painting, is a circle that's complete but also open-ended, as the brush stroke passes the beginning and moves out. Making an enzo gives the satisfaction of returning, but changed and still moving forward. In the children's game of "Drop the Handkerchief," the "it," while completing the circle once again, gains a new place in the circle, a new perspective. The circle is both familiar and changed. "The end of our exploring," says T.S. Eliot in "Four Quartets," is "to arrive where we started / And know the place for the first time."

For me, I hope for us, the journey of this course has been such a circle, of completion and awareness and growth. Thanks to you, my sister and fellow travelers, for your many gifts to me and to one another through this space and time.

Appropriately, then and now, the end, and the beginning, for contemplative writing and for all my teaching, is gratitude—for myriad rich opportunities to learn and for the many treasured companions I've walked with.

APPENDIX: SELECTED RESOURCES

Writings on nature that students have relished:
Thomas Merton, *When the Trees Say Nothing: Writings on Nature*; *"Rain and the Rhinoceros"*.
Basho, *Narrow Road to the Deep North*.
Rebecca Solnit, *A Field Guide to Getting Lost*.
Robert M. Hamma, *Earth's Echo: Sacred Encounters with Nature*.
Rita Winters, *The Green Desert*.
May Sarton, *Journal of a Solitude*.
Wendell Berry, poems.
Dennis Maloney, ed. *Finding the Way Home: Poems of Awakening and Transformation*.
Mary Oliver, poems.

Writings on the benefits of nature, useful for teachers
Barnes, S. (2019). *Rewild yourself: Making nature more visible in our lives*. Pegasus.
Keniger, L. E., Gaston, K. J., Irvine, K. N., & Fuller, R. A. (2013). What are the benefits of interacting with nature? *International Journal of Environmental Research and Public Health, 10*(3), 913–935.
Lane, B. C. (2007). *The solace of fierce landscapes: Exploring desert and mountain spirituality*. Oxford UP.
Massey, M. Encountering nature: Outdoor walks to reduce stress and increase focus in students. *Faculty Focus*, September 23, 2020. https://www.facultyfocus.com/articles/teaching-and-learning/encountering-nature-outdoor-walks-to-reduce-stress-and-increase-focus-in-students/. Accessed 11 June 2021.
Mitchell, E. (2019). *The wild remedy: How nature mends us*. Michael O'Mara.

Moore, M. E. (1998). *Ministering with the earth*. Chalice.

Nichols, W. (2014). *Blue mind: The surprising science that shows how being near, in, on, or under water can make you happier, healthier, more connected, and better at what you do*. Little, Brown Spark.

Sacks, O. (2019). "The Healing Power of Gardens," from *Everything in its Place*. https://www.nytimes.com/2019/04/18/opinion/sunday/oliver-sacks-gardens.html.

Shinrin-yoku—forest-bathing, forest therapy

Forest Therapy Society. https://www.natureandforesttherapy.org/.

Association of Nature and Forest Therapy. https://www.natureandforesttherapy.

Peck, A. (2019). *The green cure: How shinrin-yoku, earthing, going outside, or simply opening a window can heal us*. Cico/Ryland.

Song, T. (2019). *The healing nature trail: Forest bathing for recovery and awakening*. Snow Wolf.

Writings on Writing:

Dillard, A. (2013). *The writing life*. Harper Perennial.

Inchausti, Robert, (Ed.). (2007). *Echoing silence: Thomas Merton on the vocation of writing*. New Seeds.

Miller, B., & Hughes, H. J. (2012). *The pen and the bell: Mindful writing in a busy world*. Skinner House.

Powell, R. (2006). *Wabi Sabi for writers*. Adams Media.

Sher, G. (1999). *One continuous mistake: Four noble truths for writers*. Penguin.

Notes

1. My additional writings on the contemplative writing course include: "Reading the Word, the Self, the World: *Lectio* and *Visio Divina* as a Gateway to Intellectual and Personal Growth." *The Whole Person: Embodying Teaching and Learning Through* Lectio *and* Visio Divina. Ed. Jane E. Dalton, Maureen P. Hall, and Catherine Hoyser. Lanham, MD: Rowman & Littlefield, 2019. 49–60.

"Seeing mindfully: Fostering Creativity and Connection through Contemplative Photography. *The Mindful Eye: Contemplative Pedagogies in the Visual Arts*. Ed. M. Garbutt and N. Roenpagel. Champaign, Illinois: Common Ground Research Networks, 2018. 21-37.

"Noticing Deeply Through Contemplative Writing." *The Art of Noticing Deeply: Commentaries on Teaching, Learning, and Mindfulness*. Ed. Jan Buley, David Buley, and Rupert Collister. Cambridge: Cambridge Scholars, 2016. 67–77.

2. "Anatomy of the Desert," "Desert Rising," and "We have all the time we need" are from my chapbook, *Above the Eastern Treetops, Blue* (Finishing Line, 2010).

REFERENCES

Gilbert, C. (2019). *Forest bathing: Discovering health and happiness through the Japanese practice of shinrin yoku*. St. Martin's.

Li, Q. (2018). *Forest bathing: How trees can help you find health and happiness*. Penguin.

Simard, S. (2020). *Finding the mother tree*. Knopf.

Williams, F. (2017). *The nature fix: Why nature makes us happier, healthier, and more creative*. W. W. Norton & Company.

CHAPTER 7

The Self Who Teaches and Learns: Sharing the Space After a Disaster

Billy O'Steen

He aha te mea nui o te ao.
He tangata, he tangata, he tangata.

What is the most important thing in the world?
It is the people, it is the people, it is the people.

INTRODUCTION

This often used Māori whakataukī (proverb, pronounced fa-ka-tow-key) describes my focus on the people involved in education—the selves who learn and the selves who teach—and their lived experiences. Throughout my 30 years in education as a high school teacher, middle school creator and director, community college instructor, and now as a university faculty member, I have always sought, through the inspiration of John

B. O'Steen (✉)
University of Canterbury, Christchurch, New Zealand
e-mail: billy.osteen@canterbury.ac.nz

© The Author(s), under exclusive license to Springer Nature
Switzerland AG 2021
M. P. Hall and A. K. Brault (eds.), *Academia from the Inside*,
https://doi.org/10.1007/978-3-030-83895-9_7

Dewey, to design and facilitate "educative experiences" (Dewey, 1938, p. 28) by asking the question: "What is the place and meaning of subject matter and of organization within experience?" (p. 20). His guidance has influenced my decisions in the creation of curriculum and the facilitation of teaching and learning. This has included teaching outside the classroom by: working with teachers on an Outward Bound course, collecting, sorting, and analyzing roadside trash with middle schoolers, deconstructing a house to recycle materials with teacher education students, and having high school students walk barefoot through the grass in order to write poetry about combs. What happens, however, when students' experiences occur beyond the boundaries of my campus or classroom and without my design?

Like the proverbial question as to whether a tree makes a sound in the forest when it falls and no one is around, how much are free-range experiences educative on their own, or can, and should they be enhanced by me? In reconciling this potential de-centering of my role as the self who teaches, is there the possibility of a shared space with students for me to become the self who learns alongside them and for them to be my teachers? Quite unexpectedly, these considerations became central to my identity as a self who teaches and a self who learns following the 2010 and 2011 earthquakes and their effects on the University of Canterbury and Christchurch, New Zealand. To explore these intersections of my teaching and learning positions in this particular post-disaster context, it is essential to understand teaching and learning in Aotearoa (Māori term for New Zealand and means "land of the long white cloud," pronounced ah-tay-rowa).

Aotearoa New Zealand Context: Ako, Manaakitanga, and Kotahitanga

While the earthquakes were the physical manifestations of an unsettled land, Aotearoa's contemporary identity has been the cultural manifestation of an unsettled people. This tension has existed since the founding of New Zealand as a British colony in 1840 through the signing of the Treaty of Waitangi by representatives of the Crown and Māori chiefs. However, the discrepancies between the English and Māori versions of the Treaty have had long-lasting implications regarding perspectives on sovereignty, land ownership, shared governance, and biculturalism in general. The establishment of the Waitangi Tribunal in 1975 led to the successful transfer of some land back to iwi (tribes). At the same time, as this critical legal redress, a resurgence of Māori culture and language began to gain momentum such that biculturalism continues to become more and more prominent in contemporary Aotearoa New Zealand. Examples of this exist in all sectors of society and particularly in education where te reo (Māori language, pronounced tuh-rayo) and elements of tikanga (Māori culture, pronounced tea-kanga) are taught to all students in pre K-8 grades. In addition to learning the *what* of Māori language and culture, students and teachers are invited to utilize a particular Māori concept for the *how* of teaching and learning through ako (defined below, pronounced ah-co), which also represents the notion that identity is dynamic within Aotearoa.

> In te ao Māori, the concept of ako means both to teach and to learn. It recognises the knowledge that both teachers and learners bring to learning interactions, and it acknowledges the way that new knowledge and understandings can grow out of shared learning experiences. This powerful concept has been supported by educational research showing that when teachers facilitate reciprocal teaching and learning roles in their classrooms, students' achievement improves. (Alton-Lee, 2003)

Ako's direct implication in the classroom is that students and teachers are in fluid and reciprocal positions of being learners and teachers and sharing the instructional space. This is akin to Paulo Freire's idea of critical pedagogy where students and teachers learn together and from each other (2018). A practical application of this sharing of the space was Eliot Wigginton's invitation to students in his English class to write about what they knew and that led to the Foxfire publications (Wigginton, 1985). While Wigginton's actions were out of desperation—the students burned his podium—his impulse was in line with Dewey, Freire, and ako.

Outside the classroom, the idea of ako can be seen in New Zealand society where positions of leadership and followership are also always changing, layered, and mutually negotiable. This is most striking in the high reliance that New Zealand has on volunteers to perform essential services such as being the primary people on: ambulance crews, fire brigades, school boards of trustees, and surf life-saving patrols. Thus, your neighbor may hold multiple identities that alternate between leading the fire brigade, being a mom, and working a full-time job. One explanation for this ako approach of holding multiple positions, being a leader and a follower at different times, and being expected to contribute to society is related to the Māori practice of manaakitanga (ma-na-key-tanga), which translates to hospitality and kindness and encourages you to take care of your whānau (defined below, pronounced fa-now), hapū (subset of larger tribe), and iwi (larger tribe). In line with these concepts of ako and manaakitanga, Academy Award winning Kiwi filmmaker Sir Peter Jackson described his homeland as: "New Zealand is not a small country but a large village." This is further reflected in New Zealand's position as the third most giving country in the world and with more than 95% of Māori reporting that they give back to their iwi.

The belief that future generations should practice manaakitanga is directly spelled out in the Five Key Competencies in the New Zealand Curriculum (managing self, participating and contributing, relating to others, thinking, and using language, symbols, and texts). These Competencies are meant to drive everything about the curriculum, and the traditional subject areas of English, math, science, and history serve the attainment of them, as is demonstrated by their appearance at the beginning of the Curriculum document. The Competency with the most relevance to ako and manaakitanga is the "participating and contributing" one, which is described as:

> This competency is about being actively involved in communities. Communities include family, whānau*, and school and those based, for example, on a common interest or culture. They may be drawn together for purposes such as learning, work, celebration, or recreation. They may be local, national, or global. This competency includes a capacity to contribute appropriately as a group member, to make connections with others, and to create opportunities for others in the group. Students who participate and contribute in communities have a sense of belonging and the confidence to participate within new contexts. They understand the importance of balancing rights, roles, and responsibilities and of contributing to the quality and sustainability of social, cultural, physical, and economic environments. (Ministry of Education, 2015, p. 13)

> * Whānau is a Māori term that is often translated as "family", but its meaning is more complex. It includes physical, emotional and spiritual dimensions and is based on whakapapa (genealogy). Whānau can be multilayered, flexible and dynamic. Whānau is based on a Māori and a tribal world view. It is through the whānau that values, histories and traditions from the ancestors are adapted for the contemporary world. (Te Ara, 2021)

As indicated above with the definition of whānau, the Māori and Pakeha (Māori term for anyone non-Māori, pronounced pa-key-ha) bicultural context of New Zealand is critical to understanding expectations of contributing and serving society. Alongside these practices and expectations of ako and manaakitanga is another Māori idea, kotahitanga, which means unity and solidarity. Because of the small size and relative isolation of New Zealand, there is a survival instinct of needing to come together rather than oppose one another. This, along with ako and manaakitanga, came to bear following the earthquakes of 2010 and 2011 as well as the country's response to the 2019 mosque shootings and the 2020 pandemic. The responses to these tragedies, as will be described, were inherently New Zealand responses and provided the context for my re-evaluation of a self who teaches and a self who learns.

2010 AND 2011 EARTHQUAKES

While New Zealand has always been seismically active due to it straddling the meeting point of two major tectonic plates, the situation was never discussed in the same way that the San Andreas Fault in California is with "The Big One" always lurking in the background. Before 2010, the last major quake had occurred in 1931 when a 7.8 affected several cities on the North Island. Many buildings were destroyed and 512 people died. Unfortunately, this event did not spur an evolution in quake-resistant buildings as Christchurch continued to use stone and brick as main materials. This would prove to be a fatal decision with a 7.1 happening outside of Christchurch on September 4, 2010.

Fortunately, this quake took place at 4:35 AM on a Saturday morning so there were few people out in the city. Much of the damage was due to the collapsing of brick and stone facades—a British style of architecture for which the city was known, as it is with most British cities outside of England. Again, because of the time of day, people were thankfully not walking underneath those buildings. In addition to the brick and stone, another source of damage was liquefaction, which is basically a pushing up of water through the ground such that it finds any available outlets and emerges as a gray, quicksand like substance. The day immediately following the quake, many people were connecting with neighbors to see if people were alright. At my own house, two 80-year-old chimneys were severely compromised. While I was looking up at them with no idea about what to do, the Kiwi spirit of helping out showed itself in my neighbor, who is a builder, stopping by and immediately going into action to get us on the roof, secure the chimneys, and then we began to take them apart brick by brick. While up there, we saw that everyone else's chimneys up and down the street looked the same so we spent the day repeating that process regardless of whether people were home or not. This struck me as perhaps a uniquely Kiwi action where the assumption was we were going to help out no matter what.

The University of Canterbury in Christchurch was already on a mid-semester break so it was an easy decision to immediately suspend action there until we got a better handle on the damage and what post-quake life would look like both on campus and off. Because the area around campus was not that affected, students, for the most part, had water, power, and little of the liquefaction. So, their response was to quickly post up quake parties on Facebook and enjoy the extended break. One student, Sam Johnson, however, chose to do something quite different. He was studying political science and was particularly interested in how to engage young people in the political process. He also came from a farming background so had been brought up in that environment of helping your neighbor. His Facebook post invited fellow students to go out two days after the quake to an area that had been hit hard by lique-faction and help residents there clean up. With 100 fellow students on the first morning, they set out without equipment and little more than a desire to assist. They spent the day using anything that they could get their hands on to move the liquefaction from people's yards onto the street. Sam even emptied his bank account to pay for lunch. Because the day had felt productive and successful, he reposted the event and got 200 students the following day. Fast forward to a week later and he had over 2,000 students showing up and using donated wheelbarrows, boots, gloves, and meals. This Student Volunteer Army (not the original name for the movement but catchier than Student Response to Earth-quake Affected Residents) quickly captured the adoration and respect of the whole country and, alongside first responders, was seen as a real posi-tive emerging from the negative situation. I believe that it was so popular because it captured everything that Kiwis want to believe about them-selves with regard to community contribution. Once the clean-up work was completed in mid-September, the students went back to classes and people mostly wanted to put the quake behind us because no one had died and the built environment could be repaired. At the time, I felt that we could have done something to recognize the Army's efforts through an entry on their transcripts or a certificate or something. However, the moment for action passed and the students went about turning their movement into a volunteer club.

Despite the collective sense of relief that we had survived the big one in September of 2010, the ongoing aftershocks for months suggested that the seismic activity was not over. On the second day of Semester 1 classes on February 22, 2011, our fears of another big one were realized when a 6.3 struck near downtown in the middle of the day at 12:51 PM. Unlike the September one, this was prime time for people to be in the city and resulted in 185 deaths, over 80% of the city's buildings destroyed, and 11,000 homes rendered uninhabitable. Similar to the September one, everything except for the actions of the first responders ground to a halt while we figured out what to do. The Student Volunteer Army club immediately met to determine whether and/or how they would respond. Two days later, they relaunched and tallied up a quick 25,000 likes on their Facebook page, which led to over 11,000 volunteers for the next month. This time, they had the use of hundreds of donated wheelbarrows, access to as many city buses as they needed, thousands of pairs of boots and gloves, and donated food from around the country. Like with September's response, they were a bright spot nationwide amidst the rubble and liquefaction in Christchurch.

From a Student Movement to a University Response

Two days before the February earthquake, my family and I had moved out of our house for it to be repaired from the September event. Thus, we were living out of suitcases and staying on the third floor of an oceanside apartment. When the quake hit, I was in my office at the University of Canterbury campus across town from where my wife and kids were. After assisting with clearing and securing the campus, a colleague gave me a ride to our part of town. It should have taken 40 minutes and instead was 6 hours due to road closures and difficulties in finding intact bridges across the many rivers that crisscross the city. Once I got to my wife and kids, we quickly determined that we weren't going to stay in the third-floor apartment near the water as tsunamis were a threat with so much seismic activity. So, we headed to a resort area north of town with the hope that there would be places to rent. We were in luck and, like many of our friends and neighbors, decided to stay there for a few days until we were better informed.

On our second day after the quake, we were watching the news and a story about the Student Volunteer Army came on. With the backdrop of students shoveling liquefaction, the news anchor said: "Isn't it great that the students have put aside their learning to help out the community." My wife gave me a quick glance and said: "That doesn't sit well with you does it?" At that moment, I decided to do something and hastily sent an email to the Deputy Vice Chancellor (second in charge) whom I knew pretty well. I suggested to him that I had a desire to connect the SVA's actions with an academic response. To my surprise, I heard back from him within an hour that stated that the university was desperate for positive and innovative ideas. Further, I had 24 hours to develop my idea and pitch it to the Vice Chancellor. I quickly made two phone calls to Vincent Ilustre, who was the Executive Director of the Center for Public Service at Tulane University, and to Dr. Patti Clayton, who had been the Director of Service-Learning at North Carolina State University when I had been there and is my long-time mentor in service-learning. Both Patti and Vincent were great in helping me combine service-learning and disaster response, which Tulane had done following Hurricane Katrina by making service-learning a graduation requirement. While I was familiar with service-learning after having taught with it and researched it, I knew that this potential version of it would be non-traditional given our circumstances. With Patti and Vincent's assistance, I put together a pitch to the Vice Chancellor where we would create a new course with the three typical components of service-learning (academic content, service, and critical reflection) but we would let the SVA students' service count as having completed one-third of the course. Then, with successful engagement with relevant academic content and completion of critical reflection assignments, students would receive three credit hours.

When I pitched this to the Vice Chancellor, he stopped me after less than a minute and simply said, "Let's do this. What do I need to do to help you make this happen for Semester 2 (July)?" It's important to note that his background was having been the dynamic head of companies and while he had a PhD from Penn, he had a quick business-like response to implementing ideas. The typical time period for an idea to become a course at our university was 18 months so we would need his help along with the Pro Vice Chancellor of the College of Education (where I was located) to hasten the process and launch the course in 4 months.

So, amidst the majority of the campus being closed for building assessments and all of us working remotely from all over the country, a Ph.D. student, Lane Perry, and I began to put the course together. First up was to create a name for the course that would stand out on students' transcripts and signal that they had been part of something special. We settled on CHCH101: Rebuilding Christchurch, which has been shortened over the years to Christchurch 101 and implies that this is a basic course to understanding the city. As we developed the course, we worked closely with the SVA to make sure it was something they would want to take and that we were not co-opting their great work. We were very appreciative, as well, of the support of many colleagues. What we were proposing was not within the realm of many peoples' experiences and they trusted us. With the beginning of the course's launch, we settled on the following characteristics to make this elective course as accessible and desirable as possible:

- Except for the first class, there would be no whole class meetings;
- Students would meet in small tutorial groups that would be led by TAs who were the SVA leaders;
- The only requirement for the completed service was that they had a "significant service experience";
- The two assessments would be based on connecting the academic content with their service through critical reflection.

For the first iteration that July, we had over 100 SVA members take it and we received very positive feedback from them. At the time, we were not sure if we were headed down the Tulane path where CHCH101 would be mandatory for everyone, or if this would be a "one and done," or if we would land somewhere in between. We offered it during both summer school sessions and had another 200 students take it. When we were preparing to offer it for Semester 1 in February 2012, we were contacted by the International Relations Office; they had been contacted by numerous US students who were inquiring about earthquake related service-learning at UC. Sensing an opportunity to expand our class, we set up two tracks—one for the SVA students who had already done service and one for US and UC students who had not done the service. For the latter group, we would organize service within the class and both groups of students could learn alongside each other. The service within the class was focused on the earthquake and involved activities such as recycling wood from red-zoned houses for use in social innovation projects. This proved to be extremely popular and over the next few years, as the SVA earthquake students began to graduate, our portion of students doing service within the class grew. To guide us through these developments, we leaned into both Sir Peter Jackson's sense of New Zealand as a village to promote community service and the Māori concepts of ako and manaakitanga for how to teach and learn within this context.

AKO AS A PHILOSOPHY AND A PRACTICE

As defined earlier, ako is the educational manifestation of an ideal of equality through its dynamic equivalence and flexibility of the roles of teacher and learner. This is further elaborated on with:

> The concept of ako describes a teaching and learning relationship, where the educator is also learning from the student and where educators' practices are informed by the latest research and are both deliberate and reflective. Ako is grounded in the principle of reciprocity and also recognises that the learner and whanau cannot be separated. (Ministry of Education, 2021a, p. 20)
>
> Ako… is a reciprocal learning relationship wherein teachers are not expected to know everything. In particular, ako suggests that each member of the classroom, or learning setting, brings knowledge with them from which all are able to learn. (Keown et al., 2005, p. 12)
>
> Embracing the principle of ako enables teachers to build caring and inclusive learning communities where each person feels that their contribution is valued and that they can participate to their full potential. This is not about people simply getting along socially; it is about building productive relationships, between teacher and students and among students, where everyone is empowered to learn with and from each other. (Ministry of Education, 2021b)

From the onset of CHCH101, its design was predicated on placing students in the position of experts of their experiences and they were invited to teach us about what they had learned through their manaakitanga. Far from the traditional relationship in university teaching of the teacher being the knowledge holder and the students being recipients of that knowledge—Freire's "banking model" (2018)—our model sought to uplift and validate the lived experiences of the students and to place them in authority. Further, the current model of CHCH101 utilizes field trips and guest lectures by those involved with social innovation in post-quake Christchurch. Again, this sharing of the teaching and learning space with people who have contributed to rebuilding the city is to reiterate to the students that the people we are learning from are experts of their experiences. Thus, ever since the course's launch in 2011, this shared delivery of teaching and learning has invited students to frame their own experiences as expertise and to determine how they might convey that to others. The two assignments of the course below are designed to provide students with that opportunity.

Assignment	Learning outcome measured	% of final grade
Healing Proposal (up to 2000 words)	1. Apply theory critically to analyze community engagement 2. Evaluate the impact of their own community engagement experiences 3. Demonstrate an understanding of the Principles of protection, partnership, and participation of the Treaty of Waitangi with regard to community engagement in New Zealand 4. use a self-reflective approach to devising, developing, and presenting personally relevant assessment products	50%
Individual Reflection on the Group Project (up to 2000 words)	1. Apply theory critically to analyze community engagement 2. Evaluate the impact of their own community engagement experiences 3. Demonstrate an understanding of the principles of protection, partnership, and Participation of the Treaty of Waitangi with regard to community engagement in New Zealand 4. Use a self-reflective approach to devising, developing, and presenting personally relevant assessment products	50%

For the first six weeks of the course, students go on weekly field trips to both do service projects (e.g., work in a community garden, contribute to a mural, transplant plantings from red-zoned properties to newly opened childcare facilities) and to meet with social innovators who have responded to the quakes in creative and meaningful ways. These include artists who aligned their passions with community needs through manaakitanga. An example of this is an art gallery owner who saw the ugly, rusted shipping containers that were stacked two high and lined our main road for protection as a space of possibility. He got over 20 New Zealand artists to agree to have their work transferred onto large canvases and placed on the containers creating a massive outdoor gallery. Another musician offered to play music anywhere, anytime to help lift people's spirits. He and his band performed over 100 times in a month and often did several shows a day in parks, basements, and back yards. Keeping with the ako concept, students engage with the local expertise of these innovators by meeting them in their contexts—the art gallery and a bar—as that is more appropriate than bringing them onto campus and speaking in sterile lecture theaters. At the conclusion of those six weeks, students are tasked with the first assignment in the table above, The Healing Proposal, which is further described in the course outline as:

The Healing Proposal

Recognize that you have the same power and potential to affect and influence your community as the guest speakers we will have met and others we will read about (i.e., Sam Johnson of the Student Volunteer Army, Ryan Reynolds of Gap Filler, and the Neighborhood Police Team). This assignment is an opportunity for you to think critically and laterally about how you might do so.

You will come up with a feasible proposal that aims to positively affect and influence a specific community and reflects your own personal and academic interests. This can be the Riccarton Neighborhood, Christchurch, UC, New Zealand, your hometown, a primary school, wherever.

In addition to the proposal, which may take any format that you determine is effective and can reflect your area of study (e.g., an engineering report, a creative essay, a legal brief, etc.), you will create an "artistic hook" (e.g., painting, poem, poster, sculpture, song, etc.). The hook will reflect your proposal and would be something that catches the attention of an approving or funding group to whom you are presenting your proposal. You will have the opportunity to see what sharing your proposal feels like through presenting it and the hook to the class at the meeting in Week 6.

Upon their initial introduction to the Healing Proposal assignment, students are wary on a number of levels, particularly with the apparent freedom to respond to it in both the substance and style of their choosing. While they are provided with a detailed rubric about what the Proposal must address, the lack of specifics, especially engaging with the artistic hook, is often related to trusting us that we are not out to trick them and that they are, in fact, meant to be experts of their own experiences. This is yet another opportunity to use the ako concept of truly sharing the teaching and learning space among all of us and is exemplified by this student who recognized that this assignment was an opportunity to embrace his passion.

> I have submitted my Healing Proposal, but I would like you to know that it is only the tip of the iceberg. I am super grateful for this course as it has forced me to start putting my dream on paper. (CHCH101-20S2 student)

The class session where students present their proposals and artistic hooks is a highlight amidst a semester full of meaningful experiences. And, over the years, we have seen some of these proposals come to life through actual projects. For example, in the 2013 occurrence, a student's proposal aligned a need in the city with her academic and personal interests. By that year, many of the downtown buildings (of which 80% were severely damaged) had been deconstructed so that there were huge gaps between existing buildings. Rachel Dewhirst, a Fine Arts major taking CHCH101 as an elective, chose to focus her Healing Proposal on a prominent building's wall in the heart of the city alongside a pedestrian mall. Her artistic hook was a photo-shopped image of a mural on that wall and her proposal laid out a compelling case for why the building owner should let her paint it that focused on bringing color back to that part of the city. All aspects of her Proposal were outstanding and we suggested to her that she consider approaching the building owner. She did and was enthusiastically received by the owner who said he would also help her source the paint from a local company, which came through with paint, and scaffolding was provided by another company. Within a month after her presentation of the Proposal to our class, she and some friends were painting the exact mural that she had designed. It just so happens that the mural has remained highly visible for the last eight years as nothing has been built to obscure it. It has achieved her purpose of bringing color to that part of the city and has endured beyond her belief at the time that it would be more short lived (Fig. 7.1).

A year after Rachel's mural, another CHCH101 student's Healing Proposal also came to fruition in a wholly different context. Jessica Weston was a US study abroad student from the University of Illinois and was at the University of Canterbury for Semester 1 (February–June) in 2013 and took our course because of her interest in service-learning and wanting to see different sides of the city through our projects. She

Fig. 7.1 Mural of student's "healing" project. *Source* Author

was particularly inspired by a presentation by one of the SVA founders and decided to base her Healing Proposal on starting an SVA type of organization back at Illinois. When she left at the end of the semester, we pledged to stay in touch with her and support her efforts however we could. Upon her return home, she began to identify ways to connect with her fellow students and enlist them in forming a volunteer group. Two months later, she had her "SVA moment" when a devastating tornado tore through her hometown of Washington, Illinois and left many without their homes. Jessica immediately activated the networks she had been building with an invitation to help her with donations of needed supplies through a "fill the truck" campaign. Within two days, she had received $5000 in donations and enough items to fill two tractor trailers, all of which were quickly headed to Washington just a few days after the tornado. She credits her significant and substantial actions to being inspired by the SVA and CHCH101 with:

> CHCH101 gave me the urgency and empowerment to do something to help my hometown when disaster struck. I walked away from CHCH101 a better person for many reasons. I fully understood the power young adults could have in their communities and in disaster relief efforts. I understood how to take my talents and passions and contribute them to a greater cause.

The true beauty of these two Healing Proposals is that they exemplify the shared teaching and learning space that we sought to create with the course. Jessica's mention of "empowerment to do something" is really what our goal has been all along. While not every Healing Proposal has resulted in such a dramatic outcome as Rachel's or Jessica's, we have heard from other students that the ideas from the Proposals have come to life as projects in other settings and as job interview conversation starters.

After providing the students with a combination of applying ako and manaakitanga through their Healing Proposals, for the second half of the semester both of these concepts are intensified through the Team Projects. Students are placed on teams of five and are given five weeks to design and implement projects that will positively impact specific communities of their choosing. They are given nearly complete freedom as to when and how they will meet, what they will do, and how they will measure the impact. This type of teaching and learning embraces ako and manaakitanga and approaches a form of "group existentialism" where, aside from weekly check-ins with members of the teaching staff, the students are truly in control. At this point in the semester, my self who teaches becomes nervous and slightly stressed especially when some groups inevitably struggle with working together and determining what they will do. However, I push through my challenges with the belief that this will be an amazing learning experience for all of us, and that I am there to learn from them. Save for one group over the last 10 years, every other of the 50 groups has accomplished their goal and pulled off an impactful project in a short amount of time. Some of the noteworthy ones have been: facilitating a leadership day at a local school, refurbishing a community garden, making over the waiting room at a children's mental health facility, and hosting a lunch and activities at a retirement village. As noted by this student, an important outcome from the Team Project is learning how to listen to others and work with them—a key aspect of ako.

> The group project develops our project management, problem solving, critical thinking, communication, teamwork, and leadership skills, but the most important skill I learned was listening to people, building genuine connections, and understanding what they need. I was able to use these skills during an internship at the Shirley Village Project. (CHCH101-19S2 student)

The key with both the Healing Proposal and the Team Project is that they may appear to be easy for the self who teaches because students are put into a position of authority and leadership and we heavily rely on community members to serve as teachers, but they are far from easy to coordinate, facilitate, and feel the discomfort and insecurity of being less in control. As is aptly noted by this student, the overall feeling of the course is more of a journey taken together with me only providing guidance as the "guide on the side."

> Thank you very much for taking us on such an interesting journey this semester. I'm very sad that the course has finished but am hoping it is the 'beginning' of my journey into more community engagement. I appreciated your kind guidance and reframing of perspective during the course. (CHCH101-20S2 student)

AKO AND MANAAKITANGA FOR OTHER CONTEXTS

While we feel confident about our application of ako and manaakitanga in CHCH101 based on positive course evaluations, unsolicited feedback, and formal research, one question I have had is if this notion of sharing the instructional space will work in other contexts. Similar to the uncertainty felt when ceding the "sage on the stage" position, how best can I work between the self who teaches and the self who learns when I have far less control of the space. An opportunity to explore this challenge came in the unexpected situation of being involved in the aftermath of the 2018 shooting at Marjory Stoneman Douglas (MSD) High School in Parkland, Florida. From 9,000 miles away I watched the gut wrenching television footage of students hustled out of the buildings and of the shocking death toll of 17 students and staff with many others wounded and far more forever psychologically affected. Immediately following this horrific event, several MSD students began planning how they would respond. This eventuated a month and a half later with the March for Our Lives events, which took place in over 800 locations around the world and more than 500,000 participants at the main march in Washington, DC.

Through mutual connections between myself and the MSD students and staff, we determined that it could be a positive experience to bring them together with our SVA students and see what might happen given that they were both movements led by young people in response to tragedy. Thus, in July of that same year, 28 MSD students came to New Zealand for a week of collegiality and bonding. The itinerary that we designed was light on lecturing or presenting to the students and more weighted toward them interacting and sharing their experiences. By emphasizing ako and manaakitanga, the experiences of the students from MSD and New Zealand were valued and served as the content for the week. Their visit culminated in a one-day summit whereby the MSD and SVA students were left completely on their own to collectively see what they could create. The result of putting the students in charge of their own learning was a substantial document that provided details about creating and sustaining youth movements. Their presentation of it was emotional, inspirational, and proof of what people can accomplish when invited to reflect on and hold up their experiences. Despite the heavy source of the document, especially for the MSD students, it was similar to student-driven Healing Proposal and Team Project processes in CHCH101 whereby students are guided and supported but, ultimately, the outcome is in their hands and we are there to learn from them.

From Rubble to Rocking Chairs: Ako and Manaakitanga in Action

My work in community engagement following the earthquakes has provided me with incredible opportunities to learn from others such as the MSD teachers and students. Another opportunity along those lines came in 2017 when I had the immense privilege to meet with the late Congressman John Lewis. The premise for our meeting was to interview him about what it takes to answer the call of history even when doing so could prove deadly. To say that he possessed mana (Māori for spirit and power, pronounced ma-nah) is an understatement. Through his gentle and kind demeanor, he told me about several incidents in his life where he was thoroughly tested and how he made it through them. Just before we finished, I asked him what he would want me to tell the students I teach. Without hesitation, he responded with a three-part model of developing a passion, preparing yourself to act on that passion, and taking every opportunity to right a wrong. Within his three suggested actions, Congressman Lewis provided a clear way of how to implement ako (becoming the expert of your own passion and sharing that with others) and manaakitanga (righting a wrong). And, there was the implication that for an idea like the Civil Rights Movement to succeed, it required its followers to express kotahitanga in being unified for the cause even when facing daunting odds including death.

While Congressman Lewis clearly and readily provided me with a way that individuals can enact the ideas of ako, manaakitanga, and kotahitanga, what does it look when coming from an organization or institution? Thus, it is no coincidence that my conversation with Congressman Lewis led me to later visit the Highlander Center for Research and Education, a place that had been important to him, Dr. Martin Luther King, Jr., Rosa Parks, and others during the Civil Rights Movement. Situated on an idyllic property in East Tennessee that looks out upon the Great Smoky Mountains, its deceiving sublime beauty has been the constant foundation for powerful social justice movements since the 1920s. Founded by Myles Horton as a place for rural farmers, coal miners, and factory workers to come together and collectively advocate for better working conditions, it was modeled on folk schools of Europe to also preserve rural culture. The power of Highlander is in its fairly simple model of bringing people together, having them sit in rocking chairs in a round room where the positions of power are equally shared, and share their stories in order to find their own solutions. It is an ideal physical representation of ako and manaakitanga through its tangible equality of teacher/learner positions and pursuit of improving the world. An early participant at Highlander described the school's invitation to self-empowerment as:

> People were in pretty bad shape. But at Highlander we learned how to handle our daily problems, to do by organizing, by showing our power and our strength. The most important thing the people ever learned from Highlander was what we learned then – how we could help ourselves. (Adams, 1975, p. 38)

In a conversation between Horton and Paulo Freire that was recorded and transcribed into a book, Horton elaborates on this point from the early participant regarding the blurring of boundaries between the self who learns and the self who teaches with:

> I think if I had to put a finger on what I consider a good education, a good *radical* education, it wouldn't be anything about methods or techniques. It would be loving people first. If you don't do that, Che Guevara says there's no point in being a revolutionary. And wanting for them what you want for yourself. And then next is respect for people's abilities to learn and to act and to shape their own lives. You have to have confidence that people can do that. (Horton & Freire, 1990, p. 177)

Perhaps an ako approach to teaching and learning that truly has no fixed boundaries between learner and teacher is, in Horton's words, radical in that it calls for different emphases, intended outcomes, and structures. He was able to create a tangible place where love and the respect for others' abilities were central to its purpose. Maybe an important question is why is this considered to be a radical education and not more of the norm? And, if an ako and manaakitanga teaching and learning approach were more normalized, what might society look like?

Conclusion: Beyond the Classroom—A Culture of Ako, Manaakitanga, and Kotihitanga

In her book of case studies about five disasters and their aftermaths, *A Paradise Built in Hell*, Rebecca Solnit describes glimpses of utopia that occur when neighbors help each other out and, for the moment, there is a shared sense of humanity. Taking the chimneys down with my neighbor and the SVA's actions were clearly what she was describing. The sad part is that most of these situations do not last and people slip back into pre-disaster behaviors. Could an adoption of ako, manaakitanga, and kotahitanga retain aspects of utopia? Unfortunately, in addition to the earthquakes of 2010 and 2011, Christchurch had another tragedy in 2019 when a white supremacist opened fire in two mosques and killed 51 people and wounded many others during Friday prayers. For a country not well experienced in gun violence and steeped in a bicultural context, what would be the response?

The University of Canterbury and the New Zealand government took what had been learned from the earthquakes and applied them to this tragedy. One thing that was clear after the quakes was a deep desire by people to be together with others. This spirit of kotahitanga—unity and solidarity—was well recognized by both the Vice Chancellor, Professor Cheryl de la Rey, and the Prime Minister Jacinda Ardern in their immediate actions, which served as models for us all. On the Monday after the shootings, the University of Canterbury held a call to prayer and outdoor ceremony in the middle of campus. As always, the SVA contributed to the kotahitanga and manaakitanga by distributing flowers, which became part of a tribute wall. Soon thereafter, the Prime Minister donned a hajib and coined a phrase of hope that resonated with many—"Kia Kaha (stay strong) they [the victims and the Muslim community] are us." These reactions by leaders within our institution and country went far in promoting the sense of kotahitanga and manaakitanga while crafting a uniquely New Zealand response.

Both concepts have had more recent application with New Zealand's world-leading efforts against COVID-19 with the elimination of the virus through a concerted effort of hygiene, a tracking app, and wide compliance with masks, a strict lockdown, and managed quarantine. Again, the Prime Minister's leadership leaned into manaakitanga and kotahitanga with a catch phrase of "the team of five million." Like those before her, particularly the first inhabitants of New Zealand, the Māori, she was calling on Kiwis to be the villagers who are dependent on each other, love each other, learn from each other, and lead each other. While there is no definitive proof that the use of ako and manaakitanga in education has led to this society where followers are leaders and vice versa, there is at least an explicit attempt to implement Horton's idea for a radical education. However, to truly reach for that aspiration calls for a loosening up on the confines of the self who learns and the self who teaches. As noted in this chapter, it is not an easier road to travel but it is potentially a richer one.

References

Adams, F. (1975). *Unearthing seeds of fire: The idea of Highlander*. John F. Blair.
Alton-Lee, A. (2003). *Quality teaching for diverse students in schooling*. https://www.educationcounts.govt.nz/publications/series/2515/5959
Dewey, J. (1938). *Experience and education*. Simon & Schuster.
Freire, P. (2018). *Pedagogy of the oppressed* (4th ed.). Bloomsbury Atlantic.
Horton, M., & Freire, P. (1990). *We make the road by walking: Conversations on education and social change*. Temple University Press.
Keown, P., Parker, L., & Tiakiwai, S. (2005). *A final report on values in the New Zealand curriculum*. Ministry of Education.
Ministry of Education. (2015). *The New Zealand curriculum*. Ministry of Education.
Ministry of Education. (2021a). *Ka Hikitia – Managing for success 2008–2012*. https://www.education.govt.nz/our-work/overall-strategies-and-policies/ka-hikitia-ka-hapaitia/ka-hikitia-history/ka-hikitia-managing-for-success-2008-2012/
Ministry of Education. (2021b). *The concept of ako*. https://tereomaori.tki.org.nz/Curriculum-guidelines/Teaching-and-learning-te-reo-Maori/Aspects-of-planning/The-concept-of-ako
Te Ara. (2021). *Te Ara—The New Zealand encyclopedia*. https://teara.govt.nz/en/whanau-maori-and-family/page-1
Wigginton, E. (1985). *Sometimes a shining moment: The Foxfire experience*. Anchor Press.

CHAPTER 8

Holding the Space: A Teacher Educator's Poetic Representations of Pre-service Teachers Acts of Self-Care

Narelle Lemon

INTRODUCTION

Self-care is important. It is an imperative. Self-care is about being proactive. It is the future of preventative well-being—it is about what you can do to be the best version of yourself so you can flourish physically, emotionally, mentally and spiritually (Butler et al., 2019; Lemon, 2021; Reading, 2018). But in contemporary society this is not the message that is always attached to self-care. The concept has been muddied and between scattergun program approaches, social media influence with focus on hedonic strategies based around facials, massages and yoga poses, and no clear definition of self-care itself, the concept of self-care is revealing itself to be difficult to engage with. Additionally, most people

N. Lemon (✉)
Department of Education, Swinburne University of Technology, Melbourne, VIC, Australia
e-mail: nlemon@swin.edu.au

feel they do not enact or embody self-care well, and thus often feel guilty when they do engage with acts of self-care. Furthermore, in contemporary Western societies especially, those who embody self-care are confronted with resistance or judgement from others for their practices and routines.

Self-care is even more complex in the field of education; for both in-service and pre-service teachers across all contexts. To be a teacher is to care. One cares for the young people they work with as they facilitate learning in and across academic and personal growth. However, it is this act of care that is sometimes out of sync. Too often as teachers, we care for others while forgetting to care for ourselves. We know that we cannot care for others if we cannot care for ourselves. Kristen Neff reminds us, self-compassion is required and "entails being kind and understanding towards oneself in instances of pain or failure rather than being harshly self-critical" (Neff, 2003, p. 223). As teachers we must show ourselves self-compassion and fill our own bucket before we fill the bucket of others (Neff, 2011). However, we are fully aware that teachers often put their own self-care or well-being last (Ghanizadeh & Jahedizadeh, 2015; Napoli & Bonifas, 2011). This reveals a need to be able to illuminate the importance of self-care for teachers, and for pre-service teachers, and highlights the spaces and need to build bridges towards purpose, unity, peace and collective well-being.

Self-care is about the self, but, it is also about a collective. The "I", "we" and "us" are intersecting. As future teachers, pre-service teachers must learn to care for themselves in order to be able to care for the students, colleagues and wider community they are to work closely with. This significantly highlights a need to focus on the act of caring for self in partnership to teaching, and indeed caring for the students that are recipients of learning. However, this illuminates some questions. When is self-care and teacher well-being discussed, contextualized, modeled and embodied within initial teacher education degrees? How do teacher educators discuss, model, contextualize and embody self-care? If a pre-service teacher isn't caring for themself how can they truly care for the students that they are supporting? If a pre-service teacher does not have an opportunity to realize they can enact and embody self-care differently, how can they flourish? If a pre-service teacher does not experience a mentor who enacts self-care, what message is being communicated about well-being?

Teachers often place student well-being above their own. The modelling of self-care by teachers to pre-service teachers is often not present. This is complex, and does reveal the tension of being in a caring role such as a teacher. The tension is acknowledged in writing this chapter, and as such it is assumed that the promotion of self-care amongst pre-service teachers during initial teacher education is a vital element to disrupt and interrupt common patterns that ignite stress, burnout and anxiety amongst the profession of teaching. Initial teacher education can be one space that provides a scaffolding to disruption of not prioritizing self-care as a teacher.

There is a need to reframe self-care in the discipline of education. This need is required for teachers in the professions, but also for those who are becoming teachers. When working with pre-service teachers this becomes visible in their negotiation between professional and personal identity. In the journey of becoming a teacher, initial teacher education is a fundamental stage of training whereby well-being needs to be positioned as both an individual and collective action. Present though are systemic problems—primarily, that we know there is a problem with teacher attrition, mental health, high expectations, over testing, crowded curriculum, societal ideals of what a teacher is, lack of resources, etc. (Betoret & Artiga, 2010; Madaliyeva et al., 2015; Qiu, 2018; Schnaider-Levi et al., 2017; Skaalvik & Skaalvik, 2017). In initial teacher education itself, well-being is not always honoured, and there are complexities also present here with crowded curriculum, external accreditation requirements, university requirements, teacher educator identity and capacity, and indeed vision for degree foci (Lemon, 2021). Years.

Thus, for a pre-service teacher undertaking initial teacher education studies and entering the profession of teaching, there are many layers of political and systemic influences that can be rather confronting that impact well-being, while also raising the position of caring for self both hedonically and eudemonically. Often the focus can be on these aspects of the profession that are connected to a deficit way of thinking—what is wrong, negatives and issues. But what happens when we focus on flourishing and what is good? What happens when we value conversations about self-care with pre-service teachers? In this chapter, I explore this through poetry as a vehicle to explore and promote what self-care is for pre-service teachers. This form of expression is seen as a way through which we can be with, in and through an embodiment of a discovery of ideas. Poetry represents conversations that focus on how as teacher educators, we can support the preparation and participation for becoming a teacher in partnership with self-care integrated at this time in initial teacher education. Illuminated in the poems are moments of boundary setting, learning to connect with inner joy via a smile, interruptions to feelings of isolation by realizing one is not alone, embracing failure for growth, and advice to future selves.

RESEARCH CONTEXT

As the author of this chapter, I am a statistic of teacher attrition having left the profession within the first 5 years due to burnout. After a break, I did return with a focus on well-being, as underpinned by this chapter sharing my passion to highlight new ways of working. Locating and positioning conversations and learning about self-care at the forefront of being and becoming a teacher are a significant goal for me.

In this chapter, representations of pre-service teachers' voices are shared in poetry form to contribute to building bridges and placing well-being and self-care conversations at the forefront of becoming a teacher. These poems have been created from listening to critical moments for pre-service teachers. I listened, made reflective notes after class, and came back later to be with both my thoughts and my written reflections to create poetic representations of these moments in time. In this chapter poems were generated from working with Australian undergraduates over a duration of a face-to-face semester of study. These pre-service teachers worked with me in preparing for professional experience (time spent in a school or educational context) within an initial teacher education subject.

The poetry presented in this chapter emerges from ongoing reflections throughout a semester. They are representations of conversations that occurred at different times sparked by weekly workshop themes. They were not planned, nor a part of an assignment. The conversations that these poems are based on are from professional conversations that emerged from valuing authenticity in the initial teacher education classroom that values integrity, generosity and a curiosity to answer the hard questions, to disrupt silence, and to embrace reflection about how one will, can and wants to be within the profession of teaching.

In this chapter I respond through poetry to some of the tensions of becoming a teacher and in learning that self-care requires a curious stance that supports ongoing reflection. The poems are a response to pre-service teachers. I respond to their moments of sharing, the trust they had in me to open up with me and each other. There is trust in me representing their moments of professional, and personal, growth through written words presented creatively. Moments of vulnerability are showcased. These moments are invited and celebrated. From this perspective, pre-service teachers have embraced, displayed and embodied the courage to share openly about their tensions of becoming. The sharing openly is embraced and seen as critical moments to build bridges between experience and reframing that scaffold a journey of self-care for one and many to flourish physically, emotionally, mentally and spiritually. Although sharing can be cathartic, the focus of these poems is on how we can reframe and move forward, productively and positively.

Richardson (1997) argues that "lived experience is lived in a body, and poetic representation can touch us where we live, in our bodies" (p. 143). In examining the experience of pre-service teachers and the tensions they encounter in their becoming, poetic representation of data provides an entry point to considering the nature of becoming a teacher and locating self-care. Through poetry, a contemplative practice itself, and also a research reporting process (Dark, 2009; Yoo, 2019) that communicates concisely and with intensity to ignite a response from the audience, the poems are representative of both the process and outcome. This approach draws "on poetic representation as a means of displaying and disseminating research data" and provides scope to honor voices "to be heard in ways that move beyond cognitive, intellectual modes" (McDonough, 2018, p. 113).

The vulnerability as a teacher educator, a learner oneself, to engage with conversations on self-care with pre-service teachers and represent this in poetry form promotes critical moments of being present with suffering, celebrations, worries and anticipations. As a teacher educator, I am holding the space for pre-service teachers in working in this way. Poetry is, thus, seen as an entry point into accessing current reality for the pre-service teachers that have engaged with their self-care needs individually and collectively, and honors the "essence of the how, the why, the what" (Carroll et al., 2011, p. 624) of becoming a teacher. Poetic representation invites you as a reader to engage both emotionally and cognitively with the concepts (Januchowski-Hartley et al., 2018), and I invite you to enter a dialogue about what might be possible when we think about self-care.

As an initial teacher educator who has responded to moments of individuals and collectives exploring self-care, poetry is crafted as a response; a bouncing off and reaction to pre-service teachers' reflections, sharing, insights, worries, ruminations, anger and moments of tension from a space of curiosity and awareness of their lived experiences of becoming a teacher. The poems are thus artistic expressions and representations of the pre-service teacher voice. In the process of responding through writing poetry, highlighted is how the act of being grounded as a teacher educator supports and openness to explore the building of bridges between personal and professional growth, and individual and collective self-care that positions well-being at the heart of being and becoming a teacher. The space has been held for these pre-service teachers.

The poetic representations of critical moments are presented simply but effectively in conversations that interrupted ruminations or moments of what usually would be silenced. In this way, critical moments for pre-service teachers are honored and thus we "slow down and linger with memories, experiences and emotions" (Leggo, 2018, p. 15). Poetry provides a space for the author to share pre-service teacher's vulnerability (Lemon, 2021; Lemon & McDonough, 2021). The poems also provide a space for pre-service teachers to be listened to. And poetic representation provides a space for pre-service teachers to reframe. We collectively listen. We collectively build bridges to connect to lived experiences. And we collectively reframe self-care as valuable and a necessity.

The poetry is underpinned by a pedagogy of curiosity that values courage and vulnerability to promote a way for all of us, teacher educator and pre-service teachers, to learn from one another and to explore self, care and self-care. Key to a pedagogy of curiosity is locating mindfulness, specifically the mechanisms of intention, attention and awareness (Shapiro et al., 2006). By holding the space and being curious as a teacher educator, pre-service teachers are invited explicitly and implicitly to make connections to explore personal and professional well-being and these intersections. They are invited to be reflexive and self-aware. This approach draws on mindfulness as the process of self-regulating attention and awareness in the present moment, accompanied by the use of an open-minded, curious and accepting attitude (Bishop et al. 2004; Brown & Ryan, 2003).

Through the lens of mindfulness whereby the intention is set to be present with this moment in time, I as the initial teacher educator hold the space for the pre-service teachers. As I have developed and extended my own mindfulness practice, I have made specific decisions that align to the mindfulness mechanisms of intention, attention and awareness to enable the holding of this space (see Fig. 8.1). That is, being grounded oneself before working with the pre-service teachers. This is achieved via

MINDFULNESS MECHANISMS	MY PRACTICE	SPECIFIC ACTIONS
Intention *What I hope to get out of practicing mindfulness. Directing my attention with purpose.* *The why we practice.*	The strength of my intention helps motivate my practice and shapes the quality of my mindful awareness. • I am setting the intention to bring my mindfulness practice into my work life as a teacher educator. • I am setting the intention to talk about mindfulness practices, with a mutual respect, rather than hide it. • I am setting the intention to be in the moment non-judgementally for the pre-service teachers I work with. • I am setting the intention to hold a space for pre-service teachers with non-judgmentally and with compassion.	These intentions are written on a piece of paper stuck on the wall placed at eye level by my computer monitor on my office desk where I can see them and constantly connect with them. Before beginning each class, I speak out loud these intentions, almost like they are mantras. During class, these intentions are embodied.
Attention *Paying attention to the inner and outer experience.* *What we practice.*	The strength of my attention is in being centred and grounded; having an inner composure and self-assurance, whatever the situation, with a deep inner sense of calm and confidence.	Daily personal meditation practice. Before teaching, I spend 15-30 minutes undertaking a silent self-guided meditation to ground myself, to calm the breath, and to bring my attention back to my intentions to hold an open supportive space for the pre-service teachers I am working with. During class, I bring attention back to the breath as I listen. As I listen, I undertake a mini self-compassion meditation; I inhale for me, and I exhale for the individual talking at the time. This helps me be grounded, open and hold the space for the lived experienced being shared with empathy and a vulnerability while also protecting myself from wearing others experiences or emotions.
Attitude *Paying attention to certain attitudes, noticing habits of the mind and becoming gentler and more appreciative.* *How we practice.*	The strength of my attitude is the positive emotions that I engage with and embody as I am being present. I bring my signature strengths of curiosity and self-awareness to assist me to align my intentions while holding the space. I enact compassion, appreciation, kindness, acceptance, open-mindedness and gratitude.	Curiosity – showing an interest in new things, ways of supporting expression of lived experiences, and seeking out new information; being excited to learn more. Self-awareness – knowing myself and understanding my emotions and behaviours – what excites me, what triggers me, what happens if I over analyse and don't enact self-compassion.

Fig. 8.1 Mindfulness practice in action to enable holding the space for pre-service teachers

Appreciation, kindness, compassion, open-
minded, acceptance and gratitude – are
modeled and embodied in verbal and
non-verbal communication as part of
holding the space, creating a
psychologically safe learning environment,
and to foster a community with mutual
respect.

Fig. 8.1   (continued)

meditation and setting intentions for those I am working with. The aim is to be present with the pre-service teachers throughout the class; to hold the space for the pre-service teachers to also maintain awareness, being present non-judgmentally to class discussions and indeed how pre-service teachers present themselves in class (Fig. 8.1).

Mindfulness is paired with a positive psychology; a focus on what is a good life and including how one can flourish (Lomas et al., 2015; Seligman & Csikszentmihalyi, 2000). Flourishing is a state where one can be their authentic self. To flourish is to find fulfillment in our lives, accomplishing meaningful and worthwhile tasks, and connecting with others at a deeper level—in essence, living the "good life" (Seligman, 2011). Flourishing is a state where people experience positive emotions, positive psychological functioning and positive social functioning, most of the time, living within an optimal range of human functioning (Lomas et al., 2015). Mindfulness is integrated to offer the positioning of intention, attention and awareness more clearly with outcomes aimed towards addressing pre-service teachers' lived experiences of becoming a teacher. This approach builds upon intention, attention and awareness, acknowledging that this integration supports positive variables and what is good in life (Lomas et al., 2017), thus allowing a positive mindfulness cycle to be formed (Ivtzan, 2016; Young, 2016, 2019).

Integrated throughout this positive mindfulness cycle is curiosity, that motivates learning and supports one to be present and open with appreciation of novelty, challenge, and uncertainty supporting experimentation with new and interesting experiences (Biswas-Diener et al., 2011; Ciarrochi et al., 2013; Kashdan & Silvia, 2012; Kashdan & Steger, 2007). It is the partnership and interrelationship between being present and curious that sparks possibility for flourishing; to promote connections to current experiences of stress and what is possible with self-care for pre-service teachers. And it is the embodiment of these practices by myself as the initial teacher educator that enables the pre-service teacher to embrace this way of being and responding. A pedagogy of curiosity is thus formed, where negative and positive experiences of being a teacher are acknowledged, appreciated non-judgmentally, and further explored to unpack what helps one flourish with their self-care.

CREATING THE POEMS

A pedagogy of curiosity requires ongoing inquiry. One way I did this was to maintain a diary throughout a semester where I would reflect on my teaching, specifically working with final year pre-service teachers. I would reflect on what I did, how I held the space for those I was working with, and for myself. My reflective notes enabled me to both be present with my own thoughts in response to pre-service teachers sharing in class, while allowing me to disconnect, connect, ponder, rethink, honor and capture moments where I needed to hold the space for those I was working with at the time. In this way journaling became both a site for my own reflective practice as a part of my self-care and productive coping but also a place to support self- healing (Pennebaker, 2013); it was a version of quiet time or me time. Journaling to support reflective practice brings awareness to your thoughts, actions, and behaviours (Harvey et al., 2020; Hensley & Munn, 2019). It can support you to be able to reveal patterns and facilitate change. The act of "writing your thoughts out" can support the examination of different angles and examination of assumption or blockers (Chang & Lin, 2014). Journaling became an act for my self-care and spiritual and emotional well-being, helping me to assert the value of self-acknowledging there is always a way to figure things out, that sometimes we need time and methods to process; to engage with everyday realities; to respond to something happening in our life; and to look back and reflect upon growth as well as what was serving me well (Sinats et al., 2005).

I manually coded my journal entries and the subsequent reflections as a form of qualitative data and had this cross checked by a research assistant. I followed a thematic approach; searching for patterns and relationships to "find explanations for what is observed" (Boeije, 2010, p. 76) through segmenting and reassembling. Patterns were identified within a theme to find replications and or sub-themes that helped shape the poems. Trustworthiness working this way comes from the revealing of the content analysis process. Furthermore, the criterion of credibility (the research design and participant demographics are described accurately, with awareness of researcher bias); dependability (stability of data over time and under different conditions noting how the data was collected and the context); conformability (the potential for comparisons between two or more independent people about the data's accuracy, relevance, or meaning); transferability (the extent the reader can consider the findings can/may be transferred to other settings or groups); and authenticity (showing a range of realities) have been embraced throughout this research (Elo et al., 2014; Guba & Lincoln, 1994; Lincoln & Guba, 1985; Polit & Beck, 2012).

In the next section of this chapter five poetic responses to face-to-face class conversations with pre-service teachers illuminate shifts in thinking and highlight crucial moments of curiosity towards self-care and well-being. Highlighted is the complexity of emotions that pre-service teachers grapple with as they explore who they are and how they want to be. These insights emerged from my teaching, as an initial teacher educator, holding the space to honor these conversations with a curious and open stance located in awareness and attention with the intention set to encourage exploration and finding out more about one's self. They are representations of what can emerge from a pedagogy of curiosity.

The Acknowledgement

I can't do it.
Tired. Exhausted. Sleepy. Heavy. Lost. Worried.
Have to stop.

I say yes.
Then I don't feel it.
But when I say no, I get worried I am missing out.

I have a fear.
A fear of missing out.
What if? What if? What if?
It keeps going around in my head.
Yes, no, yes, no, yes, no...it's a whirlwind of decisions.

I'm tired.
Physically, mentally.
Make it stop.

For pre-service teachers the negotiation of becoming and being a teacher is always present during studies, none more prevalent during professional experience placements. During this time the pre-service teacher is required to be full time in a classroom, engaging with the learning that is seen critical in initial teacher education for connecting theoretical and practical understanding. It is also a critical moment where well-being comes into fruition. One is navigating time as a "teacher" but not with full ownership, and also still wearing the identity as a university student, while navigating life that often involves part time work, other caring responsibilities, managing living costs on low budgets, and family and friendship commitments. It is tension packed; negotiation being a critical skill. The setting of boundaries is crucial. And often the first lesson in self-care. Learning to say no is actually a yes to care for oneself, and others.

The Smile

Smile.
What makes you smile? Me? Makes me?
I have forgotten how to smile.
You think you do it.
But I realized I don't.

You asked me to smile.
I rolled my eyes.
I always smile.

You asked me to smile.
I realised I don't smile.
I haven't made time to smile.

Such a simple question.
Smile.
Smile!!!!!

The joy, the laughter.
Feeling light.
Smile, I need to smile more.

Make time to smile.
Smile for me.

Such a simple question.
When did you last smile?
When did I last smile?
How will I smile more?
I will smile more.

Learning to connect with inner joy and the power of the smile is crucial as a teacher; as a human being. When do we stop and just smile, to savor the smile? To engage with a moment, a micro-moment that ignites positive emotions. It is often something that sparks a critical moment in a pre-service teachers' moment of development as they navigate the tension of moving from being a student to being and becoming a teacher. The smile is something one can forget to do. Being so caught up with assumptions, requirements, needs, to do lists and assessment is part of the pre-service teacher identity, as too is figuring out if the roles for them and what it can and will look like. Smiling seems so natural. But as a pre-service teacher it is often missing in the journey. Stopping and smiling or even just asking the question "when did I last smile?" sparks a reminder of joy and being curious, open, aware and attentive to what it is one is hoping to achieve, do, and enjoy. A smile is a connection point to being present as part of the self-care journey. It is a simple question, but powerful in connecting to how one care for oneself.

I'm Not Alone

I've been alone for so long.
Pondering, wondering.
My thoughts going around in my head.
It's just me.

You asked me, us, to share.
To share what we find stressful.
You asked me?
You asked us?
You listened.

I shared.
They shared.
We shared.
We listened.

I am not alone.
I have felt alone…isolated…terrified…. juggling…coping, not coping.
I cry. I cry tears of joy.
I am not alone.

That moment when a pre-service teacher realizes, they are not alone, is powerful. It is a gift to one's self-care. That ruminations are indeed just that. That there is power in sharing; being vulnerable in sharing your voice is honored. That listening to others helps you process, to make connections and to share experiences. This is why sharing lived experiences is so important as educators, especially in relation to self-care and to becoming a teacher. Teaching is a stressful job, and for pre-service teachers it is not only the stress of moving into this career, but also the navigation of shifting from being a learner to facilitating learning, to forming a teacher identity, while also navigating life. Opening up the space in the initial teacher education classroom is vital for the sharing of lived experiences. Scaffolding the opportunity to problem solve what is stressful and most critically how we can approach this. The poem "I am not alone" is a representation of the power of being vulnerable in sharing a lived experience and that listening to others, and being heard is an interruption to rumination, and indeed feelings of isolation. It is a crucial moment in self-care and building bridges to resisting isolation, silence and accepting current norms and patterns of dismissing well-being in education.

Failure

Failure doesn't mean you aren't capable
It means you are learning
I too am a learner

Failure doesn't mean you aren't capable
Even when the kids tell you, you have made a spelling mistake
Read a word wrong
Don't ask the right questions
Forget to go to assembly

Failure doesn't mean you aren't capable
Even when your mentor has to intervene in a lesson
When a student refuses to work
When a student says no
When a student ignores you
When you feel totally without any authority

Failure doesn't mean you aren't capable
When my lesson goes totally off topic
When my lose sense of time
When my classroom management strategies don't work

Failure doesn't mean you aren't capable
When my organization needs some attention
When I forget to take my lunch to school
When I wear the wrong clothes for sport
When I totally forget there is a meeting after school

Failure doesn't mean you aren't capable
It means I am taking a risk
I am putting myself out there
I am trying

Failure and the place this has in initial teacher education is often gleaned over. The journey that pre-service teachers undertake as they prepare to become teachers and the place of failure is rarely discussed in the literature on teacher identity (Lutovac, 2020; Lutovas & Flores, 2021). Failure does exist, but often focus is drawn to failure of a unit, assessment task or a professional experience placement. However, failure occurs daily and is hidden, unspoken and even subtle. It is a critical part of learning (Dweck, 2017) and, also, for self-care and well-being (Lutovas & Flores, 2021). As teachers we highlight failure with students as growth opportunities, but as Armida (2019) reminds us:

> We don't talk about failure enough. Sure, we talk about allowing kids to deal with failure and how to set up an environment where failure is valued, allowing redos, and constant revision. Again, like the highlight reel, these pieces are needed. (para 6)

The way failures influence and shape who we are as teachers is important, especially if we see them as opportunities for growth (Dweck, 2017) and as a foundation for shaping teacher identities (Carmi & Tamir, 2020). Although it is assumed failure may not be discussed often in initial teacher education as an integral part of learning, what we find with this poem is that pre-service teachers think about it. And indeed, it does feature highly in their reflective practice, self-talk and conversations with each other.

The poem "failure" represents a lengthy conversation that occurred in class upon return from a professional experience placement. *"Failure doesn't mean you aren't capable"* was a mantra shared as a form of advice for peers and those pre-service teachers coming through the initial teacher education training. The mantra was acknowledged as a form of self-care; an intention and statement that forms a reminder to self. This mantra became a leading off point to share openly about experiences where failure was present, when it was not always embraced, and when feelings of inadequacy were present. This mantra became the lifting off point to both pour hearts out and to heal.

This poem represents what Brene Brown (2018) calls the rumble—when we have courage over failure, to step up and enter the arena and be ready to rumble, be real, authentic, raw and vulnerable. By holding the space for these pre-service teachers, they were able to individually share, but collectively heal at a moment in time when there was no judgement. Collectively there was an awareness that they were not alone, that each in the class had, had multiple experiences, sometimes similar, and where in this moment of time of sharing failure was embraced, celebrated and welcomed as growth.

Advice to Future Selves

Self-care can grow
Listen to your lecturers
Your mentors
Your peers
Other teachers

Pick up ideas
Watch what others do
Learn from others' mistakes

Plan
Organize yourself
Make lunch the night before
Get your clothes out for the week
Have a note nook to capture all your thoughts
Document everything
Ask questions

Walk
Rest
Eat well

Breathe
Meditate
Body scan
Use an app
  Before bed
  On the train
  Take that time out for you
  Ground yourself

Sleep
Don't scarify your sleep
Rest

Move
Keep playing basketball
Keep training
Stretch
Walk around the block
Go to the park
Walk your dog

Connect to your purpose
Remember your passion
Remember why you wanted to become a teacher
Let that drive you
Remind yourself everyday
Use it to help motivate you

To help you refocus when stressed
Cherish your passion
Let it shine
Let other see it

Find moments in the classroom to make you smile
Where you bring joy to not only your students, but to yourself as well
Laugh
Be silly
Wear bright colors
Embrace dress up days
Create moments in the classroom where you all
    Sing
      Dance
        Laugh with each other
Treasure the moments
They will boost you as much as the students

Be kind to yourself
Self-love
Care
Awareness

What we see in this poetic representation of pre-service teachers becoming and note to future selves is an embracing of a variety of self-care strategies. Essential for the enactment of self-care is daily practice that individuals initiate and perform on their own behalf that support them in maintaining life and well-being (Gbhardt Taylor & Renpenning, 2011). This requires balance between self-awareness and self-regulation (Baker, 2004), with an agency and that supports addressing imbalance to sustain equilibrium (Adkins-Jackson et al., 2019). Thus, it is suggested that the act of self-care is underpinned by awareness and reflection to support personal growth (Cook-Cottone & Guyker, 2018). Self-care is, therefore, comprised of some actions within an individual's control to manage well-being (Narasimhan & Kapila, 2019).

Key to self-care is empowerment. The feeling that one has agency and choice (Lemon, 2021). Empowerment is possible in partnership with self-compassion and awareness, where a self-kindness supports proactive decisions to be made on a daily basis that support well-being. From a positive psychology lens, agency, empowerment and choice with self-care come from the opportunity to build well-being resources from what works and is good in life. It is about connecting with what energizes you, enables you to utilize your strengths and supports you to make decisions that promotes and recognizes who you are (Lemon, 2021; McQuaid & Kern, 2017; Seligman, 2011).

Self-care requires an agency and empowerment of choice that broadens and builds resources for us (Fredrickson, 2001; Garland et al., 2015) it is more than just focusing on preventing disease, caring careers or what is wrong (Eller et al., 2018). Self-care is about paying attention to what you really need. It is about being present, assessing, observing and being curious about one's needs with a compassion that is soothing and supportive. As we inquire with ourselves, we are able to put into place practices and habits to support our needs, that lead to maintaining healthy boundaries. Self-care is a path to empowerment. Empowerment is proactive and allows for considerations of how one can be autonomous within systems of support. As we develop knowledge, we gain confidence (Ludman et al., 2013). With confidence we can become more motivated and gain self-determination abilities. This might include being able to communicate our needs, seeking professional health more proactively, and being able to express concerns or preferences (Chen et al., 2016).

Conclusion

The profession of teaching is plagued with reports of well-being issues. There are ongoing reports of stress, anxiety, burnout and continued pressure to do more with less. For pre-service teachers entering the profession this rhetoric is strong. Awareness is coupled with the tensions of experiences of isolation, retention, and own grappling with shifts from moving from learner to teacher, identity formation, entering a profession that is not always valued by our community, and where well-being and self-care are often dismissed. Conversations about self-care are often not present in these tensions of the profession. A reframing is invited, encouraged, and thus a resistance to well-being traditionally sidelined in the profession is highlighted as an imperative in initial teacher education with and for pre-service teachers.

Responding to pre-service teachers' dilemmas and tensions through poetry as presented in this chapter humanizes becoming a teacher. Through poetry, I invite you as the reader to engage with these provocations as a beginning point to position self-care as possible. This way of responding through poetic representation is "a way of presenting these tensions [and] exposes the felt, emotional dimension of the tensions, and provides an insight into the way emotions mediate the work" (McDonough, 2018, p. 113). It highlights how we can approach the valuing of voice, and lived experience. It also reveals that conversations about self-care are an intrinsic part of the act of self-care itself. The pre-service teacher conversations captured in this chapter are raw, however representative of the lived experience and complexity of self-care and becoming a teacher. They are important. It is these moments that we as initial teacher educators can embrace as critical moments of learning through a lens of curiosity.

Holding the space as an initial teacher educator requires one to listen and to reiterate that pre-service teachers know they will be heard. Holding the space for pre-service teachers interrupts traditions of dismissing self-care. Listening is at the heart. An initial teacher educator doesn't always have to provide an answer; however, we can listen, and we can collectively support, be aware and present non-judgmentally.

Creating a safe space ignites possibility when a stance of curiosity is paired with locating self-care and well-being as a part of the conversations of becoming and being a teacher. By holding a space for these conversations to occur a teacher educator must be aware themselves, grounded and fully present non-judgmentally as they listen, facilitate conversations and provide scaffolding for reframing what can be done differently.

A pedagogy of curiosity is underpinned by exploring new ways of being. It has foundations in mindfulness and positive psychology whereby flourishing is the stance that supports opportunity to explore, be open-minded and problem solve new ways of being and embodying being a teacher and being a future teacher who embraces self-care. In this act self-compassion is required, a kindness and understanding when one is confronted with challenges, ups and downs in life and perceived personal failings. As a pre-service teacher, self-compassion forces one to think about how one treats oneself during the journey of becoming a teacher. This can make one vulnerable. However, pre-service teachers are encouraged to be curious and aware of what is coming up, to share, to reflect and to respond to emotions, fears and uncertainty. This occurs when a safe space is enacted, including a teacher educator who is grounded and holds the space. They too embrace vulnerability.

Through a pedagogy of curiosity, vulnerability is honored, encouraged, and enables one to explore and embrace love, belonging, joy, courage, empathy and creativity (Brown, 2012). There is a reclaiming of being, rather than a stance of distance (Ergas, 2017). It is the holding of a space that establishes, supports and scaffolds conversations on self-care and that embraces an intention within a safe space to share and be vulnerable, an awareness to honor the place of self-care and attention to what is real and lived that honours the voice to be shared. Infused is a sense of warmth, curiosity and compassion, that fosters a sense of self-acceptance (Fulton, 2005). This is a conscious aim of a pedagogy of curiosity that promotes approaching dilemmas with a framing to ignite new possibilities. The "I", "we" and "us" are placed carefully in navigations of self-care illuminating individual and collective self-care that positions well-being at the heart of being and becoming a teacher.

References

Adkins-Jackson, P. B., Turner-Musa, J., & Chester, C. (2019). The path to better health for black women: Predicting self-care and exploring its mediating effects on stress and health. *The Journal of Health Care Organization, Provision and Financing, 56*, 1–8. https://doi.org/10.1177/004695801987 0968

Armid, G. (2019). *Facing failure in the classroom.* https://theteacherandthead min.com/2019/09/29/facing-failure-in-the-classroom/

Baker, E. K. (2004). Caring for ourselves: A therapist's guide to personal and professional well-being. *American Psychological Association.* https://doi.org/ 10.1037/10482-001

Betoret, F. D., & Artiga, A. G. (2010). Barriers perceived by teachers at work, coping strategies, self-efficacy and burnout. *The Spanish Journal of Psychology, 13*(2), 637–654.

Bishop, S. R., Lau, M., Shapiro, S., Carlson, L., Anderson, N. D., Carmody, J., Segal, Z. V., Abbey, S., Speca, M., Velting, D., & Devins, G. (2004). Mindfulness: A proposed operational definition. *Clinical Psychology: Science and Practice, 11*(3), 230–241.

Biswas-Diener, R., Kashdan, T. B., & Minhas, G. (2011). A dynamic approach to psychological strength development and intervention. *The Journal of Positive Psychology, 6*(2), 106–118.

Boeije, H. (2010). *Analysis in qualitative research.* Sage.

Brown, B. (2012). *Daring greatly: How the courage to be vulnerable transforms the way we live, love, parent and lead.* Penguin Putnam Inc.

Brown, B. (2018). *Dare to lead.* Random House UK.

Brown, K. W., & Ryan, R. M. (2003). The benefits of being present: Mindfulness and its role in psychological well-being. *Journal of Personality and Social Psychology, 84*(4), 822–848.

Butler, L. D., Mercer, K. A., McClain-Meeder, K., Horne, D. M., & Dudley, M. (2019). Six domains of self-care: Attending to the whole person. *Journal of Human Behavior in the Social Environment, 29*(1), 107–124.

Carmi, T., & Tamir, E., (2020). Three professional ideals: Where should teacher preparation go next? *European Journal of Teacher Education,* 1–20. https://doi.org/10.1080/02619768.2020.1805732

Carroll, P., Dew, P., & Howden-Chapman, P. (2011). The heart of the matter: Using poetry as a method of ethnographic inquiry to represent and present experiences of the informally housed in Aotearoa/New Zealand. *Qualitative Inquiry, 17*(7), 623–630.

Chang, M. M., & Lin, M. C. (2014). The effect of reflective learning e-journals on reading comprehension and communication in language learning. *Computers and Education, 71,* 124–132. https://doi.org/10.1016/j.compedu.2013.09.023

Chen, J., Mullins, C. D., Novak, P., & Thomas, S. B. (2016). Personalized strategies to activate and empower patients in health care and reduce health disparities. *Health Education and Behavior, 43*(1), 25–34. https://doi.org/10.1177/1090198115579415

Ciarrochi, J., Kashdan, T., & Harris, R. (2013). The foundations of flourishing. In T. B. Kashda & J. Ciarrochi (Eds.), *Mindfulness, acceptance, and positive psychology: The seven foundations of well-being* (pp. 1–29). Context Press.

Cook-Cottone, C., & Guyker, W. M. (2018). The development and validation of the mindful self-care scale (MSCS): An assessment of practices that support positive embodiment. *Mindfulness, 9*(1), 161–175. https://doi.org/10.1007/s12671-017-0759-1

Dark, K. (2009). Examining praise from the audience: What does it mean to be a 'successful' poet-researcher? In M. Prendergast, C. Leggo, & P. Sameshima (Eds.), *Poetic inquiry: Vibrant voices in the social sciences* (pp. 171–86). Sense Publishers.

Dweck, C. (2017). *Growth mindset: Changing the way you think to fulfil your potential.* Little Brown.

Eller, L. S., Lev, E. L., Yuan, C., & Watkins, A. V. (2018). Describing self-care self-efficacy: Definition, measurement, outcomes, and implications. *International Journal of Nursing Knowledge, 29*(1), 38–48. https://doi.org/10.1111/2047-3095.12143

Elo, S., Kääriäinen, M., Kanste, O., Pölkki, T., Utriainen, K., & Kyngäs, H. (2014). Qualitative content analysis: A focus on trustworthiness. *SAGE Open, 1–10.* https://doi.org/10.1177/2158244014522633

Ergas, O. (2017). Reclaiming "self" in teachers' images of "education" through mindfulness as contemplative inquiry. *Journal of Curriculum and Pedagogy, 14*(3), 218–235.

Fredrickson, B. L. (2001). The role of positive emotions in positive psychology. The broaden-and-build theory of positive emotions. *The American Psychologist, 56*(3), 218–226. http://www.ncbi.nlm.nih.gov/pubmed/11315248

Fulton, P. R. (2005). Mindfulness as clinical training. In C. K. Germer, R. D. Siegel, & P. R. Fulton (Eds.), *Mindfulness and psychotherapy* (pp. 55–72). Guilford Press.

Garland, E. L., Farb, N. A., Goldin, P., & Fredrickson, B. L. (2015). Mindfulness broadens awareness and builds eudaimonic meaning: A process model of mindful positive emotion regulation. *Psychological Inquiry, 26*(4), 293–314. https://doi.org/10.1080/1047840X.2015.1064294

Gbhardt Taylor, S., & Renpenning, K. (2011). *Self-care science, nursing theory, and evidence-based practice.* Springer International Publishing. https://doi.org/10.5860/choice.49-2104

Ghanizadeh, A., & Jahedizadeh, S. (2015). Teacher burnout: A review of sources and ramifications. *British Journal of Education, Society & Behavioural Science, 6*(1), 24–39.

Guba, E. G., & Lincoln, Y. S. (1994). Competing paradigms in qualitative research. In N. K. Denzin & Y. S. Lincoln (Eds.), *Handbook of qualitative research* (pp. 105–117). Sage.

Harvey, M., Lloyd, K., McLachlan, K., Semple, A-L., & Walkerden, G. (2020). *Reflection for learning: A scholarly practice guide for educators.* Advance HE.

Hensley, L. C., & Munn, K. J. (2019). The power of writing about procrastination: Journaling as a tool for change. *Journal of Further and Higher Education, 44*(10), 1450–1465.

Ivtzan, I. (2016). Mindfulness in positive psychology: An introduction. In I. Ivtzan & T. Lomas (Eds.), *Mindfulness in positive psychology: The science of meditation and wellbeing* (pp. 1–13). Routledge.

Januchowski-Hartley, S. R., Sopinka, N., Merkle, B. G., Lux, C., Zivian, A., Goff, P., & Oester, S. (2018). Poetry as a creative practice to enhance engagement and learning in conservation science. *BioScience, 68*(11), 905–911. https://doi.org/10.1093/biosci/biy105

Kashdan, T. B., & Silvia, P. J. (2012). Curiosity and interest: The benefits of thriving on novelty and challenge. In S. J. Lopez & C. R. Snyder (Eds.), *The Oxford handbook of positive psychology* (2nd ed., pp. 366–374). Oxford University Press. https://doi.org/10.1093/oxfordhb/9780195187243.013.0034

Kashdan, T. B., & Steger, M. F. (2007). Curiosity and pathways to well-being and meaning in life: Traits, states, and everyday behaviors. *Motivation and Emotion, 31*(3), 159–173. https://doi.org/10.1007/s11031-007-9068-7

Lemon, N. (2021). Wellbeing in initial teacher education: Using poetic representation to examine pre-service teachers understanding of their self-care needs.

Cultural Studies of Science Education, 2021(2), 1–20. https://doi.org/10. 1007/s11422-021-10034-y

Lemon, N., & McDonough, S. (2021). If not now, then when? Wellbeing and wholeheartedness in education. *Educational Forum, 85*(4), 1–20. https://doi.org/10.1080/00131725.2021.1912231

Lincoln, S. Y., & Guba, E. G. (1985). *Naturalistic inquiry.* Sage.

Lomas, T., Hefferon, K., & Ivtzan, I. (2015). The LIFE model: A meta-theoretical conceptual map for applied positive psychology. *Journal of Happiness Studies: An Interdisciplinary Forum on Subjective Well-Being, 16*(5), 1347–1364. https://doi.org/10.1007/s10902-014-9563-y6

Lomas, T., Hefferon, K., & Ivtzan, I. (2017). *Applied positive psychology: Integrated positive practice.* Sage.

Ludman, E. J., Peterson, D., Katon, W. J., Lin, E. H. B., Von Korff, M., Ciechanowski, P., Young, B., & Gensichen, J. (2013). Improving confidence for self care in patients with depression and chronic illnesses. *Behavioral Medicine, 39*(1), 1–6. https://doi.org/10.1080/08964289.2012.708682

Lutovac, S. (2020). How failure shapes teacher identities: Pre-service elementary school and mathematics teachers' narrated possible selves. *Teaching and Teacher Education, 94*(2020), 103120. https://doi.org/10.1016/j.tate.2020.103120

Lutovac, S., & Flores, M. A. (2021). 'Those who fail should not be teachers': Pre-service teachers' understandings of failure and teacher identity development. *Journal of Education for Teaching, 47*(3), 379–394. https://doi.org/10.1080/02607476.2021.1891833

Madaliyeva, Z., Mynbayeva, A., Sadvakassova, Z., & Zholdassova, M. (2015). Correction of burnout in teachers. *Procedia - Social and Behavioral Sciences, 171*, 1345–1352. https://doi.org/10.1016/J.SBSPRO.2015.01.252

McDonough, S. L. (2018). Inside the mentors' experience: Using poetic representation to examine the tensions of mentoring pre-service teachers. *Australian Journal of Teacher Education, 43*(10), 98–115.

McQuaid, M., & Kern, P. (2017). *Your wellbeing blueprint: Feeling good and doing well at work.* Michelle McQuaid Pty Ltd.

Napoli, M., & Bonifas, R. (2011). From theory toward empathic self-care: Creating a mindful classroom for social work students. *Social Work Education, 30*(6), 635–649. https://doi.org/10.1080/02615479.2011.586560

Narasimhan, M., & Kapila, M. (2019). Implications of self-care for health service provision. In *Bulletin of the World Health Organization, 97* (2), 76–77. World Health Organization. https://doi.org/10.2471/BLT.18.228890

Neff, K. D. (2003). The development and validation of a scale to measure self-compassion. *Self and Identity, 2*(3), 223–250. https://doi.org/10.1080/15298860309027

Neff, K. D. (2011). Self-compassion, self-esteem, and well-being. *Social and Personality Psychology Compass, 5*(1), 1–12. https://doi.org/10.1111/j.1751-9004.2010.00330.x

Pennebaker, J. W. (2013). *Writing to heal: A guided journal for recovering from trauma & emotional upheaval.* Wheat Ridge Co.

Polit, D. F., & Beck, C. T. (2012). *Nursing research: Principles and methods.* Lippincott Williams & Wilkins.

Qiu, H. (2018). Research on the burnout of high school teachers based on teacher professional development. *Open Journal of Social Sciences, 06*(12), 219–229. https://doi.org/10.4236/jss.2018.612019

Reading, S. (2018). *The self-care revolution: Smart habits & simple practices to allow you to flourish.* Aster.

Richardson, L. (1997). *Fields of play: Constructing an academic life.* Rutgers University Press.

Schnaider-Levi, L., Mitnik, I., Zafrani, K., Goldman, Z., & Lev-Ari, S. (2017). Inquiry-based stress reduction meditation technique for teacher burnout: A qualitative study. *Mind, Brain, and Education, 11*(2), 75–84. https://doi.org/10.1111/mbe.12137

Seligman, M. E. P. (2011). *Flourish.* Random House Australia.

Seligman, M. E. P., & Csikszentmihalyi, M. (2000). Positive psychology: An introduction. *American Psychologist, 55*(1), 5–14. https://doi.org/10.1037/0003-066X.55.1.5

Shapiro, S. L., Carlson, L. E., Astin, J. A., & Freedman, B. (2006). Mechanisms of mindfulness. *Journal of Clinical Psychology, 62*(3), 373–386. https://doi.org/10.1002/jclp.20237

Sinats, P., Scott, D. G., McFerran, S., Hittos, M., Cragg, C., Leblanc, T., & Brooks, D. (2005). Writing ourselves into being: Writing as spiritual self-care for adolescent girls. *International Journal of Children's Spirituality, 10*(1), 17–29.

Skaalvik, E. M., & Skaalvik, S. (2017). Dimensions of teacher burnout: Relations with potential stressors at school. *Social Psychology of Education, 20*(4), 775–790. https://doi.org/10.1007/s11218-017-9391-0

Yoo, J. (2019). Creative writing and academic timelessness. *New writing: The International Journal for the Practice and Theory of Creative Writing, 16*(2) 148–157. https://doi.org/10.1080/14790726.2018.1490776

Young, T. (2016). Additional mechanisms of mindfulness: How does mindfulness increase wellbeing? *Mindfulness in Positive Psychology: The Science of Meditation and Wellbeing,* 156–171. https://doi.org/10.4324/9783157547217

Young, T. (2019). Mindfulness based flourishing program: A mutually enhancing fusion of positive psychology and mindfulness. In L. E. Waters (Ed.), *6th World Congress on Positive Psychology, 2019*. Retrieved from http://wcpp2019.p.asnevents.com.au/days/2019–07–20/abstract/58437

Dancing with the Other: Esthetic Experience and Ethical Responsiveness in an Education for the Self Becoming

Paul Moerman

Dance is not about being able, at all times,
and without any pain, to stand on your feet,
like a grain of dust whirling around in the wind.
Dance is about you rising above both worlds,
while your heart is torn to pieces and you give up your soul.
—Rumi

INTRODUCTION

This chapter is an invitation to look at education through the arts, specifically dance. In this, I suggest a turn away from thinking arts *in* education,

P. Moerman (✉)
Södertörn University, Stockholm, Sweden
e-mail: paul.moerman@sh.se

University of Jyväskylä, Jyväskylä, Finland

M. P. Hall and A. K. Brault (eds.), *Academia from the Inside*,
https://doi.org/10.1007/978-3-030-83895-9_9

in favor of bluntly looking at art *as* education. Rather than concerning the arts as esthetic *expression,* I wish to explore what the mere *doing* of artwork, like dancing, may teach us, that is, what we possibly may be *taught* by dancing.

I spin a thread of thought from educational theorist Gert Biesta's ideas on art and education, subject-ness and democracy, twining in educational philosophers John Dewey's and Maxine Greene's thoughts on art as experience, esthetic literacy, education and democracy, and weaving in dance scholar and pedagogue Sue Stinson's stands on dance education and dancing as becoming. Throughout the reasoning, I emphasize the relational dimensions of education and dance, specifically relationships charged with otherness. School, like academia, is viewed as a sphere where children, pupils, students, scholars, with a diversity of life experiences meet and come into the world through their actions, an area where dance may operate as transgressing action and show a way to benefit from difference—to learn from the Other.

The theoretical framework is probed in a field study, reviewed below, featuring a creative dance program, *Dancing with the Other*, which I developed through years of teaching dance in preschool, elementary and secondary school and in teacher education in Sweden and other international settings. Analyzing findings, I discuss the relevance of looking at education through the dancer's gaze, as a challenge and a contribution to the development of educational theory and practice. Not least, I underscore how intimately the esthetic and the ethical are intertwined, in educational and artistic contexts alike.

Simultaneously, I invite the reader to look at dance through the educator's eyes, as there are apparent resemblances between what dancers and pedagogues do. Ultimately, this essay is about what we may be taught by dancing, if we let dance precisely do that—teach us.

ART AND EDUCATION—TWO SIMILAR FIELDS OF ACTIVITY

Educational theorist Gert Biesta's (2017) point of departure in reasoning on art and education, and on letting art teach, is an assertion of a number of striking similarities between the two fields of knowledge: While the arts deal with queries about what it means to be in dialogue with the world, pedagogy fundamentally deals with efforts to enter into and maintain a dialogue with the world. To Biesta (2006, 2017), existing as subject is about being in dialogue with the world in a grown-up way, i.e. not aspiring to be in the center of the world, but to be in the world with other subjects, unalike one-self, to exist in a world of plurality—diversity being a precondition for democracy.

Biesta highlights German artist Joseph Beuys's 1965 iconic happening, *How to explain pictures to a death hare*, as a vigorous staging of an educational scene. What the artist puts on there, says Biesta, is firstly the archetypical form of teaching: to *show* something, to *point out* something "out there" in the world to someone—something perceivable, something that may be good, important and worthwhile paying attention to, something that makes more sense than other things. The teacher's pointing gesture is both profoundly pedagogical and thus relational, and situated: It goes from this very teacher to this very child or pupil and that very thing in the world that might be significant.

Secondly, says Biesta, Beuys shows us the archetypical modality of teaching: to *explain*, an invitation and an initiation into the realm of sense-making. Thus, the showing and explaining gestures add up to an act of "double-truth giving", a term Biesta borrows from philosopher Kierkegaard: to offer the truth as well as the criterion to recognize something as true. Thirdly, what is explained in Beuys's performance is pictures, Biesta remarks, the *picture* being the archetypical object of teaching. Biesta reminds us of Comenius, who in 1658 in his *Orbis sensualium pictus* ceremonially aimed at presenting the world of perceivable things in an ordered fashion, the first textbook including pictures as tools of explanation. Comenius envisaged a school for every child, poor or rich, girl or boy.

Biesta concludes that Beuys the artist and Comenius the (first) pedagogue both show us the essence of teaching. Through the archetypical gesture of teaching, to *point*, and its archetypical modality, to *explain*, the teacher offers the keys for the search for meaning, which, stresses Biesta, is a gift without claim for return: The learner, eager for meaning, pays attention and steps forward as subject, or declines and stays behind as object. In the introduction to *Orbis sensualium pictus*, the "invitatio", the pupil accepts the teacher's offer to be shown around everywhere, be shown everything and be named everything. Thus, the pedagogue's gesture, akin to the artist's—to show something in the world to someone—entails a turning of the learner towards the world, by pointing—"Look, there!"— trying to awake a longing in the learner to be in the world in a grown-up way, i.e. not to be in its center, but to ask the world what it might expect from one.

The latter is a far more arduous path to walk, Biesta argues, calling forth disturbance and resistance. A pathway calling for a discernment amongst one's desires towards the world, as to which of these might be less or more desirable from the world's point of view, a world unable to accommodate all our desires, a world where I am not alone, but with others. In return, it is a more rewarding and enlightening way in the long run. I will argue that the work in an art form such as dance can show us such a path, can teach us how to enter into such a dialogue with the world.

Education and Dance as Acts of Becoming

Dance as a mode of art is a distinct way of being in the world, or, as dance educator and scholar Sue Stinson (1990) words it literally, a way of *moving* through the world. For Stinson, dance is action, relating to the world outside the studio, the stage, school, be it preschool or higher education. Thus, dancing is a way of moving in relation, and not seldom in opposition, to views on art and dance (who can/may dance?), on body and gender, on knowledge and power, on education and democracy—which is all in the bargain when dance is brought into the realm of education, not least ethical aspects ensuing from esthetic aspects of dancing in front of and with each other.

When exploring education's relational dimension, intersubjective action is central. The subject, i.e. the child, the pupil, the student, the teacher, is seen as agent, capable of action, interplaying with other agentive subjects. When Biesta (2006) emphasizes education as fundamentally relational, he advocates an education not solely concerned with transferring pre-defined knowledge, skills and a fixed set of universal values from one generation to the next, following a pre-defined curriculum. Rather than an education occupying itself with the task of fostering the individual in fulfilling universal ideas of humanity or citizenship—commonly the Kantian ideal of the autonomous rational individual—he propounds an education concerned with each and everyone's subjectivity and uniqueness as human being, a space of otherness.

We reveal our uniqueness and singularity, Biesta says, through the way we respond to the Other, more so, in the very way we take responsibility for the Other to emerge in her or his otherness. Biesta refers to Emmanuel Levinas (1992) and his philosophy of alterity, viewing the Other as infinitely unknowable, not an *alter ego*, but everything I am not. The least of pretension to a deeper knowledge about another human is equal to making her an object of my own understanding of being in the world—an objectification. Between the one I am and the Other for whom I assume responsibility, there is a bottomless abyss of difference, which at the same time constitutes the in-difference of responsibility and the closeness to my fellow being, the grounds for my affinity with the Other and for the unity of mankind, says Levinas (2003). Assuming unconditional, ethical responsibility for the Other's otherness, subordinating to difference, is how we become as subjects—we are *for* the Other before we are by ourselves—a Self. In turn, not until school truly is a space of otherness, Biesta concludes, can school be a space where becoming as human subject is possible—and where democracy can arise.

Biesta further leans on Arendt's (1954) thoughts on the individual's capability of action, to initiate, to launch an *initium*, a new beginning, like a new birth, adding something to the world that wasn't there before. However, what we bring into the world is not "realized" until it is received by others, why the subjective capacity at stake assumes both the power to act and the willingness to subject to others' reactions to one's actions. This is Arendt's definition of freedom—the freedom to *act* and initiate new beginnings, which presupposes an intersubjective space, like the public space, preconditioned by plurality, in turn a precondition for democracy. Freedom is *in the act*, Arendt stresses, referring to the scenic arts, where the accomplishment is in the *performance* itself, not in an end product outlasting the initiative taken, the dancers and actors depending on each other's *re-actions* here and now, and on an audience to witness these momentary *acts*.

Rather than learning as acquisition and internalization of predefined knowledge and values, including presumed knowledge of whom we meet, based on affiliation or representation—identity/the identical—Biesta envisions a learning ensuing from the confrontation with the unexpected, from disturbance and strain, from the response to the unfamiliar and the otherwise, the unique and the uncommon—, learning from the Other. This way, education's first concern becomes the pupil's *subject-ness*, the solicitude to create contexts where the pupils can bring their beginnings to the world and take place in the social fabric of difference with their own thoughts and emotions, bringing their own, unique answers to the world.

Contemporary dancers interact with the world through dance as an act of resistance against any objectification of the body: as commercialized item, as lifestyle fetish, as projection surface for esthetic, social, political, gender and even biological codes, or as puppets in the hands of genius choreographers. Philosopher and cultural theorist Manchev (2011) conceives an esthetics of resistance to such manipulations, back to the body's original potentiality to explore experiences not yet "one's own", the dancer interplaying with other dancers as subject-body, engaging in corporeal, sensuous communication, as a living window wide-open to the world.

So does the dancing child, says Stinson (1988, 1990), exploring the magic of movement, breaking into the world by force of imagination, a body eternally becoming as subject. The dance pedagogue's task, she argues, is to create spaces for such discovery and exploration, without given outcome, for freedom of trial, and for a process where all involved learn about themselves, each other and the world we live in. To dancer and philosopher Erin Manning (2009), every movement in itself is a beginning through which the very body becomes, dancing "the not-yet"—every movement is body and dance coming into being. The images of the child dancing into the world and the dancer going along with the movement both capture dance as open-ended, body-sensuous action and experience preceding consciousness, cognition and knowledge.

ESTHETIC EXPERIENCE

Experience as the outcome of activity, i.e. the interaction between the individual and the physical and social world is the key concept in pragmatist philosopher and progressive educationalist John Dewey's (1926) epistemology. Interaction, communication and participation are central in the interplay with the world through which the individual gathers knowledge on what it is to be a human being, in the ongoing process of *doing* and *undergoing*, of acting and subduing to the consequences of one's actions, a process of participation in which both the self and the surrounding world develop and transform. Thinking and knowing come out of endless interplay with the world—*learning by experience*.

In *Arts as Experience*, Dewey (1934) elaborates on the experience notion in esthetic terms, the object of an *esthetic experience* being a work of art, architecture, poetry, music or stage art which the beholder engages in and deepens into, trying to grasp its form and content. The interactions constituting the experience are situated, corporeal and social. They include events, initiatives, disturbance, dissolvement and suffering.

Not the least, they include sensation, cognition and consciousness, which Dewey all regards as action—sens*ing*, mind*ing*, know*ing*. Through the work of the senses, the esthetic penetrates the experience from without, from the object of the experience, the artwork. The esthetic consists of the clarifying and intensifying treats of the consummation of the experience, as a whole is created from the particular and the disparate, an understanding evolves and meaning is communicated. Resistance, tension, excitation and dissolvement are converted into appreciation, fulfilment, participation, insight and growth as the experience consummates.

Elaborating on Dewey's thoughts on esthetic experience, communication and meaning making, educational philosopher Maxine Greene (1986) develops her ideas about *esthetic education* and *esthetic literacy*: a fostering through intense, receptive, reflective intercourse with the arts, probing unfamiliar lines of thinking, new ways of symbolizing and structuring experience, allowing the child and the young to see more, hear more, feel and sense more, to make unexpected connections and investigate deeper levels of meaning. The space where such an education can take place, Greene argues, reminds us of Arendt's *public space*, presupposing the presence of others, appearing in front of each other with the best of their abilities. Hence, Greene considers the opening of such spaces in school as a precondition to develop esthetic literacy, spaces which only active, growing human beings can establish, who can achieve their individuality while coming together with others, and through action and speech initiate new beginnings.

Greene (1995) views imagination as a social capacity which helps us to get a grip of a complex world, which enables empathy, helps us to cross the empty spaces between ourselves and "the others", allows us to make alternative realities credible, break off that what we take for granted and lay ingrained distinctions aside. Esthetic education enhances a reflective response and the capability to experience such a response from another human being, a response Greene denotes as ethical and which opens for change.

In *Art as Experience*, Dewey expands on experiences in the encounter with works of art, architecture or poetry created by artists, architects or poets. Greene advocates engagement in the raw material of arts, canvas and colors, poetry, or bodies in motion—to move with dancers, balance one's weight, to sense the *effort-shape* of an outflung arm—in order to more profoundly perceive what unfolds in a dance work performed on stage. However, neither elaborate on esthetic experiencing in the individual's own work in the arts. Dewey scarcely discusses art as experience in educational settings, more than in general terms and in concluding notes.

In his reasoning on what the arts can teach us, Biesta (2017) deepens all the more into the pupil's very experience of resistance doing art work, the point at which education begins. The encounter captures the premises for dialogue between "self" and "other", a process through which we come out to the world and the world comes to us. Resistance causes disturbance, *interruption* and *suspension*, offering golden opportunities to scrutinize and sort out which desires in the individual are more "desirable" than others when meeting the world. The teacher's task is then, Biesta argues, to encourage the young to linger in this difficult *middle ground* between going about too hard or shying away and refrain altogether, between destroying the world we seek to exist in and self-destruction, obliterating our very existence in the world.

The teacher's task is to "stage" this encounter, making the encounter between the pupil and the world possible, and to *support* the pupil to endure and cope with the labor it takes to exist in and with the world, not in its center, but in dialogue, sensitive to what the world may ask from one, not least to be *with others*—a world-centered take on education rather than a student- or self-centered one. The middle ground, Biesta underscores, is a thoroughly worldly and educational space; it allows us to meet the world's realities and even the realities and limitations of our own existence in the world, it teaches us we are not alone. Working in the arts, meeting the realities of paint, stone, sound, body—in the British curriculum earlier called "resistant materials"—offers golden opportunities for play and to try out limits of ideas and aspirations, to find out what it is to be in dialogue with the world and find forms for this dialogue.

Kinesthetic Experience and the Ethical

The dance teacher's grateful task is to guide the child through a rich repertoire of play and exercise, encouraging imagination of movement, offering the young dancer a bounty of opportunities to develop *kinesthetic awareness*. Stinson calls it a sixth sense, and precisely that what turns movement into dance. Kinesthesia comes from Greek *kiné*, to set in motion, and *aisthesis*, sensation, which emphasizes power of action, to *initiate* movement, as well as a sensuous and sensitive capacity to *experience* movement, one's own as well as co-dancers'.

Thus, Dewey's concept esthetic experience is rendered a *kinetic*, corporeal, dynamic dimension, yet another aspect of *doing* and *undergoing*, a quintessentially relational one. Movement, Stinson (1988) argues, becomes significant, and is literally given significance in itself, by *attending* to it. Thus, Biesta's view of the archetypical form of teaching, the pedagogue's pointing gesture, drawing the pupil's attention to something that might be meaningful, is charged with a kinesthetic dimension—to attend to movement and just like that turn it into dance.

For a long time, Stinson (2016) struggled to formulate the relationship between the ethical and the esthetic dimension of human existence related to dance education. After a walk pausing from writing, laying down to rest, she came upon a theoretical framework for her research: It all came down to the difference between the vertical and the horizontal position of the body. The upright position stands for activity, power of action, control and mastery—to be *on top*—the extended position stands for passivity, receptiveness and docility—to be *with* other people.

We may view also the vertical body posture in the walk break as beneficial to relaxation and release of tension, allowing both free flow and suspension of thought. Biesta (2017) introduces Roth's (2011) denotation "passibility": the capability to be affected, to be "moved", crucial in daily experience and in gathering knowledge and understanding. It denotes a capacity to move and to be moved, for motion and emotion, a blend of agency to act and a radical passivity to be permeated through the senses by the not-yet-known and even the unknowable, a capacity preceding cognition and even making cognition and understanding possible.

The capacity to be affected—to be *moved*—by movement is at the core of kinesthetic experiencing and may help us understand what dancing can teach us. We may backtrack from Roth's "passibility"—also a term in Christian theology, denoting the susceptibility to sensation and passion, derived from the Latin verb *pati*, to *suffer*—to Stinson's passive extended position and to Levinas' stances on ethical responsibility and the vulnerability of the Other. Levinas (2003) views vulnerability as passivity more passive than all passivity, and thoroughly corporeal—a nakedness more naked than skin. Assuming ethical responsibility calls for assertion and receptivity for the Other's vulnerability, in pain and sorrow as well as in enjoyment.

Levinas (1992) speaks about the Other as a *face* emerging, not in a metaphorical sense, but in the flesh, a living face approaching, calling upon me. I can chose to slay and annihilate it, or submit to its vulnerability. By letting the Other call on me and engage in a dialogue—command and privilege—I can become a self. Ethics precede the ego. I am *for the Other* before I am *by myself*—a Self. The encounter with the Other's face, Levinas continues, unfolds in proximity, in dialogue, through listening and speaking, with body language, facial expression, glances. The eye that sees is body which is hand and ear, which creates action and speech. A bodily gesture is no discharge in the nerves, but a celebration of life, poetry, he adds. When children and pupils—and teacher students—talk about dance, as in the case study below, they often emphasize on the interplay, described as a wordless, tender dialogue between bodies, which creates a feeling of community and closeness, even when the dance is powerful, a cool "uglydance" or a *battle*.

This touches the radical power and potential of dance in education. Kinesthetic experience presupposes the capacity to sense and surrender to movement, to move along with an arm's swing, to follow the motion and let the arm, the shoulder, the torso, the hip be affected by the move, to let it twist and take a turn into a new direction, and on, and on, before thought enters and steers the next gesture or step. In the dancing interplay between two children, pupils or students, it is impossible in the end to tell who is steering and who is following. What is at stake is knowledge, capabilities and skills different from predefined rational knowledge, it concerns pre-cognitive sensing and acting.

A kinesthetic experience is a sensuously internalizing of movement through which we can feel other's dance and our response to it, Stinson (1988) says. We become participants, we breathe with those we see dancing, we feel the stretch extending from the fingertips, feel the body softly landing after a jump. Or, as modern dance pioneer and choreographer Cunningham (1955) puts it, just stand still and with timely means condense the sensation of "movement action". Kinesthetic experience is the active part of working in the dance art mode, which, in Biesta's (2017) terms is, amongst art modes, a specific channel for dialogue between the self and the world. Spaces are created for esthetic experiencing and ethical being with others—spaces of becoming.

Field Study—Dancing with the Other

In order to gain insight in how teachers in education experience and understand "doing" dance, and its relevance in education, I conducted a case study in creative dance in an *educare* teacher education program (preparing students for teaching in- and after-school curriculum activities grade 1–4) at Södertörn University (Moerman, 2014). The overall purpose of the study was to examine conditions of possibility for dance in its own right in education and the relevance of dancing in school settings. Partial questions studied were how the participants described dance generally as well as dancing with and in front of each other in this educational context, and in which way relational, esthetic and ethical aspects of working in the dance mode were expressed.

The study was designed as a series of seminars where creative dance was introduced from its basics in two seminar groups of twelve resp. fourteen students during a five-week course on children's play and existential questions. Participants' age varied, from early 20's till late 30's, as well as to ethnic background, gender, functional variation and earlier dance experience, ranging from little to leisure pursuit.

The activities, following my teaching and learning program *Dancing with the Other*, were aimed at introducing dance hands-on, encouraging participants to create dance together on the floor, from scratch. No steps were presented, no theme was suggested. During improvisation and composition exercises, the participants were instructed to investigate whatever dance they had in themselves. Stinson's exploratory teaching method *Dance for young children* was implied (1988): The students inventoried physically possible movement on the floor—stretching, bending, twisting—and steps—jumps, gallop, turns, walking, sneaking, skipping, standing still, etc. They deepened and expanded the material by exploring movement quality through variation according to the parameters *space*, *time*, *body* and *force*. Single steps, turns, jumps, arm or hip movements or sequences of moves were varied as to how much room or floor space could be used or forms could be shaped, how fast or slow they could be done, with repetition or sudden stillness, how much body parts were engaged, isolated body parts or radiating out to the whole body, and also how much muscular intensity was used, forceful or withholding, "holding" an arm or a leg, pending for a continuation, an unexpected movement or a stop. Patterns were explored on the floor, lines of bodies, crowding on one spot or helter-skelter all over the floor, a dancer individually moving out of a circle or a quartet joining in a corner in a synchronized movement sequence. The skills were trained in whole group exercises, in smaller groups, in pairs and individually, all applicable to children and the young in the ages the pre-service teachers would meet as trainees and in their profession.

Following group composition tasks four by four, the participants eventually created solos, which they shared and instructed to peers, interpreted and integrated in a joint choreography taking shape along the way. The entire explorative and choreographing work was mere movement based. The participants were not urged to and did not bring in any narrative, illustrative nor dramatized aspects.

In subsequent semi-structured group discussions, the participants were asked to define dance, to describe their creative dance work, and to formulate the relevance of dance in education. The talks were transcribed and discursively analyzed with Wetherell's (1988) tool *interpretative repertoire*: lexicons of terms and metaphors speakers use to construe, evaluate and signify their actions. Four thematic repertoires were identified and analyzed: *what dance is, me and the others in interplay, security and vulnerability, what we learn from this*. Below, terms inventoried in the repertoires are reviewed within quotes.

As to what dance *is*, the dancer's agency was generally claimed to be decisive: how one chooses to "charge movement", including everyday gesture or even stillness, with "intention", "meaning" or "feeling". Important to many was finding one's "own expression", one's "own dancing" through improvising and exploring variation and quality of movement, beyond notions or categories of "beautiful" and "foul", "esthetic" and "artistic". Probing possibilities of movement in an open-ended fashion was stated to create a sense of "freedom" to further explore "one's own dancing", find inspiration in "others' ways of dancing" and also, notably, to discover earlier unimagined own ways of moving, skills and capacities to create dance: "I never imagined I had this in me".

The sense of open-endedness, of nothing being given beforehand, was further worded and appreciated under the *interplay* headline. The creative work was said to visualize different layers of exploration and interaction. New possibilities opened in the leap between having found one's "own dance" to "dancing with the others", described as a "bodily dialogue" in a "sense of community", "cooperation" and "communication of meaning". The dialogue was called "wordless", "explorative" and "affectionate", in an atmosphere of "trust", "wonder", "closeness" and even "intimacy". Shifting between "me" and "the others" was experienced spatially: "There you are, here I am", "give space and take up space", "spheres to enter into and leave", "vanish into own spaces and join assembling spaces", "dwelling in the periphery, moving into the center".

Ethical aspects of doing dance came to the fore in the utterances about *security and vulnerability*. Dancing in front of each other was formulated as "fragile". Feelings of "security", "safety" and "trust" were contrasted to "fear", "vulnerability", "shyness", "exposing oneself", "standing naked", an "intimacy" which caused "resistance". Feelings of "hesitancy" or "disinclination" were related to an "anxiety" for "inner and outer judgement". Spatial metaphors reoccurred, such as "barriers", being "in the center", as opposed to "comfort zones" or staying in the "periphery".

An "allowing", "caretaking" and "receptive" atmosphere was said to help overcome resistance and give opportunities to "develop" and "grow", "a struggle between fear and courage", "to dare and gain". Particularly sensitive instants mentioned were those moments just when someone was about to "step forward", especially in the solo work, which may be understood as new beginnings, tentative initiatives of movement which the dancer had composed and then emerged through. The welcoming atmosphere of caring and attention may be seen as a way of ethically responding to the Other, appearing with her or his esthetic resources in situations perceived as delicate and vulnerable.

Overcoming resistance was consequently considered as "transgressing" action, literally *"an experience"*. Esthetic treats of such an experience were pronounced in descriptions of a state of intensified "seeing", "listening" and "reading" one another, including "seeing" oneself and the others "anew" or "in a new light". The heightened perception was clearly sensorial and thoroughly corporeal, triggering new sensuous and kinesthetic scanning, and intensifying the interaction through which the esthetic object, the very dance work created, was built on. The process was evidently communicative and brought about intense participation, entailing in sharing and learning from each other's different ways of moving, which was cherished and eventually constituted the common choreography. The participants' choreographing work was experienced as going from distinct, individual inputs to an experienced whole: "It all melted together". Resistance and tension were converted into fulfilment, wonder and joy.

ANALYSIS AND DISCUSSION

What was analyzed in the collected data, was the meaning constituted by the participants through "speech-in-action" in the very social context of the case study, "the inner meaning of the interaction", that which amongst the infinitely many possible perspectives of what had occurred was relevant, meaningful and probable to them (Wetherell, 1988). How the informants worded and viewed what was visualized in the dance activities, is what it was. This concurs with dancer and choreographer Merce Cunningham's (1952) view on modern dance: What we see is what it is, what the dancer does is the most realistic of all possible things. So which meaning did the participants create? How do their utterances "speak back" to the theoretical lines of thinking on (kin)esthetics, ethics and becoming?

(Kin)esthetic Experiencing

The students' use of language indicate a deepened understanding of basic elements of movement and how these can be rendered dance qualities in the improvising and composing processes. They discovered their *own dancing* and abilities to move beyond rules and views on beauty and ugliness, to create with a sense of freedom and to charge movement and stillness with their own significance. Dance was explored as an *own expression* and as a mode of communication, in the creative work on the floor and in the conveying of meaning—in Dewey's (1934) terms: An interaction of doing and undergoing unfolded in which meaning was created and communicated, giving the *experience* body and distinction.

A heightened level of perception, attention and receptiveness was created, beneficial to imagination, allowing the participants to enter "as if" worlds, in Greene's (1986) words, and, in the students' terms, a space to "vanish" into and discover unexpected assets. A flow arose in time and space, alike the continuum Cunningham (1952) describes when disparate parts interplay and create movement sequences, fully visible to anybody. Literally step by step, with each and everyone's distinct contributions, the dance evolved and developed to a whole, experienced in wonder. The esthetic, in Dewey's (1934) sense, came out of the clarifying and intensifying traits of the interaction with the work of art, which in this case was the participants' own dance work, their choreography.

Ethical Relationships

Throughout, the dance work was described in relational terms. As interplay with the self, exploration of *oneself* together with others, exploration of relationships infused with affect, trust, wonder, tenderness and intimacy, speechless relationships, bodies talking, cooperative relationships. The participants entered an empty floor, at times hesitantly, eventually with a readiness and agency to send out impulses from within and take in impulses from without, establishing a boundless, unforeseeable space. Through imagination and initiative, the students brought their new beginnings to the world and took place in the social, creative interplay. Biesta (2006) reminds us of the teacher's consequential preparedness, "a responsibility without knowledge" of what may be expressed in emotionally charged situations. Greene (1986) reminds us that in relating one's own actions to others, and in facing the unexpected, the individual develops her or his ability to be present, for judgment, imaginativeness, possibilities of choice, initiative and capability of action.

The dancing and interplay was described in existential terms as well—a *self* "took up space" and was "scrutinized" while dancing with the others, "something existential" took place. Possibly, the course in the teacher training program during which the field study was undertaken, Children's existential questions, may have influenced the utterances. However, the design of the study, limiting instructions to merely discovering and exploring the basic building stones of dance art through improvisation and composition, included no outspoken ties to existential themes, which is why the students' choices of words and descriptions must be considered as independent.

Did the students engage in ethical encounters? *Seeing* and *listening* was related to taking consideration, showing respect and building a sense of reassurance. As the work deepened, participants stated they got a grasp of themselves and of each other, they came closer to one another, "dancing and revealing one's self". They *saw* each other, not in a recognizing way, but "anew", in Dewey's (1934) distinction: in a pregnant way of seeing, at this very point of time, in this very place: "There you are". First, everyone danced *with one's self*, in one's "own spot", denoted as "here I am". Gradually, the space for "giving and taking, dealing with oneself" was extended to a space for interplay where "whom I am" was reinterpreted.

Appearing in front of each other in dance solos, overcoming hesitation and resistance, allowed for each and everyone to step forward as a unique being, adding something to the world that had not been there before, breaking into the world amongst others. Sharing and probing each other's material of movement evolved in a sensitive response to otherness, through active saying and doing as well as passive listening and waiting. The gradual integration of the movement material into a joint choreography evolved through intensified seeing, turn taking, speechless reading and listening, a dialogue between bodies and faces with small means of communication, glances, gestures, poses. The Self, in close proximity to the Other, was modified and rediscovered: "This *may* be me". Eventually, "everything was flowing together". Encounters evolved in vulnerable exposure, care and trust, openness and receptiveness, courage and risk taking. The raw material were the bodies in motion, the encounter occurred *in* the art work itself, the encounter *was* the creative work.

Summary—Dancing as Becoming

Creating spaces in education for esthetic experience is about making room for imagination, the capability to act and the capacity of receptivity, for participation and intercourse, for intense presence and perception, seeing and listening. Imagination opens for the unforeseeable and for new perspectives on the world, the otherwise and the others. Spaces open up for experiencing, knowledge shaping, meaning making—in Greene's (1986) terms: spaces to enter into, observing, sensing, reflecting, to see what there is to see, to experience what there is to experience—irresistible spaces for new beginnings.

In dance education, spaces are created for kinesthetic experiencing, for initiative and docility in movement. Children, pupils and students appear in front of each other with their esthetic resources, meeting each other anew and building fragile, ethical relationships imbued by otherness, proximity, trust, participation and communication, a wordless dialogue of giving and taking. Worlds of dance arise where things may appear in a different light. With their imagination of movement and their ability to take action, they break into the world. They take place in their education, they literally secure room for maneuver on the world stage that school or higher education represents. Such spaces are indispensable for an education concerned with providing possibilities for each and everyone to become as subject in plurality, and thus also for democracy to become.

Teaching, Biesta (2017) says, is about turning the gaze of the pupil to the world and to arouse a desire in the young to exist in the world as subject in a grown-up way—not in its center, but with others. Dance, with its immediate kinesthetic power and call for responsiveness, invites us to let go of the familiar and step into the unknown and the unforeseeable—a pedagogical opportunity. In the open-ended creative dance work, play and joy of discovery blend with the experience of resistance in meeting the unknown and the other—a *not-knowing* in a broad sense—opening for interruption and suspension, for dialogue, for being with others, and for becoming as self.

There is a decisive distinction between Dewey's notion of esthetic experience and Biesta's ideas about working in the arts. Both Dewey and Biesta underscore the value and the necessity of resistance in the self's dialogue with the world. But whereas the former stresses the self's labor through dissolution towards re-integration and synthesis, the latter insists on the subject becoming again and again, through interruption and suspension—not towards a consummated whole.

In Dewey's (1934) concept, the object of an esthetic experience is a work created by an artist, architect, poet, etc. In order to be able to observe and assert it as a work of art, perception must be action, a re-creation in which the viewer creates her or his own experience through interactions comparable to the creator of the work, a selective arranging of the elements towards clarity and synthesis. In both creative processes, Dewey states, a discernment of meaning is made, of something meaningful, an understanding, as physically fragmented parts and particularities are put together into an experienced whole.

Biesta (2017, 2018) reasons in another direction, away from what he calls an *expressivist* conception of art, where the focus is on the idea, the feeling, the concept, the *meaning* the artist tries to express in the artwork. The "receiving side"—the spectator, the listener, the viewer, the reader—is thus locked into the position of trying to understand what is expressed. Biesta rejects the logic and the dichotomy intention-reception in favor of the making-of-art as such, a never-ceasing exploration of its raw material through the work of the head, the hand and the heart, and hence of the encounter with the otherwise and the others, showing us what it is to exist in and with the world.

This is where this essay took its point of departure, in Biesta's ideas on letting art teach, letting art point out a way to enter into a dialogue with the world. I related this line of thinking to his plea for an education beyond the learning of predefined knowledge, skills and values, towards a good and democratic education providing for each and one's unique, distinctive subjectivity and eternally becoming. I wove these threads of thought together with Dewey's ideas on esthetic experience, Greene's thoughts on esthetic literacy and Stinson's stances on dance as kinesthetic experience and becoming.

Do these threads of thought converge? Despite distinctions, they suggest similar ways to knowledge and meaning making, to pre-knowledge and pre-cognitive action and to receptiveness and dialogue with the social and natural world—when working in an art mode such as dance. I have proposed a way to expand Dewey's esthetic experience concept, as well as Greene's ideas about esthetic education, giving them a more profound dignity in this inquiry on children's, pupils', students and educators' singular, own work in the art of dance. I have probed Biesta's thoughts on art as teaching in a reflection on what dance may teach us. There are other possible points of connection between these thinkers for continued study from dancing and pedagogical, ethical and esthetic perspectives.

Meanwhile, Dewey (1934) bluntly states that art, through its way of communication, appears as education's incomparable mode of instruction, lifting art high above how we think instruction, if we think education free from imagination, not touching the desires and emotions of human beings. He concludes that art's moral function is to take away prejudice, to brush off the scales that hinder the eye from seeing, to tear down the veils of habits and randomness and sharpen our capability to perceive. Biesta (2006), in turn, refers once again to Arendt, who argues that we need imagination to put things in their proper distance as well as to bridge the abysses to others (Disch, 1994). Stinson (1988) highlights kinesthetic experience as a internalizing of movement through which we can imagine the other one's dance and our response to it.

Greene (1995) sees esthetic experiencing as research and support in the work for social justice, and encourages discussions about artwork relating to concrete phenomena in society, rather than discussing social problems starting from abstract ideas and ideals. In the case study, the students themselves created a dance work which can lead on to personal conversations about esthetics, ethics, plurality and coexistence. In preschool, elementary school, high school and college, children, pupils and students encounter other's stories with radically different experiences, often marked by suffering. In dance and in consequent talks, they can stay close to each other and with feelings of solidarity, empathy and guilt make themselves "hosts"—in educational scholar Sharon Todd's (2002) wording—for the Other's narrative presence.

Works of art, Dewey posits, are the only media of complete and unhindered communication between humans that can occur in a world full of gulfs and walls that limit community of experience. What potential is there not then, artistical and pedagogical, if we give children, pupils and students opportunities to enter the relational world of dance, with all their imagination and power of creative action, on equal conditions, a magic world, as Stinson's youngest dancers call it, of becoming. The conclusion is that dance *is* educational and that kinesthetic experience is democratic *Bildung*. All this, dance can teach us.

REFERENCES

Arendt, H. (1954). *Between past and future: Eight exercises in political thought.* Penguin Books.

Biesta, G. (2006). *Beyond learning: Democratic education for a human future.* Paradigm.

Biesta, G. (2017). *Letting art teach: Art education "after" Joseph Beuys.* ArtEZ Press.

Biesta, G. (2018). "What if? Art education beyond expression and creativity." In N. Christopher, B. Gert, & D. R. Cole, (Ed.), *Art, artists and pedagogy: Philosophy and the arts in education.* Routledge.

Cunningham, M. (1952). Space, time and dance. *Transformation, 1,* 3.

Cunningham, M. (1955). *The impermanent art* (7 Arts No. 3, 69–77).

Dewey, J. (1926). *Democracy and education: An introduction to the philosophy of education.* Macmillan Publishers.

Dewey, J. (1934). *Art as experience.* Penguin/Perigee Books.

Disch, L. J. (1994). *Hannah Arendt and the limits of philosophy.* Cornell University Press.

Greene, M. (1986). The spaces of aesthetic education. *Journal of Aesthetic Education, 20*(4), 56. https://doi.org/10.2307/3332600

Greene, M. (1995). *Releasing the imagination. Essays on E=education, the arts, and social change.* Jossey-Bass Public Health.

Greene, M. (2007). *Aesthetics as research.* Maxine Greene Center for Aesthetic Education and Social Imagination.

Levinas, E. (1987/1992). *Time and the other and additional essays.* Duquesne University Press.

Levinas, E. (2003). *Humanism of the other.* University of Illinois Press.

Manchev, B. (2011). Vermögen, Ausbeutung und Widerstand der Subjekt-Körper. Für eine trans-versale Veränderung. In *Inventionen* (pp. 197–213). Diaphanes.

Manning, E. (2009). *Relationscapes: Movement, art, philosophy.* The MIT Press.

Moerman, P. (2014). Dansen och pedagogiken: En undersökning ur ett estetiskt och etiskt perspektiv av dansens möjlighetsvillkor i sökandet efter kunskap och mening. Södertörns högskola. http://sh.diva-portal.org/smash/record.jsf?pid=diva2%3A848664&dswid=9677

Roth, W.-M. (2011). *Possibility: At the limits of the constructivist metaphor.* Springer.

Stinson, S. (1988). *Dance for young children: Finding the magic in movement.* American Alliance for Health, Physical Education, Recreation and Dance.

Stinson, S. W. (1990). Dance education in early childhood. *Design for Arts in Education, 91*(6), 34–41. https://doi.org/10.1080/07320973.1990.9934836

Stinson, S. W. (2016). *Embodied curriculum theory and research in arts education: A dance scholar's search for meaning (Landscapes: The Arts, Aesthetics, and Education, 17).* Springer.

Todd, S. (2002). Listening as attending to the "echo of the otherwise": On suffering, justice, and education. *Philosophy of education yearbook*, 405–412.

Wetherall, M. (1988). Discourse analysis and the identification of interpretative repertoires. In J. Potter (Ed.), *Analysing everyday explanation: A casebook of methods* (pp. 168–183). Sage.

PART III

Humanizing Education

'The Wound is Where the Light Enters': Bringing our Impure, Journeying Selves into our Teaching

Agnes B. Curry

I said: what about my eyes?
He said: Keep them on the road.

I said: What about my passion?
He said: Keep it burning.

I said: What about my heart?
He said: Tell me what you hold inside it.

I said: Pain and sorrow.
He said: Stay with it. The wound is the place where the Light enters you.
—Jalal al-Din Rumi (1207–1273)

A. B. Curry (✉)
University of Saint Joseph, West Hartford, CT, USA
e-mail: acurry@usj.edu

© The Author(s), under exclusive license to Springer Nature Switzerland AG 2021
M. P. Hall and A. K. Brault (eds.), *Academia from the Inside*,
https://doi.org/10.1007/978-3-030-83895-9_10

INTRODUCTION

This reflection on teaching and authenticity in conversation with Parker Palmer is prompted by aspects of my selfhood I have often found troubling and difficult to describe, yet are deeply implicated with who and how I am as a teacher. One aspect is my family history and personal embodiment as a 'mixed' Latina and Anglo, with physical traits that can register variously, depending on context. The other is my experience of childhood sexual assault (CSA). Both of these experiences, in complex relation to my academic journey, have shaped my approach to my field, philosophy, and my relationships with students and colleagues.

The chapter is also shaped by the public health and political circumstances under which I wrote it. The ongoing COVID-19 pandemic has laid bare for all the horrific race- and class-based health disparities and the unfair distribution of risk that structures US society. The murder of George Floyd crystalized the horror into anti-racist protests worldwide. The January 6, 2021 storming of the US Capitol Building was a further reminder that a return to a pre-pandemic status quo is unacceptable. Philosophical questions about meaning, purpose, justice, freedom and facing death went from being socially marginal to being wracking issues for most people. This includes our students. While this made for generally more immediate, sometimes desperate connections to my class material as students searched for answers and lifelines, it also made for daily heartbreak for me, witnessing their struggles along with those of the world. At the same time, knowing the public health implications of their trauma, and the trauma of younger children, steeled my resolve to write.

The pandemic opened many previously secure children and young people to a barrage of disruption and loss. For many, it demolished safety nets that had held abuse at bay, or exacerbated adversities they were already facing. If we consider the pandemic in light of the watershed 1999 study by the Centers for Disease Control and Kaiser Permanente on Adverse Childhood Experiences, we can infer that many of these children and young people will bear its effects for a lifetime. As the American Academy of Pediatrics (2014) notes, "adverse childhood experiences (ACEs) can contribute significantly to negative adult physical and mental health outcomes and affect more than 60% of adults. This continues to be reaffirmed with more recent studies." While my household and I weathered the pandemic without job loss or illness, I know these are markers of my privilege, as is the fact that my life has offered so many opportunities for healing around adversities I have experienced. As one so privileged, I must speak.

I have learned through both my academic work and my life outside the academy that healing is real—and wondrous—but it involves integrating and witnessing, not 'getting over' the traumas or their causes. It involves full-bodied plumbing of wells of shame and resultant impulses to secrecy. At their best, such explorations flower into openheartedly naming the reality—and ubiquity—of the wounds and the domination systems perpetuating injury—and the openings into healing. My self-care and integration has included recognizing that nothing is simple: my sense of vocation as a teacher is a guiding thread, but it is also, undeniably, a complex response that is at once functional and dysfunctional, at once resistant to and complicit with domination systems. This is the paradox of human existence: nothing is pure.

Looking back on my own journey, I see why I turned first to philosophy but then within philosophy to feminist explorations of corporeality. I see why my teaching techniques have for two decades included the sorts of meditative and other contemplative activities that helped save my life. At the same time, it is not surprising that only in recent years have I directly named my experiences with CSA, very sparingly, in relevant teaching contexts. Nor is it surprising that I have never heard any faculty colleagues publicly disclose experiences of sexual violation, other than graduate school or workplace sexual harassment, in any professional context. I too have most directly practiced the courage of vulnerability about CSA in contexts outside school, particularly in Interfaith spiritual companioning circles. But growth there pushed me to consider more deeply my responsibilities to be more direct with my students and colleagues, in spite of the risks. This essay is a start to making such considerations more public.

Philosophizing from Where We Really Are

For me, philosophy loses its life when divorced from its ancient and cross-cultural depictions as a search for wisdom prompted by our life circumstances and relationships. What I teach in my courses, no matter how current the topics, is grounded in the equally ancient concern about inquiry and teaching as dialogical relationships. While due to the biases, fears, and shames of its practitioners through the ages, philosophy has so often attempted to flee or control our human condition of fragile embodiment, the ancient call of wisdom can help keep us grounded.

My main aim when teaching is to help my students see where this call is operative in their own lives, and to encourage their steps heeding this call. My students' philosophical work includes personal self-reflection and listening-oriented dialogue, where the point isn't to argue but to hear. They experience philosophy as inherently multicultural, as involving contemplation of the arts and the natural world, and as unconcerned about triumph in debate. Whether the ways the call of wisdom is alive for my students align precisely with current practice in professional philosophy is not my main concern. My ability to be less concerned is a luxury that comes from working exclusively with undergraduate students taking one or two philosophy courses as part of their general education. In that context, connecting philosophical inquiry to their explorations of their relationships, vocations, and identities is paramount.

"What Are You?" and Why Speak?

Regarding my own racial and ethnic identity, I am one of those persons who has had strangers approach to ask flat out, "What are you?" Other strangers have assumed I am Jewish, Middle Eastern or Balkan. No one has assumed Mexican. With my father's Anglo surname as my own, the fact that I also identify as Latina and Xicana in important respects is not obvious. In our racially stratified sociopolitical environments, inadvertently 'passing' for Anglo has given me huge advantages. At the same time, it has put me into positions of witnessing the sort of racist habits of speech and action to which even well-meaning White people can revert when they think they are not in the company of Others. This ability to 'pass' in many contexts has thus afforded me information and insight that is less accessible to most highly privileged people. At the same time, it creates dilemmas demanding significant cognitive and emotional labor.

Regarding my experiences of CSA, I want first to note that survivors' personal responses to sexual violations vary. My main aim is to describe aspects of my own responses insofar as I can; both the thickness of memory and the immediacy of some continued reactions can be difficult to decipher. And barriers of fear and shame dog me (and many survivors) even when we know cognitively that our victimization was not our fault. These reverberations can pop up unexpectedly in spite of significant healing.

In academic contexts, the axes of experience I describe in this chapter remain subject to what Viet Thanh Nguyen (2018) describes as "narrative scarcity"—the situation where there are relatively few narratives available due to systemic economic constraints facing the tellers of such narratives. First of all, philosophy is predominantly a male field. According to 2020 demographic data compiled by the American Philosophical Association (APA), around 28% of US philosophers identify as female. Philosophy is overwhelmingly White and my career path was eased by my Whiteness. Of the 2580 APA regular members who gave identifying information regarding their race and ethnicity, 128 (5%) of any sex or gender identify as Hispanic/Latino and even fewer identify as Black (88, or 3%). These figures reflect academic philosophy's culture of gate keeping and justification, which is notoriously unfriendly to women of all races and BIPOC philosophers of all genders. Utilizing the work of Gayle Salaman (2009), Kristie Dotson (2012) characterizes: "To say that philosophy has a culture of justification, then, is to say that the profession of philosophy requires the practice of making congruent one's own ideas, projects and....pedagogical choices with some "traditional" conception of philosophical engagement" (p. 6). Philosophy's culture of justification means that philosophy is at heightened risk of screening out just those questions and perspectives *most* needed for more adequate, comprehensive truths. Narrative scarcity thus links to epistemological scarcity, which in turn links to patterns of ignorance and epistemic injustice (Fricker, 2007).

Despite the ubiquity of sexual assault, I know of only two academic philosophers, both women, whose work on sexual violation includes accounts of their own experiences: Linda Martín Alcoff and Susan Brison. Tellingly, while Brison has written extensively since the early 1990s about her rape by a stranger when she was in her mid-30 s, it was only in 2014 that she disclosed an earlier rape, at age 20, by an acquaintance. From what I can tell, Alcoff started publishing about her experience of CSA after securing tenure.

Along with narrative scarcity and epistemological scarcity, these topics are also fraught with narrative peril. There are patterns in how some types of narratives feel especially dangerous to disclose—because in most circumstances they *are* dangerous to disclose. Alcoff (2018) characterizes rape cultures as producing frames for knowledge and inquiry that constrain, from the start, the sorts of questions that can be asked and the sorts of answers that can register as intelligible in both public and private spaces. These frames are not organized by argument or evidence, and especially not by listening to those victimized. Yet they sort out who is and is not a credible victim, who can and cannot be accused of assaulting, plausible versus nonsensical narratives, and in what contexts sexual violation may be spoken about at all. White supremacy produces its own multifarious frameworks that reinforce sexism and other axes of oppression.

At the same time, life for everyone, no matter how advantaged, brings with it inevitable heartbreak (Palmer, 2009). There is the further paradox that only through heartbreak are we opened to becoming more fully human in the richest, most positive sense. How do these dimensions weave together for us as we interact with our diversely situated students and colleagues? In a world riddled with what Brison (2008) characterizes as "everyday atrocities and ordinary miracles" (p. 188), how do we bear witness in ways that respect both the unfathomably individual and the all-too-common patterns?

THINKING WITH AND ALONGSIDE PARKER PALMER

Parker Palmer (2017) reminds us of what deep down we know all along, that what we bring as teachers has far less to do with pedagogical techniques than with our listening to ourselves as human beings on ongoing quests for wholeness. Wholeness, he reminds us, means recognizing and becoming friends with all the parts of ourselves, including our shadowy wounds and limits—the confusions, complexities, and compromises concealed beneath the "brave faces" (p. 44) we so often wear in academia. For me personally, this is impossible without devoting time to early morning silence. Through a mixture of meditating, praying, journaling, I have to take time to welcome what comes in all areas of my life, scanning for their implications on my showing up for my students and colleagues that day, and accepting the variable, ragged edges of my response. At times this effort at welcoming can feel like a traipse along the spiral-path of familiar issues and responses. I welcome the subtle exhilaration of resentment, the sour taste of apprehension, the carload of trickster-teachers accompanying grief as they hearken sometimes to clarity and other times to the lure of false innocence (Alison, 2001). At other times, welcoming can feel like a lightning bolt of newness, bathed in light, or an unfathomable joy. Whatever the day's guests may be, I have learned through failure that if I skimp on these morning practices of noticing, welcoming, and releasing, I needlessly risk hurting others and damaging my integrity. At the same time, paradoxically, I have learned to hold judgments of my failure with gentleness, as situations I have deemed failures have sometimes turned out to be vital openings for others. Thus for me to teach is to say yes to mystery—to the mystery of contact, the mystery of selves in communication, the mystery of timing in the encounters, and the great Mystery backlighting all we think we know.

Palmer describes integrity as wholeness, in contrast to self-division. I agree that there is a difference between self-integrity and fragmentation but do not assume integrity is necessarily the same as wholeness. I leave open the possibility that in some instances, integrity may mean noting that some structures of psychological rupture, for example, what W.E.B. DuBois (1903/2019) characterizes as double-consciousness, may be inescapable as long as the social systems perpetuating them remain in place. Alternatively, integrity may involve recuperating a positive sense of what Chicana theorists such as Gloria Anzaldúa (1987), Edwina Barvosa (2008), and Maria Lugones (1992, 2003) characterize as mestiza consciousness, borderland subjectivity, or even further, multiple selfhood. Mariana Ortega (2016) articulates both the ontological uniqueness of each self and the existential multiplicity experienced by many immigrants, exiles, and multicultural beings. For at least some, selfhood may be constituted by states of liminality—of being neither wholly one identity nor another, but rather an ambiguous sense of both and neither. A sense of irreconcilable multiplicity may be an authentic, sane, even wise response to being existentially situated at intersections structured by not just differing but opposed ways of living and sense-making, but to which those situated must still respond.

What I think can be said is that integrity involves discerning the difference between fragmentation and openings to mystery and possible creative multiplicity. My criterion in discerning the difference is my recognition of what medieval mystic Hildegard of Bingen called *viriditas*: "greening" or the sacred flow of life-givingness. In what ways does the situation invite me to feel compassion and awe at the irreplaceable dignity of others? Does it invite me to foster appreciation of the sacramental dimension of each moment? Does what I am considering invite me to see opportunities for creative response to whatever situation I am facing? Does it pull me into attempting to communicate and build community? Or does it replay old tapes of fear and self-isolation, which I associate with dampening of the force of life? I take the things that give life to be relational and communicative even in silence—the silence of soil, which too is comprised of many things, each of which is needed. Following the line of this discernment helps me move beyond the self-division that circumstances inflict on everyone to varying degrees, to honoring "every major thread of one's life experience" and "creating a weave of such coherence and strength that it can hold students and subject as well as self" (Palmer, 2017, p. 48). Only such a self, according to Palmer, can venture and sustain the connections outward—the openness to *meeting* otherness in all its manifestations—that characterizes liberatory teaching and learning.

While there is a discernible difference between fragmentation and integrity, the world always has an Infinity of lessons in newness and otherness to offer. Thus, we need continually to process. Our human worlds—the ones we have laden with structures to house (and thus hide) our fear and pain—are ongoing construction projects, always presenting new (or revisiting) dilemmas to repair. With respect to losing heart in academia, here are many reasons: as Palmer notes, under the rumbling symptoms of academia's illnesses, which are but a reflection of larger social ills, "teaching is a daily exercise in vulnerability" (Palmer, 2017, p. 50). Even if our institutions are atypical havens, and even when we don't have secrets, "teaching is always done at the dangerous intersection of personal and public life" (Palmer, 2017, p. 50). With that inevitable crossover into personal life it is tempting to respond to the tenderness of that intersection with bandages. What's harmful about that approach is that we are still overcompensating: those bandages we proactively use to conceal and protect can leave us both encumbered and numb.

As a starting point to the vulnerabilities I explore, I turn to the story of Eric and Alan with which Palmer opens *The Courage to Teach*. Readers are told that both men come from families of working-class skilled craftspeople, "rural folk, with little formal schooling but gifted in the manual arts" (Palmer, 2017, p. 47). As they grew, each developed a sense of self and value in which "pride of craft was key" (Palmer, 2017, p. 47). Since it is unsaid, I wonder if we can presume that both are White. The seeds of Eric's downfall seem to have been cast when he let his culture shock at being thrust into an elite college environment get the best of him. From there he took on the persona of an 'intellectual,' sustained by the more deeply adversarial stance one can assume when the ground of one's entitlement feels shaky. His failures as a teacher are summed up as being 'driven by a need to inflict on his students the same wound that academic life had inflicted on him—the wound of being embarrassed by some essential part of one's self" (Palmer, 2017, p. 47). His love of craft (and by implication the integration of his working-class identity) stayed ensconced in his private life. Alan spared himself some culture shock by his choosing a less elite, land grant university. In contrast to Eric, Alan was able to integrate more of his ancestral sense of craft into his teaching and mentoring by feeling less need to defend who he is—still in some ways a foreigner in the halls of academia—but a little more comfortable by virtue both of some personal resilience and of not venturing quite so far above his station.

Palmer notes that the self-protective split is encouraged not just by the inherent vulnerability of the teaching situation, but also by the simplistic understanding of objectivity regnant in academia. While the problem of objectivity is a difficult one, it is both unrealistic and harmful to think the problem is solved by enshrining a dualist model that sees knowledge of the world 'out there' possible only when the personality of the knower is bypassed. This has been recognized in many fields, including the natural sciences. Even still, however, budding practitioners are still socialized into thinking that objectivity involves removing all vestiges of the personal identity of the knower from the situation, a point brought home to me repeatedly when discussing epistemology with science majors. Insofar as many academic fields reward disconnected, depersonalized speech as reflective of a more objective standpoint, those selves who are already marked as more 'leaky' by virtue of their social location or personal history have additional vulnerabilities and dilemmas. As Palmer's vignette about Eric and Alan suggests, self-development, no matter how mysterious its spiritual depths, can never be divorced from the cultural and socio-political forces of the communities in which we live. Along with the spark that can never be reduced to description, our individuality is always at the same time a collaborative affair involving elements of happenstance, historical constraint, and implicit as well as explicit choice. Anyone in a leadership position needs to rely on this point of intersectionality within and at the same time recognize that others' points of intersectionality may be configured very differently from theirs. As teachers, how does this inform our intellectual framework and approach to our subject matter? How does it shape how we share our understandings, whether with students, faculty colleagues, or administrative staff?

Faced with both intrapersonal and interpersonal complexity, it is easy to understand the temptation to academic cultures where "the pathology of speech disconnected from self is regarded, and rewarded, as a virtue,"

(Palmer, 2017, p. 51). This temptation can encourage forms of self-alienation for everyone. At the same time, however, there are patterns that hang up some people more than others. How many academics are of rural working-class background? What fields are they clustered in? How do they stay true to themselves when their presence is so often regarded as an anomaly? Palmer characterizes teaching in generally positive terms, as one of the professions people choose for "reasons of the heart." This truth is extraordinarily complex: while our hearts are vastly more mysterious and powerful than we know, I want to give due to the forces of circumstance. I wonder how many of us who entered and remained in academia had parents who were academics, and whether those in academia who identify more fundamentally as teachers than as scholars or researchers had family members who taught at the K-12 level. I wonder how many of the women who have managed to persist in academia initially saw higher education as a break from tradition but later in life recontextualize it as also in part an ambitious variation on family-sanctioned themes.

In *A Hidden Wholeness* (2004) Palmer charts how our fear and demoralization upon confronting a world that seems to prize inauthenticity works to silence what he variously characterizes as our inner teacher, inner light, or soul. The impetus to self-division develops early—by mid-late childhood, sometimes earlier. "Afraid that our inner light will be extinguished or our inner darkness exposed, we hide our true identities from each other. In the process, we become separated from our own souls. We end up living divided lives," (Palmer, 2004, 92–93) characterized by denial, equivocation, cowardice, and avarice (Palmer, 2004). Much of Palmer's work on teaching is describing how in contemporary life educational institutions sadly and ironically foster divided lives for those working within them, and how we can follow the stirrings of soul to craft better lives and better institutions. For me, academic work was a vital step in the journey of living divided no more, of nurturing the flicker of light from childhood while pursuing a life of doing decently to myself and others. At the same time I see my choice as also exhibiting the weavings of circumstance and the lure of self-alienation.

Unlike Eric and Alan, I was socialized into some middle-class entitlement. While my parents were nowhere nearly so entitled (which manifested in patterns of resentment in my father and an air of striving in my mother) both earned their bachelor's degrees and embarked on middle-class careers. While it took my mother almost a decade, alternating school and work and bucking the pressure to major in Spanish, she earned her degree in Elementary Education and taught intermittently through my childhood. She was a very good elementary teacher and found particular joy in fostering literacy. Her own mother taught piano in Hispanic and Indigenous communities in southern Colorado and New Mexico from her early 20s until her death in her mid-80 s, first as a contribution to the ranch's variable coffers, later as a way to assert her own personhood.

Both my parents revered teachers. Even after my parents' marriage imploded, my father continued to express admiration for my mother's skills as a teacher. Two of my maternal grandfather's sisters had shown such promise as students that my great-grandfather invested the family's limited funds in their education rather than my grandfather's. While he was pulled from school after eighth grade, my great aunts went on to earn teaching certificates from teacher-training institutions called Normal schools. They taught for periods in rural southern Colorado. Decades after they'd become farm wives with many children and grandchildren, they took pride in these certificates. My paternal grandmother had also earned some sort of teaching certificate in Alabama in her early teens. While her marriage at age 20 consigned her to a hardscrabble life in the sawmill camps of the Florida panhandle and she didn't survive the birth of her seventh child at age 42, her pride in that certificate spurred three of her daughters to college by any means necessary. One eventually earned a Ph.D. in mathematics and taught at the college level (spurring her daughter to do the same), while my other aunts served K-12 education, one as a librarian and the other as a teacher in international schools. My father was the only boy of the lot to go to college. While neither parent particularly envisioned the life of a professor for any of their children, my father's pride in his sister led him to be more open to my decision to go to graduate school in a scholarly field than my mother was. For once I had a taste of college, I never doubted that I would go on to graduate school in hopes of teaching at the college level. The question was in what.

To help reintegrate the sundered parts of ourselves, Palmer (2017) advises us to reflect on our recognized mentors, whose lessons to us about who we are may not be clear to us for many years. Even more difficult is to see how adversaries, both personal and circumstantial, can also serve as mentors, challenging us to dig deeper to find our sources of integrated response rather than flailing reactivity or further compartmentalization. Finding and fostering communities in which both differences and overlapping convergences are recognized demands yet another layer of effort that can take longer still, as determining common ground for communication becomes more challenging. These axes of difference shape what is communicable regardless of speakers' and listeners' intentions. The subtleties of class differences among those sharing the same racial identities are just one such axis. The divergent senses of identity operative for members of subordinated and marginalized communities are perhaps even more salient, but even less noticeable because the terms for articulating selfhood are those of the majority. When Palmer (2017) talks about the pain of dismemberment in an academic context, he emphasizes that this pain has both spiritual and sociological dimensions but insists that ultimately, this pain stems from our own spiritual turning away from our authenticity. While surface pain can come when academia turns out not to be community of concord but instead an arena of competition, "deeper down, this pain is more spiritual than sociological: it comes from being disconnected from our own truth, from the passions that took us into teaching, from the heart that is the source of all good work" (p. 55). However, at the very least, these types of pain are experienced in our lives as interweaving. In the following narrative, I try to illuminate some of the connections between these two dimensions,

Storytelling as Re-membering and Reanimating

As Palmer says, we teach out of who we are. Our selfhood cannot be sidestepped; it 'leaks through' for good or ill. And Palmer's point is that authentic teaching only emerges through owning who we are. Childhood is lived navigating the shoals of self-discovery and others' impositions, guided by the varying signs offered by our fallible and usually wounded elders. While all familial and social milieu are complex once we start to notice, some of us were situated in places and times where intersectional complexities emerged from the fog of childhood at a relatively earlier age.

By the time I was four in late-1960s Gainesville, Florida, I had been given precise instructions for answering the "What are you?" question that my parents knew their children would regularly face. Eager to start kindergarten and always aiming to please, I had taken to the task of memorizing a two-part response and remember practicing it in a mirror. To the opening question, I was to respond, "I'm Spanish and Scotch-Irish." I was taught to anticipate a follow-up question as well: "Spanish from Spain, or Spanish from Mexico?" to which I was to respond, "Spanish from Spain." Although I have no doubts about parents' sincerity in trying to equip us with knowledge for navigating life in our socio-politically cleaved world, neither answer was true in any simple sense. Both labels by which I was taught to identify myself simultaneously mark and obscure centuries of settler-colonialist class, race, and religious conflict.

Although I had no clue at the time what it meant, I have since learned that the term "Scotch-Irish" connects to the wanderings of people from the English/Scottish borderlands, largely descendant from the fifth-centry Angle invaders to the British Isles. After the Protestant Reformation they were predominantly Presbyterian. Many were pressured to emigrate to Northern Ireland in the early 1600 s as part of the British Crown's efforts to subdue or displace the Irish Catholic inhabitants from their ancestral homelands (McKinney et al., 1992). From Northern Ireland, about a quarter million of these recent immigrants journeyed further to other British colonies in the eighteenth century. While they and their descendants had not initially objected to being known as 'Irish' upon landing in North America, the subsequent mid-nineteenth-century waves of impoverished Catholic immigrants fleeing Ireland's famines changed that. As Jay Dolan (2008) characterizes, "in no way did Irish Protestants want to be identified with these ragged newcomers" (p. x) and thus 'Scotch Irish' gained currency as a term of distinction. While 'Scotch Irish' meant something when used in Florida—something that prompted knowing nods from listeners but left intact my ignorance about its full meaning—it registered much less in northeast Kansas, where my family moved when I was thirteen. In that context, among classmates of largely German and Scandinavian stock, my looks raised an entirely different set of associations, and I was known initially as "the girl who looks like Anne Frank." By that time, too, my father had become interested in genealogy and it turned out that his ancestors were largely from more southern regions of England.

With respect to the other side of the answer, "Spanish...from Spain, not Mexico," even my four-year-old self registered and absorbed the layering of unease it marked, for it conflicted with a piece of my small stock of geographical knowledge. I knew my grandparents lived in a place called New Mexico and that when I described visiting them to other children, I sometimes had to explain that New Mexico was in the United States. But I was confused: how did "from Spain" relate? I knew Spanish was the name of the language my mom knew and grandparents knew, that they spoke intermixed with English, and that my mom tried to teach us in fits and starts. I knew my mother had been born in Colorado and that my grandparents and ancestors had been in New Mexico and Colorado for hundreds of years, since before the United States was born. But how did New Mexico and Mexico relate? Whether I asked and was rebuffed or sensed the fence around the question so didn't voice my question has been lost to memory.

What I learned, regardless of parental intention, was that Mexico was a place I should not let myself be associated with—a place marked with flags of shame. Spain, in contrast, was a more acceptable, if utterly abstract, imagined homeland, though in elementary school I started to recognize that people didn't necessarily know what to make of the 'from Spain' response. In particular, the Cuban kids scoffed. I saw these scions of the first and second waves of post-Castro emigration as moving with an assurance I couldn't place, their tawny skin a point of fashion, their bilingual abilities likewise a cachet. In contrast, my mother's efforts to teach us Spanish were inconsistent, stymied by my father's lack of fluency in spite of what I now see as valiant efforts and by the way we children sometimes responded with resistance. In addition, I was by far the lightest of my siblings, sheathed with the sort of skin that burns and freckles but never tans. While merely a point of remark for my extended families, my coloring was occasion of some derision at school. At the time I was jealous that I was not darker. I have since recognized the advantages my ethnic ambiguity has afforded me.

I have also since learned that the Spanish-speaking people in the lands ceded from Mexico to the United States in the 1848 Treaty of Guadalupe Hildago were initially known as "Mexicans" no matter their economic level. But historian Charles Montgomery (2001) documents how after decades of economic and political standoff between residents and Anglo arrivals to the territory, both sides deployed the term "Spanish American," but for different aims. Leaders of the Spanish-speaking communities initially used the term "Spanish American" as a term of unity across classes to evoke "both a proud Spanish colonial past and an elusive American future, a future in which they might still realize the promise of equality amid Anglo intolerance" (Montgomery, 2001, p. 65). Anglos, on the other hand, deployed the Europeanized term in a dual effort to garner national respectability for the territory while also courting Spanish-speaking voters. However, in the early twentieth century, when discourses supporting racism solidified and then metastasized across the US, the term "Spanish" played into the construction of White supremacy. Its use exacerbated class divisions among the Spanish-speaking people in

New Mexico and southern Colorado, while proving ineffectual against encroaching Anglo dominance. Meanwhile, the project of constructing "Mexicanness" along a racial hierarchy that had started in the nineteenth century continued unabated:

> as English-speaking army officers, missionaries, travel writers, and settlers passed judgment on New Mexico's people, they constructed, layer by layer, the term's practical meaning. The "Mexican" was said to be primitive and uninventive, lazy and apathetic, politically corrupt and privately immoral, impoverished and ignorant. The most abject attribute and the apparent root of all evils was mixed blood: as the offspring of Spaniards and Indians, the "Mexican" was irreversibly tainted by racial impurity....To the typical Anglo observer, a "Mexican" was inferior in mind, body and spirit; there was no need to belabor the matter. (Montgomery, 2001, p. 65)

On the other hand, there was no gain belaboring the distinction in cases where business collaboration or intermarriage might be useful, so both Anglos and Spanish-speaking elites colluded in infusing the distinction with both racism and classism. For both Anglo residents of the territory and outside observers, racializing Mexicans bolstered not just the right but also the moral duty to overrun the continent and reshape it according to Anglo Saxon institutions and norms. (Montgomery, 2001). Thus, while "Spanish American" garnered some token surface respect in the early part of the twentieth century, it was a salvo in a battle already lost.

The generations before and after my mother's grew up being called "dirty Mexicans" while wanting to be "Spaniards," their desires entrenching spurious doctrine of purity. At the same time—the first half of the twentieth century—the stakes of impurity became increasingly fraught for Spanish-speaking people, no matter when they or their ancestors arrived to what is now US soil. In the 1930s, when my mother was a child, Colorado and other western states arranged for mass deportations to Mexico—including deportations of US citizens (Florido, 2015; McIntosh, 2016). Francisco Balderamma (2006) conservatively estimates that 60% of the over one million people deported during this period were US citizens. To enforce the removal of people from northern Colorado, the governor of Colorado set up a blockade of the southern border of the state. As historian Marjorie McIntosh (quoted in Dobbs & Dyer, 2014) describes, "The governor sent troops to set up barriers and stop trains, buses, and automobiles; anyone who looked suspicious was questioned by the soldiers, asked about their origins and financial situation." Road maps from both 1896 and 1841 indicate that one of these blockades likely would have been on Highway 285, which connected the Texas/Mexico border with Denver and ran through my mother's childhood home of La Jara, twenty miles from the Colorado/New Mexico border. Later, as a young wife traveling cross-country by car to Florida at the tail end of Jim Crow, my mother faced stares no matter which public restroom she tried to use.

My parents maintained close ties with their families, so we had some sense of the difference college degrees made in late twentieth-century life. Not all my father's siblings made it out of the pine forests, while the fortunes of our maternal relatives varied. Some older cousins went away to college and came back briefly identifying as Chicano to the incomprehension or horror of their parents, until the bitterness of some internecine conflicts within the movement was too much for them to ingest. A few others got caught up in low-rider culture and the post-Vietnam influx of heroin that has since resulted in multigenerational cycles of death. Visiting the Española, NM, trailer home of my maternal aunt and our five closest cousins, I saw differences of opportunity made even more obvious when they came to visit us. While my mother spent years nostalgic and lonely for home, I could see why she left.

Perhaps loneliness for multigenerational extended family—and having four children in seven years—makes some sense of my mother's receptiveness to the overtures of the older, childless couple who moved across the street when I was about eight. They lavished us with treats and gifts; it was a special privilege to be the child chosen to accompany them on the Sunday drive in their sea-green Cadillac, or to deliver to them a gift of bread or cookies. Gradually the privileges started to come with the price of being hugged by Mr. L. a little too long, a little too closely, a little too much in the front, then kissed in ways that gradually oozed from grandfatherly familiar to uninterpretable, to creepy. But the grooming was subtle, and he was patient, lavishing similar attention on other little girls throughout the neighborhood. When he crossed the line to what I could understand as attacks, I did my best to squirm away and within weeks tried to tell various adults in whatever terms I had at the time. I also went on a spree of breaking small objects. Whatever the adults' response from their perspective, which has been lost to time through my parents' deaths, I got the message that I had created difficulty for my parents' relationship between themselves and with the neighbors. I remember muffled conversations about whether to call the police. Instead, we moved to another part of the neighborhood within a year.

The second assaulter was a cousin on my father's side, in his late teens whom I recall meeting only once. That encounter compounded the damage of the initial assaults because I took the fact that I was targeted by someone I barely knew as evidence that something was terribly, visibly wrong with me. In contrast to the earlier situation where snippets of the felt-memory of physically struggling have functioned as both jagged intrusions into my consciousness and also tiny nails onto which to pin some self-respect, this time I completely froze and became mute. I told no one for years.

Within three years we had moved from Florida to Kansas, to the smallish town where my mother had attended college and done her first years of teaching. It was only a day's drive to New Mexico and there was a long-standing Mexican–American community who knew my mother from her teaching days. The community was comprised mainly of families whose elders had followed railroad work or pushed north to escape Revolution-era instability along the Texas border. Some regarded my mother as "uppity" while others admired her. More importantly, they understood her. My parents had decided to relocate to the town in large part because of the high school there, a Catholic boarding and day school with a sizable international program that included students from Mexico and Latin America whose complexions partook of a broad palette of hues. My own lightness was far less notable than in Florida. My brothers, all darker than me, had more racist incidents than I did.

While my parents allowed me to apply to colleges all over the US, it ultimately became clear that the only realistic choices were those that I, as the eldest child, could pay for myself. The most generous scholarship was for the Catholic college run by the same community as the high school; it maintained a solid record of medical school placements. I'd initially planned to major in "pre-med" although I was getting some maternal pressure to consider something with a more feminine career path. Nevertheless, I started out majoring in biology, then tried to combine that with music for a time. I eventually switched wholly to music even though I knew I did not want to teach music in k-12 schools and did not especially like to perform.

My relation to music was complicated, wrapped in the double layers of authentic connection and familial expectation. Although my grandmother had taught piano for most of her life, she had not taught my mother to play—for reasons now lost in the mist, though it felt to my mother like neglect. To compensate, I started piano lessons by age five. I took to it better than most children, and as I grew, playing the piano was one of the organizing features of my life. It was a pillar of an identity built predominantly around pleasing others. However, along with approval and attention, it offered me solace and a vehicle for exploring emotions that were inexpressible or unwelcome otherwise. It was also a vehicle for losing myself in work. My talent was not of the caliber needed for a professional career and college study, even at a tiny institution, made that clear. While perhaps a mistake in a practical sense, I see that I chose the major because in my relation to music I could sense a way to leave open the possibility that some questions are not answered in words. At the same time, it afforded an avenue for my own personal expression even though many parts of myself were still locked in the debilitating silence of shame and abasement. These differing types of the unspoken can dwell in close proximity.

As a music major, I was initially drawn into philosophy though questions about the meaning of music and the intention of artistic expression. This turn, from the doing to the wondering about the doing, helped me take hold of my ambivalence about performing, and to see more clearly that one could have various relationships to music. At the same time, I found another kind of both attention and solace in philosophy classes, where I was surprised to find myself enjoying philosophy and performing well. Ironically, the philosophy department offered a context of traditionalism and sexism so pervasive and self-assured that it need not erect any defensive walls against bright women. The dominant voice in the department—wielded by the most hidebound of the professors—assumed that we understood and assented to the 'special' dignity offered by a traditionalist, complementarian view of the sexes. And if nothing else, he saw the need to educate some women to be appropriate helpmeets for some men. Ironically, this insularity and leisure of low expectations opened a space of freedom. In philosophy I could at least see my biggest perplexities taken seriously. All the same, I saw it as a diversion, not anything with a future for myself, until late in college, when a course syllabus included the first philosophy book by a woman included in our curriculum—Hannah Arendt's *The Human Condition*. That book, then meeting a Benedictine sister who taught a few upper-level courses as a sideline to her Deanship, made women's presence in the discipline at least conceivable.

When the time came to decide my post-baccalaureate plans, I wanted to branch away from performance to music theory or composition and had managed to secure an assistantship to a regional university. But a combination of misgivings about music and greater readiness to move more into the realm of words prompted me to defer the assistantship and consider philosophy instead. The department Chair was supportive and recommended I apply to Catholic University in Washington, DC, while the Dean suggested I add some Jesuit schools to the mix. While as the sole daughter my moving from home for its own sake would have been utterly unthinkable, moving away for school was understandable, and I left Kansas for what my mother understood to be a limited span of years in New York City to attend Fordham University.

This initial interest in pursuing a career in philosophy mixed several motives: some full-hearted interest in the questions, particularly those offering differing accounts of religious and aesthetic issues; excitement about college teaching; some investment in proving myself in a field where I knew women were under-represented. While I followed an instinct to seek graduate departments employing at least one woman, I was naïve about the ferocity of gate keeping in the field and blissfully unaware that my "irenic" turn of mind had been flagged as a point of weakness in my recommendation letters. Later, I happened to be present in a conversation where my recommender expressed his opinion that it was impossible to do philosophy in Spanish because the language allowed only for poetic expression, which in turn reflected the fact that overall, Spanish-speaking people lacked reasoning ability. This remark prompted a re-evaluation of the professor, whom I had admired, but also the sort of self-reflexive turn that erodes trust in oneself and one's judgment—like the time at age 19 when, a few weeks in to my first intense romantic relationship, something I said prompted the guy to exclaim, "I didn't know you were a Spic!" as I watched the interest in his face visibly drain.

While I entered graduate school with a default stance of vigilance on both the professional and personal fronts, graduate study was nonetheless a step into fuller authenticity. I had applied to Fordham not only because it had two women in the philosophy department, but also because unlike most Ph.D. programs in philosophy, it included a seminar in teaching and a structured introduction to classroom teaching. The fact that it was Fordham to which I was being directed became clear through a number of odd incidents: I'd initially turned down the assistantship, bowing to some pressures to attend Catholic University instead, but the postcard got lost in the mail. By the time the department secretary called to check on my decision, I was regretting my decision and jumped at the second chance. When I got there, the fact that the obviously most brilliant student in the program was a young man, half Puerto Rican, half Austrian, with a Spanish surname, was another watershed. Our friendship, then love, was a gift.

From the start as a graduate assistant I saw myself as primarily training to be a teacher. Only later did I realize that I was an outlier and most of my peers saw themselves as scholars. The department was determinately pluralistic and more humane than many, a fact made abundantly clear as I became acquainted with students and faculty from other area schools and started teaching for New York University. Nonetheless, even at Fordham, the norms and schemas of academic philosophy, tagged by philosopher Sally Hanslanger (2008) as "hyper-masculine" (p. 217) remained dominant. These norms include competitiveness, quickness to judgmental position-taking, individualism even among those espousing more relational philosophies, and baseline hostility to femininity. They were not the only reasons why, of the dozen or so students in my starting cohort, including three other women, only four finished and I was the only woman. But they were contributing factors. My weathering them says less about my philosophical acumen than about skills picked up in my prior socialization, as suggested in Hanslanger (2008): "Those women and minorities succeed who are good at adjusting to or managing dysfunctional social environments, or who can conform to a milieu governed by certain masculine norms" (p. 217). In spite of feeling increasingly alienated from the questions and approaches I was supposed to be learning, I was so invested in succeeding that I did not consider quitting. Luckily, I was introduced to the work of Maurice Merleau-Ponty and feminist philosophy; the first philosophical work that I encountered that even broached the topic of race was in feminist philosophy. At the same time, I worked other jobs to support myself and help my youngest brother with college expenses and was buoyed by good teaching reviews.

The self I had assembled in my 20s and early 30s, through work and love relationships (one good, one bad), had some strengths but was also, even still, firmly gravitated and orbiting around my mother. So this self unraveled in the wake of her death, which occurred while I was trying to pull together my dissertation proposal. I couldn't write my dissertation until I took care of myself and got some therapeutic help for my grief at my mother's death—grief that was pinned in place by a well of anger for which I hated myself. It was almost easier to die than to face that. Although I didn't see it at the time, my dissertation topic, on feminist interpretations of Merleau-Ponty's account of corporeal subjectivity, was an inner call to greater truth and self-integration. It was no wonder that after getting the proposal approved in something of a fog, I fell into an ineradicable writers' block. The cliché that writing one's dissertation forces you to face yourself was true for me. The self I had to befriend in new ways had never repressed her memories of being sexually violated, nor of speaking up in whatever confused language available to her at the time. But having not felt heard, she had by adolescence dusted herself off and told herself that these events did not define her. That's a story I still hold as true, though in vastly more complicated fashion. But back then it was a mainly intellectual truth, and while those can be glittering lodestars, they're not homes in which we can live.

And I wanted a chance for a home—a chance for a home in academia where I could teach and contribute, and a chance for a partner and children. After years of seeing myself as unsuited for and unworthy of committed love and seeing a family and intellectual life as opposed, my inner self was listening to its deeper desires. At the time, these desires were submerged in the more immediate question of life itself: one afternoon by the Bronx River, I caught the felt shift of my inner background tapes from familiarly dysthymic to something more vividly dangerous. Within 24h, I had begged for an appointment with the campus counseling services. Whatever was happening and whatever feminist skepticism I'd garnered regarding some psychologies, I knew I needed help. I'm grateful for each of the counselors and midwives from those years: for the Masters candidate on her first internship, whose wide-eyed silence was a canvas on which I could at least lay out some colors and shapes; for the Jungian grandmother who suggested I expand that canvas to the night and the Unsayable; even for the Anglo postmodernist who chirpily informed me that "women don't exist" at the same time I was reading bell hooks' take on that idea; finally for the gifted practitioner whose deep understanding of race and trauma was made accessible by a sliding fee scale. I also worked with a Spiritual Director—a woman from a Christian tradition other than my own, a minister and a CSA and incest survivor. I also meditated and did yoga, laying the ground for practices that have been life sustaining in the decades since, even when relegated to brief moments of busy days.

Eventually I could write from a place that blended analysis and exploration of the personal stakes of my analysis. It took work with all my mentors—philosophical, psychotherapeutic, and spiritual. But I was also afforded a moment in a scholarly conversation opened up in feminist theorizing, that was relatively more open to at least some self-naming and accountability. In broader parts of my life, I was also more able to act out of a place that was both loving and open to love, and more accepting of the particular style I brought to my teaching.

In that first flush of greater overall health, my determination to live a relatively undivided life was apparent in choices I was able to make. Feminist philosophy was starting to become established and mine was the second feminist philosophy dissertation to come out of Fordham. When one college touted its on-campus day care center as an integral part of its identity, I was sold. In my first faculty bio uploaded to the college server, I identified myself as mixed Latina and Anglo in an effort both to be up front to students and set some parameters for my encounters with colleagues and the public. As the lone philosopher on campus but charged with revitalizing the philosophy major, I could develop courses and craft a curriculum with relative freedom. I added a course on philosophy of race and approached all my classes with concerns about gender and race apparent in my choices of texts. I added courses about the philosophy of food and food ethics, because food is such a potent way to bring in questions about identity, culture, and systems of oppression in a way that speaks to most everyone. I could use my stories about my family's traditions and ties to land in a way that helped students illuminate their own worlds.

Within weeks of starting my position, September 11 and its aftermath transformed my personal life, sending my partner overseas during my pregnancy and for long stretches of our son's childhood. This narrowed my priorities: after encountering problems scheduling service for a local sexual assault center, I took the path of least resistance and stopped calling. Activism on that front waned and with it direct exploration of myself as a survivor, but for some of those post 9–11 years, I was at least able to bear publicly my intertwined identities as academic and mother, bringing my son along on student trips and academic conferences. Through my son's first ten years, much of my self-care and connection with my spirit took place indirectly: through walks and kid-yoga; through some scholarly projects; through fewer formal sitting sessions on my own and more moments of leading students—with my pretending that breaths noticed while washing dishes or cleaning toilets sufficed for myself. Gradually I recognized that my successes as well as my failures of connection (as colleague, teacher, parent, and spouse) had unsustainable costs when I wasn't simultaneously caring for the ground of myself in relation to the larger Ground.

In 2013, a window opened when one of my upper-level classes did not run. I was reassigned to research an NSF call for grant proposals on "cultivating ethical cultures in STEM." In considering possibilities, my department mate was energized by the Charter for Compassion and Campus for Compassion movement that was then gaining a foothold in Connecticut, while I wondered whether questions about the relation between meditation and ethical growth had made it to science classrooms. This led us to initiate conversations on making our institution a Campus for Compassion and committing to a campus culture more consistent with our written mission. We had variable success changing our institutional culture, but the efforts were catalysts in my growth. Our twice- or thrice-weekly on-campus meditation sessions found us alone in the room more often than not, but we held to them until the pandemic closed campus.

COMMUNITIES OF CONVERGENCE

I'd had an uneasy relationship with Christianity ever since my kinder-garten teacher at Heritage Christian School told me that the Jews were all going to hell because they had killed Jesus. This taken-for-granted anti-Semitism may not have registered to other children as troubling if they knew no Jewish people or if anti-Semitism was reinforced in their homes. But for me this was world-shattering news, as my first childhood friend—my first love for anyone outside my immediate family—was Jewish. Her parents and mine both saw the friendship as an opportunity for teaching about religious pluralism: Donna and I went to each other's houses of worship and celebrated each other's holidays. While my parents pulled me from school as soon as they discovered the catalyst of my nightmares, the spell of childhood belief that religion tells truth was broken. If believing in or loving Jesus was premised on hating Jews—or anyone—then I had no genuine interest, though I feigned belief for all those years in Catholic education. The fact that in Catholicism the sacrament of Confirmation, taking place when one is twelve or thirteen, was presented to me as marking the moment of adult assent into one's faith (but with no genuine opportunity to refuse) just meant that as years progressed, I felt more and more inauthentic. At the same time, the constant immersion in a religious milieu was doing its work. I found the topic of religion interesting even if not the particular stories and lessons that were my inheritance.

As I grew through my later teens and had conversations with a few people who were both religious and unafraid of questions, I started to peer between the lines for the unsaid presence that I could glimpse at moments in music. A little later, philosophy and courses in Asian religions offered more possibilities, and I started finding my own way to the Holy. By graduate school, I was comfortable in my stance of finding familiarity in Catholicism but taking none of it literally. Years more of encountering more people whose faith exploded both doctrinal and discursive boxes encouraged that tendency.

Encountering *church* in its most mysterious flowering happened when I started taking part in interfaith spiritual companions groups. These intentional communities of people from all perspectives can clear away chaff with remarkable efficiency. Then a watershed development occurred when I ended up in a group in which almost all the members had experienced childhood sexual assault. This wasn't intentional for any of us: complete strangers to each other, we had each simply signed up for the day and time that fit into our schedules. After my therapeutic work before marrying, I had not sought support for aftereffects except for brief stints with individual therapists. I had never even considered participating in a survivors group. Nor do I think that a therapeutically inclined or led survivors group would have had nearly the same effect. This is because the point of group spiritual companioning is that no one is a leader or authority, and no one is any more 'broken' than anyone else. While there may be a more experienced facilitator, everyone is on equal footing and equally an opening for the action of what is beyond and between us. We weren't seeking to be fixed, nor were we aiming to fix anyone else, yet in that difference healing finds a way. We held space for each other's pain while always seeing each other as so much more wondrous and mysterious than any chronicle of moments or years can convey. Most significantly for me, I saw in various ways how many of the questions and lessons of life that frighten people, hang them up, and lead them to reject rather than accept seeing some things about the world because acceptance confronts us with our vulnerability, didn't have the same kind of pull on us.

This group, and subsequent conversations, ground my determination that somehow, the stories I tell, including the stories about my theorizing and teaching, have to include, as a part, my history and experiences of

CSA. I resist the framing, particularly the language of purity and cleanliness permeating Christian culture that lends additional force to racist tropes and consigns sexual violation to the unspeakable. Like at least some other survivors, I also question the power of therapeutic discourses in shaping experience and undermining the epistemic authority of those with experience, and I recognize the double-effects of some survivor-speak in reinforcing the power of these discourses and the voyeuristic pleasure of shock and horror. But because "silencing was (and still is) the universal tactic of perpetrators, imposed on victims of this crime unlike any other" (Alcoff, 2018, p. 232), I think it is important that more people speak so that we grapple with the scope of the situation in moral and sociopolitical terms in hopes of shaping a world that doesn't normalize abuse. By now I suspect that the prevalence of sexual violation of boys and young men is even more undercounted than for girls and infects the marrow of all our institutions, public and private.

It gets tiring to have to speak to the complexity of my ethnicities and family history. In a world organized by what bell hooks (1984) terms imperialist White supremacist capitalist patriarchy, the stakes of each term reverberate differently in different contexts. Each choice of ill-fitting terms can confuse or alienate someone with whom I want to be in community, entrenching the powers that be. While it is always impossible fully to understand another human being, I know that there are differential patterns of both emotional labor and material effect in the hermeneutic gaps (Fricker, 2007) dogging others' perceptions of me and my ability to make sense of myself to others. Bringing this to teaching is never easy but it is much easier than speaking about sexual assault.

So far, on campus, most instances of speaking to my experiences of CSA have been cloaked. I can talk readily about the prevalence of childhood sexual abuse and the inadequacy of reporting statistics across all demographics, and I can talk readily about having experienced "traumas," " adverse events," and some "sexual violence" in my own life. I can assure students that things can get better. I can talk to the importance of campus mental health services and my own use of them and benefits. In a few situations, the topic has come up directly in live "teaching moments," for example in discussions of sexual violation in Feminist Theories but also in discussions of accountability, moral repair and forgiveness in Contemporary Ethics. I still have moments of panic when it happens when I do not expect it. I have to take some breaths, then turn my face to trust that these moments open when they do for reasons I need not understand, and that the seeds of teaching fall where they need. In some instances, material I present may offer openings that some students take while others do not. For example, some have reacted strongly when introduced to Thich Nhat Hahn's poem "Please Call Me by My True Names" when studying Buddhism. They hone in on the lines where he identifies both with a twelve-year-old girl driven to suicide after a rape and the sea pirate who raped her, and they usually assert that Hahn is wrong. These responses have opened to difficult but fruitful conversations about both Buddhism and sexual assault. In other instances, students pass by these lines or other classroom dynamics suggest that the time is not ripe. It is a little easier (never easy) to present the issue in writing. One class in which I have regularly brought it up, as a relevant part of the topic to which I'm responsible, has been in my online course in food ethics, because of the high prevalence of disordered eating among students and the etiological links between disordered eating and CSA. I speak about these links and to having veered briefly into anorexia in high school before the wisdom of my body issued a course correction. I speak in memory of a college roommate who lost her life to bulimia by age 25.

With respect to race, racism and social stratification, I am much more comfortable bringing up my own personal stance and stakes from the start in all my classes. In philosophy of race, I try to model how discomforts and feelings of dangers can be openings to greater insight. I use my own ambiguity, and my family's experience with education gaps and health disparities, to anchor ideas and arguments in the concrete, then invite students to do the same with their own diverse situations. I try to make clear how the personal is political, and ethical, and, ultimately spiritual. I try to make clear how we need to cultivate both critical, large-scale thinking and compassion. In addition, I try to make clear how we have to balance a sense of urgency in responding with a letting go of the desire for quick fixes. With respect to letting go, I try daily to remind myself of what I have come to see as the most important mystery of teaching—a deeply humbling but also inspiriting one. As students and colleagues respond to their own calls of wisdom, what they need to take from their encounters with me may have little to do with course topics under discussion, aims as articulated in syllabi outcomes and assignments, or items on a committee charge or agenda. This is an opening to more ease about the whole endeavor and more courage in showing myself.

While movement toward showing more faces of who I am as a teacher has been in fits and starts, I continue to try as the situations call forth. I journey toward richer and more seamless integration of my own personal narratives into my teaching. I speak to both these sources of silence, secrecy and shame because of the life and death stakes involved. I speak because my ability to survive and persist in academia has been sustained by others' efforts to speak and write about related experiences and situations. My efforts—and the openings brought from beyond my own efforts – have increased my resilience, patience, hope, and determination.

REFERENCES

Alcoff, L. M. (1996). Dangerous pleasures: Foucault and the politics of pedophilia. In S. J. Hekman (Ed.), *Feminist interpretations of Michel Foucault* (pp. 99–135). Pennsylvania State University Press.

Alcoff, L. M. (2000). Merleau-Ponty and feminist theory on experience. In L. Lawler & L. Evans (Eds.), *Chiasms: Merleau-Ponty's notion of flesh* (pp. 251–272). State University of New York Press.

Alcoff, L. M. (2018). *Rape and resistance*. Polity Press.

Alison, J. (2001). *Contemplation in a world of violence: Girard, Merton, Tolle*. http://girardianlectionary.net/res/alison_contemplation_violence.htm.

American Academy of Pediatrics. (2014). *Adverse childhood experiences and the lifelong consequences of trauma*. https://www.aap.org/en-us/documents/ttb_aces_consequences.pdf.

American Philosophical Association. (n.d.) *Demographic statistics on the APA membership, fy2018 to fy2020*. https://cdn.ymaws.com/www.apaonline.org/resource/resmgr/data_on_profession/fy2020-demographicstatistics.pdf.

American Psychological Association. (2013). *College students' mental health a growing concern, survey finds*. https://www.apa.org/monitor/2013/06/college-students.

Anzaldúa, G. (1987). *Borderlands/la frontera: The new mestiza*. Aunt Lute Books.

Balderrama, F. E. & Rodríguez, R. (2006). *Decade of betrayal: Mexican repatriation in the 1930s*. University of New Mexico Press.

Barvosa, E. (2008). *Wealth of selves: Multiple identities, mestiza consciousness, and the subject of politics*. Texas A&M University Press.

Bingen, H. (2001). In Atherton, M. (Trans.), *Selected writings: Hildegard of Bingen* (1st Ed). Penguin.

Bingen, H. (1998). In Throop, P. (Trans.), *Hildegard Von Bingen's physica : The complete English translation of her classic work on health and healing*. Healing Arts Press.

Brison, S. J. (2002). *Aftermath: Violence and the remaking of a self*. Princeton University Press.

Brison, S. J. (1993). Surviving sexual violence: A philosophical perspective. *Journal of Social Philosophy*, *24*(1), 5–22.

Brison, S. J. (1997). Outliving oneself: Trauma, memory and personal identity. In Meyers. D. T. (Ed.), *Feminists rethink the self* (pp. 13–38). Westview Press.

Brison, S. J. (2008). Everyday atrocities and ordinary miracles, or why I (still) bear witness to sexual violence (but not too often). *Women's studies quarterly*, *36*(1/2), 188–198. Stable URL: https://www.jstor.org/stable/27649746.

Brison, S. J. (2014). Why I spoke out about one rape but stayed silent about another. *Time*. https://time.com/3612283/why-i-spoke-out-about-one-rape-but-stayed-silent-about-another/.

Colorado highway maps (n.d.) http://www.printsoldandrare.com/colorado/384co.jpg.

Dodge, J. & Dyer, D. (2014). Eracism: Unwanted latinos deported from boulder county in the 1930s. *Boulder Weekly*. http://www.boulderweekly.com/news/eracism-unwanted-latinos-deported-from-boulder-county-in-the-1930s/.

Dolan, J. P. (2008). *The Irish Americans: A history*. Bloomsbury Press.

Dotson, K. (2012). How is this paper philosophy? *Comparative Philosophy*, *3*(1), 3–29.

Du Bois, W. E. B. (1903/2019). *The souls of black folk: Original classic edition*. G&D Media.

Florido, A. (2015). Mass deportation may seem unlikely but it's happened before. *National Public Radio*. https://www.npr.org/sections/codeswitch/2015/09/08/437579834/mass-deportation-may-sound-unlikely-but-its-happened-before.

Fricker, M. (2007). *Epistemic injustice: Power and the ethics of knowing*. Oxford University Press.

hooks, b. (1984). *Feminist theory: From margin to center*. South End Press.

Ignatius. (1991). In Ganss, G. E. (Trans.) *Ignatius of Loyola: The Spiritual exercises and selected works*. Paulist Press.

Lugones, M. (1992). On Borderlands/La Frontera: An interpretive essay. *Hypatia*, *7*(4), 31–37. Stable URL: https://www.jstor.org/stable/3810075.

Lugones, M. (2003). *Pilgrimages/peregrinajes: Theorizing coalition against multiple oppressions*. Rowman & Littlefield Publishers.

McIntosh, M. (2016.) Conflict, racism, and violence, 1910–1040. *Latinos of Boulder County, Colorado*. http://teachbocolatinohistory.colorado.edu/wp-content/uploads/2016/02/Volume1-Chapter4.pdf.

McKinney, G., Cowan, E., Cunningham, A. W., & Fischer, D. H. (1992). Culture wars: David Hackett Fischer's Albion's Seed. *Appalachian Journal*, *19*(2), 161–200. https://www.jstor.org/stable/40933452.

Montgomery, C. (2001). Becoming "Spanish-American": Race and rhetoric in New Mexico politics, 1880–1928. *Journal of American Ethnic History, 20* (4), 59–84. https://www.jstor.org/stable/27502746.

Nguyen, V. T., & Tran, V. (2018). Narrative plentitude. *Talks at google*. https://vietnguyen.info/2018/viet-thanh-nguyen-and-vu-tran-narrative-plentitude-talks-at-google.

Ortega, M. (2016). *In-between: Latina feminist phenomenology, multiplicity, and the self*. State University of New York Press.

Palmer, P. J. (2004). *A hidden wholeness: The journey toward an undivided life*. Jossey-Bass.

Palmer, P. J. (2017). *The courage to teach: Exploring the inner landscape of a teacher's life*. Wiley.

Palmer, P. J. (2009). The broken open heart: Living with faith and hope in the tragic gap. Reprint from *Weavings: A journal of the Christian spiritual Life* XXIV(2). https://www.couragerenewal.org/PDFs/PJP-WeavingsArticle-Broken-OpenHeart.pdf.

Ruíz, E. F. (2016). Linguistic alterity and the multiplicitous self: Critical phenomenologies in Latina Feminist thought. *Hypatia, 31*(2), 421–436. https://doi.org/10.1111/hypa.12239

Salaman, G. (2009). Justification and queer method, or leaving philosophy. *Hypatia, 24*(1), 225–230. Stable URL: https://www.jstor.org/stable/20618140.

CHAPTER 11

Who Am I?: Relational Pedagogies for Fostering Creativity and Reflective Practice

Bronwen Wade-Leeuwen and Kath McLachlan

INTRODUCTION

Disrupting traditional academic approaches to teaching and learning in higher education, we position ourselves as reflective practitioner/educators, to challenge views of teaching and learning as transactional, that is, as the transmission of knowledge. We explore how Arts-based inquiry and experiential learning can facilitate the development of critical, creative, and reflective skills to foster transformative learning and teaching.

B. Wade-Leeuwen (✉)
School of Education and Environmental Sciences, Macquarie University, Sydney, NSW, Australia
e-mail: bronwen.wadeleeuwen@mq.edu.au

K. McLachlan
Macquarie University, Sydney, NSW, Australia
e-mail: kath.mclachlan@mq.edu.au

M. P. Hall and A. K. Brault (eds.), *Academia from the Inside*, https://doi.org/10.1007/978-3-030-83895-9_11

Palmer (2017) in his support for integrative education, urges an onto-logical and epistemological shift to understanding the relational, interde-pendent nature of being and becoming, in the world. The importance of integrative education in particular, 'fostering creativity' in teaching in higher education, has been neglected. The Australian Curriculum: The Arts (ACARA, 2020), explicitly identifies the need to focus more on modeling approaches for developing twenty-first-century skills of critical and creative thinking skills, deep reflective practice, and problem-solving/finding. These skills are increasingly sought by employers seeking work-ready graduates, however, the school and higher education curricu-lums are increasingly threatened by systemic challenges and disruptions. Institutional leadership focuses on standardizing course content and assessment outcomes, rather than providing environments for engaging learners in creativity and reflective practice to develop lifelong learning capacities.Traditional academic approaches to teaching and learning in higher education, often viewed as the transmission of knowledge, are being challenged. Under current paradigms of educational practice theory (praxis) perspectives, creativity, and reflective practice are becoming more familiar and accepted approaches to fostering well-rounded graduates, as well as a conduit for enhancing the professional development of teacher educators.

The design of learning environmentsthat facilitate creativity and reflec-tive practice is of critical importance for fostering transformative learning (Mezirow, 2006), in preference to transmission approaches. Transforma-tive learning raises self-awareness, challenging worldviews through critical self-reflection. Scaffolding participant learning along paths of personal and professional development leads to a greater understanding of self, by exploring: "who am I"?

As practitioners/educators, we aim to provoke a re-thinking and ques-tioning of personal and professional values and beliefs, in relation to teaching and learning, seeking an integrated approach that positions the learner as central. In a constantly changing, complex world, the challenges for all learners, both students and educators living with increasing soci-etal trauma and resistance to change, are moderated through self-care, self-realization, and the willingness in finding radical re-enchantment in awakening our sense of our interrelatedness and interdependence.

Re-connection has become an imperative, for self and 'other' under-standing, which is at the heart of the relational aspects of the learning experience. In this context, people's response to events or activities is determined by internal (dispositional attributes - traits, abilities, feelings) as well as external (situational) variables.

In this context, establishing educational praxis fostering creative and reflective practices, acknowledges a primary goal of education (Bloom, 1956; Krathwohl, 2002), through the lens of three interconnected domains: knowledge, psychomotor and affective. However, limited attention has been given to the importance of psychomotor and affective domains in higher education. To address this gap, we investigated approaches to teaching creativity and reflective practice by building on Krathwohl (2002), and integrating two interconnected typologies; the five levels of creativity (Wade-Leeuwen, 2016a) and deep-reflective practice (McLachlan, 2014), with the aim of shifting learners towards a new transformative pedagogical approach.

The basic aim of this research is to use Arts-based inquiry research to investigate learners' situated knowledge, experiences, and implicit theories using empirical and interpretive data. In order to understand how creativity and reflective practice is fostered in adult learners, artist-led intercultural experiential workshops are used in both formal and informal settings. These experiential workshops, scaffold (systematically structuring experience and knowledge) and embed these into all aspects of the learning environment. The framework is conceptualized as participant's inward journeys 'moving' through (in and out of), levels of doing and reflecting.

Reflective processes where we consider our thoughts and feelings in relation to knowledge and experience, encourage an opening up to self-expression, using imagination to explore all five levels of creativity. Imagination plays a critical role in valuing and exploring alternative spaces that enhance creativity and reflection. New pedagogical insights emerge for learners as they explore ideas and concepts through self-reflection, and in dialogue with others. Workshops aim to foster transformative ways of thinking, interacting, and being, where embodied experiences are purposeful, contemplative, and learner-centered (Hall, Jones & O'Hare, 2018).

Praxis Context

Higher education institutions, such as Macquarie University (MqU) in Sydney, Australia, are under increasing pressure to develop well-rounded graduates, who acquire not only discipline-specific knowledge, but also life and employability skills such as creativity, critical thinking, and reflection (McLachlan et al., 2017).

Within the Academy, and the Australian Curriculum, Assessment and Reporting Authority (ACARA, 2020), there are moves towards rethinking pedagogies by reframing and redefining the understanding of 'how and why' students learn, and 'how and why' teachers teach. Accordingly, students need to develop twenty-first-century skills of creativity, critical thinking, and reflection, to negotiate and manage the inconsistency of change in the workplace, along with the stress, incongruities, and ambiguities of teacher professional practice.

The traditional siloed nature of university teaching, as referred to in chapter 1 of this book, along with excessive workloads, meeting accreditation requirements, and the pressure of maintaining formal assessment processes, can restrict the opportunity for educators and learners alike to explore and integrate opportunities for learning through creativity and reflection. Moves to 'improve' the quality of teacher education in Australia and integrate these skills, have resulted in reforms to policy, with the subsequent development of a set of professional teacher standards (ACARA, 2020).

In line with the standards, an expectation of the Australian Curriculum: The Arts (ACARA, 2020), is that learning opportunities incorporate the General Capabilities, such as critical and creative thinking, intercultural understanding, and personal and social capability, are integral to making and responding to artworks and artifacts. Teachers are required to reconsider possibilities and make choices that assist their students to become curious with risk-taking attitudes in order to clearly express their ideas, concepts, thoughts, and feelings creatively and reflectively supporting their human potential.

However, this approach to standardization doesn't always allow for creativity in teaching and learning. In efforts to measure learning, the actual learning becomes narrowed. Rather than facilitating innovative learning environments, Savage and Lingard (2018) claim the changing modes of governance may be problematic in supporting divergent approaches to teaching. This raises concerns for the propensity of standardizing to maintain transactional models, rather than encouraging and supporting creativity and reflective practice, as transformative learning objectives of teacher education.

This situation is further compounded by Australian Universities becoming 'corporatized' through a continual reduction in government funding, resulting in a competitive business model that is focused on increasing student recruitment and retention. This reinforces the dominant discourse of a neo-liberal framework of compliance, and narrow definitions of improved praxis. Referring to the foundational purpose of this book (Introduction, p. 4): How can teachers and learners in higher education prepare themselves to tackle these issues and learn on these journeys?

We recognize the challenges facing leaders and practitioners, when cultivating contexts that challenge the dominant paradigm in Australian Higher Education. Shifting away from the transactional singular disciplinary approach towards a more transformative facilitated approach to learning, requires reframing pedagogical and ontological perspectives. We see an urgency in recognizing the need for embedding critical and creative thinking and reflective practice to assist teachers and learners in higher education to explore their values and beliefs in relation to their personal and professional practice: "Who am I, when I teach?"

Building transformative capacities require, as (Freire, 2018) asserts, a certain set of attributes, or creativity dispositions that embraces action and change. Equally, the creation of innovative learning environments support experiential learning, acknowledging, and building on our interrelatedness and interdependence, as essential to the notion of human flourishing, which according to Autry & Walker (2011), fosters professional and personal development through creativity and reflection.

Bloom's Taxonomy (Krathwohl, 2002), emphasizes the importance of the cognitive, practice, and affective domains for developing whole-person learning. However, as McLachlan (2014) claims, little attention is given to reflection to encourage embodied approaches to holistic learning. Our pedagogical approach has been to integrate the dispositional attributes as they relate to creativity and reflection through the development of a typology of five levels of creativity (Wade-Leeuwen, 2016a, b).

Adopting an Arts-based approach, where learners are active participants in the process, provides an opportunity for transforming and co-creating contextual worldviews and understandings, through continuous reflection as a lifelong learning process.

While reflection is acknowledged by Heyler (2015, p. 16), as the capacity "to hone their reflective skills in order to critically appraise what has been experienced via practice", there are complexities, however, in dealing with different levels of reflection. These complexities require a scaffolded approach to reflection (Coulson & Harvey, 2013; Schön,

1987) to facilitate deep and critical higher-order thinking [metacognition] skills to deal with issues and practice, thereby empowering transformational learning.

Scaffolding reflection into our framework aims to develop the capacity for deep reflection, thereby deepening awareness and provoking shifts in consciousness not easily facilitated in traditional curriculum. In our experience, reflection can be superficial, failing to critically challenge assumptions, or question values and beliefs, thus limiting the potential for critical and creative thinking. Harvey & Coulson (2013), argue that reflection, as a practice, and even when embedded in curriculum, may be difficult to achieve in highly governed contexts.

Critical reflection builds the capacity for applying theory in practice. According to Dewey (1934) it is at the point of doubt, confusion, and dissonance that reflection and thinking begin. This discomfort leads to questioning and increasing self-awareness, and through experience confidence and personal integrity increase. Because context is integral, there are inevitably inherent tensions and complexity in the lens of inquiry into 'self', hence the need for supportive frameworks to enhance skill development.

Systemic Change for the Academy

Seminal educational theorists have long espoused the need for a new system of education that supports higher order thinking skills, including reflection and creativity. Dewey (1934) supported the notion of experiential learning claiming that "works of art are the most intimate and energetic means of aiding individuals to share the art of living" (p. 336).

Herbert Read envisioned art should be the basis of education and that the aim of education is the creation of artists (Efland, 1990). Art was interpreted as a creative aesthetic activity, which should be placed at the core of the curriculum. Greene (2010) advocated for an educational system where learners are effective and productive in their various modes of expressions and that learning requires a space of playful relaxation (spirit of play), where imagination is an important component of heightened self-awareness, demanding both reflection and praxis. Palmer (2017), in his support for integrative education, urges an ontological and epistemological shift to understanding the relational, interdependent nature of our being and becoming ("who am I?"), in the world.

The importance of developing artists and teaching for creativity, in accordance with the Australian Curriculum: The Arts (ACARA, 2020), emphasizes the need for modeling approaches that develop twenty-first-century skills like problem-solving/finding, critical, and creative thinking skills, and deep reflective practice. Increasingly, higher education curriculums are threatened by teaching in an overcrowded curriculum, with limited time and space allowed to provoke these valuable skill sets.

Teaching for Creativity: From Transmission Teaching to Transformative Learning

The idea of knowledge being transmitted from teacher to learner rather than an active learning process, remains entrenched in education systems for various reasons. Bureaucratic, hierarchical systems, which are highly governed and standardized, have led to overcrowded curricula, as experienced in Australia and globally, and is characterized by high levels of stress and burnout, (Burnard et al., 2018).

While many of these stressors are considered external, and beyond the individual control, there is a growing recognition of the need for adaptive responses, from internally driven foci. Processes for addressing these challenges, engage self-efficacy and resilience for both teachers and students, as a way of connecting with one's inner world, not just one's intellect.

In response to the growing concerns of stress and burnout and recognizing the need for helping educators manage their well-being, The NSW Department of Education and Communities (DEC) developed the Wellbeing Framework for Schools (2015). The aim is to create quality learning opportunities for strengthening cognitive, physical, social, emotional, and spiritual development. The framework identified three core themes: Connect, Succeed, and Thrive, which focus on the development of adaptive systems that are resilient and responsive to the contexts in which they operate.

Higher education programs in Australia, however, generally do not systematically support students' well-being or professional identity, but, rather, transactional approaches that focus on content-based knowledge construction and technical skills (Trede et al., 2011). Institutional leadership maintains a preponderance for emphasizing course content and assessment outcomes, rather than an integrated approach to the care, creativity, and well-being of the learner, despite rhetoric to the contrary. This narrowing approach to higher education diminishes the focus on well-being and flourishing, (Acton & Glasgow, 2015) and inhibits the shaping and development of teacher identity and self-efficacy.

One example of a transformative evidence-based program designed to support student well-being and professional practice in higher education, was established at MqU in 2009. The Professional and Community Engagement program (PACE) is a university-wide, award winning, work-integrated learning (WIL) program, underpinned by principles of mutual benefit, reciprocity and collaboration between the university and a wide range of partner organizations (Sachs & Clark 2017). These experiential learning units are designed to facilitate creativity, critical thinking, and reflective practices.

Uniquely, Teacher Education (TED), Professional Practicum Units at MqU, are designated as PACE units, facilitating students' application of WIL skills and knowledge in their professional practice. However, research shows many teachers have little experience in teaching and embodying critical and creative thinking and reflection (Coulson & Harvey, 2013; Wade-Leeuwen, 2016a). Despite the embeddedness of reflection in both the well-being framework (DEC, 2015) and Higher Education PACE units, most students require further support and scaffolding to become self-reflective learners.

As Arts Educators and Reflective Practitioners in higher education, we have developed an innovative model for facilitating creative and reflective workshops, to address the challenges outlined above, stressing the importance of self-care, and self-knowledge. Creating safe, contemplative spaces for nurturing twenty-first-century dispositional attributes, such as risk taking, curiosity, and boundary breaking, are necessary for today's professionals.

The researchers approach to learning and teaching encourages all learners to seek out new ways of knowing, thinking, doing, and being. Our pedagogical approach in higher education is shaped by our deeper understanding of the cross-curricular priority areas of the Australian Curriculum (ACARA, 2016) that is required in schools.

In this context, the working definition of creativity is adapted from Sternberg and Lubarts's (1999) definition. They mean that creativity involves making new ideas and actions, mastering a practice before transforming it. What has emerged from the literature is that more emphasis could be placed on opening up the imagination and a deeper understanding of creativity as a way of being. This chapter explores ways of fostering creativity in learners in higher education through Arts-based workshop sessions that emphasize intercultural and cultural engagement.

The Arts-based workshop sessions developed specifically for higher education, are usually conducted within two to three hour sessions, involve extensive interaction between the facilitators and the participating learners centered around a "big idea" The "big idea" is expressed through multimodal forms such as drawings, paintings, sculptures, fresco, or new digital media technologies in hands-on experiences of practice. These sessions also take the form of a reflective practice in dialogue with all involved and substantial interactions throughout the sessions.

These active learning spaces provoke the learners to find new ways of being critical and creative and offer opportunities to foster their own creativity, imagination, and reflective practice, through intercultural workshops and Arts-based inquiry practice. The facilitators of the workshops are committed to developing a person-centered approach to learning and teaching in higher education drawing on the 5 C's: communication, creativity, critical thinking, collaboration & cooperation (Wade-Leeuwen, 2016a, b).

The facilitators believe open communication is of utmost importance in developing trust and creating a supportive active learning environment where all learners feel valued and safe. The facilitators approach to teaching and learning has always been one of developing creative dispositions of openness to curiosity and risk-taking, particularly drawing on the personal qualities of the learner, such as uniqueness, flexibility, fluidity, and elaboration in their personal responses while providing space for dialogue and reflection.

These intercultural workshops can also be built upon to form a Community of Practice (CoP) (Wenger, 2000) model that can be easily adapted into higher education courses in a variety of interdisciplinary areas. For example, the facilitators have worked with learners from sciences, arts, humanities, and community education. The facilitator's depth of knowledge and capacity to mentor students and other colleagues through a CoP model in a variety of learning and teaching environmentshas been a strength of this research program.

Research Question

The research question asks: How can creativity, critical thinking, and reflection of teacher practitioners be fostered and evaluated during higher educational workshops? What role does self-care, self-knowledge, and dispositional attributes play in nurturing learning environments? An Arts-based inquiry method explores new ideas, approaches, and actions (Wade-Leeuwen, 2016a), to create innovative learning environments supporting teacher education practitioners and others.

Arts-Based Inquiry Framework:

The Arts-based inquiry framework presents an approach to learning and teaching using a socio-cultural approach to education where creativity, artistic knowledge, and intercultural communities of practice are integrated through reflective practice to incorporate the different theories discussed. The proposed effects of the workshop, Fig. 11.1, depicts

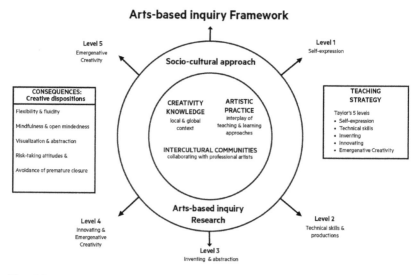

Fig. 11.1 Arts-based Inquiry framework model of creativity and reflective practice

the centrality of the learning environment for establishing a safe and supportive space in which to encourage creativity and reflection.

The five levels of creativity that will be discussed in this paper, include: Level 1- self-expression, Level 2- technical skills, Level 3- Inventing, Level 4- innovation, and Level 5- generative creativity. Through these teaching strategies, learners can experience creativity, dispositions of flexibility and fluidity, mindfulness and open-mindedness, visualization and abstraction, risk-taking attitudes and avoidance of premature closure, which is having the capacity to continue on a task for long periods of time.

Workshop Model of Creativity and Reflective Practice

The model informs the design of studio-based workshops to foster creativity (Sternberg & Lubart, 1999) and reflective practice in participants as they learn about applying new and old technologies in diverse contexts. The role of the workshops is to provide opportunities for participants to engage in material exploration through choice and discovery.

These active learning environments mean discovery and exploration of innovative art practices are experienced through a "spirit of play" (Wade-Leeuwen, 2016b). Using the analogy of a "spirit of play", which holds a free-spirited safe space that stimulates experiential learning, and provides opportunities to shift towards new innovative artistic reflective responses.

Methodology

The uniqueness of this study combines Arts-based inquiry and reflective practice research, adapted to contemporary cultural contexts. Arts-based research inquiry (Barone & Eisner, 2011), builds on the works of prominent researchers who promote the value of experiential learning in Arts education. Eisner (2017) envisaged creativity and reflection as a key component of this inquiry, focusing on the inter-relationship between the individual, the visual arts and the sociocultural context. The research aims to facilitate transformative learning, which influences pedagogical understandings, and improves educational practice and enhances student learning. We provide new perspectives on teacher education designed to enhance learners' capacities for risk-taking, curiosity, and boundary breaking for developing self-knowledge and self-care.

Re-thinking Arts-based approaches can lead to new ways of learning and deep transformative understandings. The outcomes of the studio-based workshops are reflected in the quality of insights that document practice, together with the critical discourse that is an adjunct to the work. Participants are provoked to blur the edges and break boundaries by inventing new ways of interacting with the material exploration through mark-making, molding, generating a variety of 2D and 3D dimensional images with an informed understanding of reflective practice.

The iterative process facilitated in workshops scaffolds the learning through four relational phases of the experience-based reflective learning cycle (Schön, 1987). The first of these phases, learning to reflect, may start before engagement in a learning experience and continue through and beyond the experience. Reflection for action usually occurs prior to engaging in an experience-based learning activity.

Phase 1 is about preparing for an experience through reflecting on issues such as:

- what do I hope to get out of this
- what might others (e.g. teachers, peers, on site supervisor, recipients of your efforts) expect of me
- what experience do I have
- what do I most need to learn
- how will I use what I learn from this experience?

Exploring the many reflective tools and ways to reflect is useful at this stage to further develop reflective skills and help identify the reflective processes that will best support learning.

Phase 2, reflection in action, as the term suggests, occurs during the experience. Participants explore putting theory into practice (praxis). New experiences, even the most positive ones, however, may stir up emotions or present issues participants are not immediately sure how to address. Reflective tools and processes can support participants to make sense and meaning of the experience.

Phase 3, reflection on action, is facilitated through self-reflectionas an internal exploration and through dialogue as a way of engaging with others through deep listening to consider diverse perspectives. During this phase reflection is most valuable in assisting a review and synthesis of learning and consideration for future application. This may involve debriefing or discussion of events, issues, emotions, and lessons that may have arisen during the experience. A three-stage process of:

1. Returning to the experience;
2. Attending to the feelings; and
3. Re-evaluating the experience;

To support this experience-based learning framework, we utilized a suite of 'Reflection for Learning Resources' (Harvey et al., 2020). The resources are based on universal design principles, disrupting the notion of text based reflection, to incorporate Arts-based, music, photography, technological and embodied approaches to resource development.

Multimodal Methods

Our inquiry is situated in different cultural contexts, where we explore two creativity and reflective practice workshops, which were conducted outside of regular curriculum offerings. One experiential workshop (Case Study One) at MqU was compared with a similar workshop offered at Giessen University, Germany (Case Study Two). The case study approach (Yin, 2014), systematically compared and contrasted participants' creative, critical thinking, and reflective responses through open dialogue, to explore how these concepts may change and transform their initial understandings and practice.

Data collected for this study used multi-modal methods through unique personal drawings, paintings, sculptural forms, photographs, video, and audio recording of participants' interaction, as well as regular feedback to the participants before, during, and after each level of the workshop. Reflective responses recorded during the workshops included self/peer-interpretation of the artifacts created, and knowledge and understanding of emergent learnings contributing to personal and intellectual growth.

Application of the Innovative Model

The working definition of creativity has been defined by Wade-Leeuwen (2016a) as extending across the creative person, process, product, and environment. Creativity involves developing new ideas, approaches, and actions, in a process of becoming sensitive to problems, gaps in knowledge, and disharmonies. Personal insight emerges through reflection, highlighting the relationship between creativity and reflective practice.

Drawing on Wade-Leeuwen's (2016a) creativity typology developed during studio-based workshops, and weaving together reflective practices (McLachlan, 2014), we illustrate how five interrelated levels of creativity and reflective practice differentiate dispositions to evaluate the diverse range of artifacts created in the workshops. The five levels of creativity are not time related, can occur in a variety of forms, and have different dimensions.

The first level of creativity reflects self-expression, and is seen as child-like improvisational play. The second level is the development of techniques and skills referred to as reproductions. This level is used when learning new technical skills, such as how to hold a Chinese brush or charcoal pencil in a specific way. The third level is inventing, which involves discovering old things in new ways. For example, recycling materials to create new possibilities happens at this inventing third level. The fourth level is innovation which aims to move from new discoveries into a more abstracted unknown area of visual arts. This fourth level is rarely achieved, and is where more complicated arts and reflective practices become simplified or abstracted to achieve a unique response. The final fifth level of creativity is a deeper level of generative and emergent creativity. This level of creativity is seldom seen, and an example would be the artmaking of Pablo Picasso. The artist is demonstrating curiosity and open-mindedness, and their critical and creative thinking skills have the potential to change the way society perceives art and culture.

The five levels of creativity and reflective practice in Table 1 are identified as: Self-Expression, Technical Skills Building, Inventiveness, Innovation-Transformative, and Generative & Emergent Creativity. Attempting the fourth and fifth level of creativity, shifting towards innovation- transformative learning was problematic in these workshops. The research found generative and emergent creativity (level 5), which is the ability to change cultural awareness and transform lives, was extremely difficult to achieve in the timeframe of the 2–3 h workshops. Level 5 requires continual support over a longer period of time (Table 11.1).

Table 11.1 Creativity and reflective practices typology

Creativity & Critical Thinking skills	Collaborations	Reflection
Self-Expression- Being in the 'Flow' ● Self-expressive creativity is the fundamental level of creativity. This fundamental level communicates through spontaneity, freedom of expression	Being with 'others'	**Level 1** Letting go, allowing – opening to & disruption
Technical Skills Building Mindfulness activity ● Development from the self-expression level to the technical level of creativity. This level is where learning new ideas; approaches and actions are explored to develop finished artworks, artefacts or products	acknowledging 'others'	**Level 2** Felt knowing, sensing, situated (affective, cognitive, contextual)
Inventiveness Mirroring: reflective practice ● This level is about developing new relationships where creativity reaches a new level of accomplishment. This is an area where the artwork or artefact may be different from others as the artist is moving from a known area to an unknown area	seeing 'others'	**Level 3** Presencing, embodiment, focusing
Innovation-transformative 3D Modelling: reflective practice		**Level 4**

(continued)

Workshop Process

Workshops begin with creating a safe space through gentle music, and a short mindfulness meditation, encouraging openness and attentiveness. Exploring how the materials led us, as educators and artists, to further our

Table 11.1 (continued)

Creativity & Critical Thinking skills	Collaborations	Reflection
● This innovative level of creativity shows transformative learning and flexibility in perceiving new and abstract ways of thinking ● The artworks are shifting from a space of unknown to another unknown, which offers new insights	connecting with 'others'	Crystallizing, actualising,emergent, always in the process of becoming
Generative & Emergent Creativity Transformative practices		**Level 5**
Changing the way we perceive and do things Deep reflection question ing assumptions and beliefsconnecting self to systemsEmbodied cognition, integration of mind,body & spirit	connecting self to systems	Embodied cognition, integration of mind,body & spirit

own inner knowing was an important aspect of this research, and we have documented the creative and reflective process below. Moreover, the act of reflecting through writing and discussion on the experience of creating art, is associated with a deeper understanding of one's own creativity.

From this space we move into a drawing activity, drawing with two hands, drawn from the suite of educator resources (Harvey et al., 2020, p. 64). Participants draw with both hands simultaneously using three different approaches, each linked to a level of the typology. Table 1 Participants engage in personal and group reflection after each approach. This conscious attempt to draw with both hands requires attention and focus, encouraging mindful attention to what is generally an automatic, or habitual activity.

Resources

Three pieces of unlined paper, as large as practicable for the workspace, with at least two differently colored biros (ballpoint pens), felt pens, crayons, or pencils, etc. are allocated per person. The time allotted for the whole activity is 35–40 min.: five minutes for each of the three approaches (total of 15 min); five minutes for personal reflection; and at least 10 min for group reflection.

Activities

Level 1. Self-Expression: Being in the "flow"

During the first approach learners are encouraged to develop a creative free-flow of ideas through initial warm-up exercises and exploring ideas using their imagination. Free expressive creativity is the fundamental level of creativity. This fundamental level communicates through spontaneity, freedom, and self-expression. At this level, the focus is on the creative process and not on the end production and the characteristics being developed are learning through a spirit of play.

Beginning with a clean page, participants allow both hands to draw freely in whatever unique way feels comfortable. Learners use the whole page and vary the speed at which they draw, continuing the process for at least five minutes. Personal and group reflection on the activity follows (Fig. 11.2).

Level 2. Drawing from the Imagination and Learning Technical Skills

The second approach to the activity involves building new technical skills. Some activities include: "follow the leader" that aims to mindfully explore visual conventions of drawing while developing technical skills where the dominant hand leads and the other hand follows. Participants proceed from the expressive self-expression level to the technical level of creativity, to develop concentration and dexterity. This level is where learning new ideas; approaches and actions are explored to develop finished artworks, artifacts or products. In this second level of creativity, learners reflect in and on the experience (Schön, 1987) using both hands simultaneously.

Fig. 11.2 Level 1. Self-expression, being in the 'flow' mark making

Taking a pen in each hand, participants draw with both hands at the same time, not letting the hands touch each other. The dominant hand leads and the non-dominant hand follows (copies) the lead hand around the page exactly and at the same time. Encourage learners to try switching lead hands so that the non-dominant hand also leads. Encourage learners to use the whole page and to continue the process for at least five minutes. Personal and group reflection on the activity follows (Fig. 11.3).

Level 3. Inventiveness: Exploring New Materials

The third approach is about developing new relationships, where creativity reaches a new level of accomplishment. This is an area where the artwork or artifact may be different from others as the artist is moving from a known area to an unknown area. This transition is characterized by new diverse relationships and the majority of participants remain in

Fig. 11.3 Level 2. Drawing from the imagination and learning technical skills

these more limited levels of creativity as discussed earlier. In this reflective activity, they use a variety of artistic materials to encourage discovery and imagination to make artworks and designs (Fig. 11.4).

Level 4. Innovation-transformative: Shifting into 3D modeling: reflective practice

This additional 3D modeling approach was added to the initial resource activity to encourage the innovative nature of level 4, where creativity becomes transformative, encouraging participants'.

imagination for perceiving new and abstract ways of thinking. The artifact responses demonstrate a shift from a space of unknown to another unknown unexplored space. The activity goal is developed over time, shifting through dimensional space to offer new insights and new

Fig. 11.4 Level 3. Inventiveness—exploring using different materials

unexplored possibilities experienced through this process of divergent thinking.

> **Level 5: Generative and Emergent Creativity**: transformative practices

Generating creativity is extremely difficult to achieve. Material exploration opens new possibilities for transformational learning, where insights emerge through emotional responses, giving deeper meaning and understanding to participants' personalities and lives. The participants pondered deeply and then adopted roles as risk-takers, creators, and playmates (Wright, 2010) as well as inventors. Once the participants were aware of how to explore using the new materials, they could identify using the definition of creativity, create artworks/artifacts, and reflect more deeply on the experiential process.

Personal Reflection

On completion of the whole activity, learners reflect in writing on their experience. This can include a free flow of reactions, ideas, and thoughts, as well as suspension of judgment for the first few minutes. Allow at least five minutes for personal written reflection. The emergence of insight and "aha" moments is sought. As one participant reflected:

> For me it's all about experimenting. And then you can either get ideas from other artists or yourself. The first brush stroke is always the hardest and once you get that done the rest should be easy because you're just going along, experimenting and that's what I think too, like, I love it when I make mistakes, because that can enhance your art work. (p. 1)

Another participant said: "Feeling a little nervous, confident of creativity not confident of finished work but my love of drawing and more practice should carry me through" (p. 2).

Acknowledging the benefits of creativity and reflection and its importance in education, was one of the key themes emerging from our reflective analysis of feedback from both workshops. For example, the participants considered having space to explore over the 2–3 h workshops helped them relax, so they could gain greater depth of meaning during the creative and reflective process. Participants voiced: "Just having that broad space", "allowing space", "open minded and supportive, allowing space", "a little bit of time and space for children to explore" as what is needed in a quality education program (p. 3).

Another participant said:

> Pensive-uncertain—getting excited and working fast—it's starting to flow, I feel wonderful and go again, I don't want to stop.

Reflecting on the process:

> Yes, I need to be more creative in my drawing, especially compositions. It may be a hurdle to let go of old methods but this is not difficult to contemplate. I am open to change in a number of directions and have the ability to attain the possible by extending the given'. She goes on to say: 'Feeling a bit freer. Found it difficult to "restructure the known"—I think this is the point that I would like to work from- the insight into the known—CHANGE. (p. 4)

These insightful reflections showed that most of them opened up a space for creativity and they had nearly all experienced a feeling of being 'in the flow'. They seemed to express a wide spectrum of emotions from a lack of confidence to ones of joy and a desire to embrace the changes that were naturally occurring. It would be fair to conclude that they felt their creativity had been transformed through a 'spirit of play'.

Researchers' Reflections

Dialogue throughout the activity was critical for generating new ideas and outlets for expression. Participants were encouraged and led through an exploration of making meaning of their experiences, within groups and with each other. Creating the space in the learning environment for imagination, or spirit of play, provided a scaffolding in which to encourage participants in a safe and inviting manner. Building connection by connecting participants to self and others was achieved through rituals such as mindfulness practices of breathing and active listening before practice, during, and after practice.

The researchers encouraged the participants to be open to the experience; highlighting the importance of understanding phenomena from an Indigenous perspective, to connect to the Indigenous way of 'being on country', connect to self, to others, and more broadly, to the world. Listening is an Indigenous cultural practice that is essential for connection, for being in the moment. Taking those moments to reflect and be aware of what is happening during the process, provided a grounding for the participants; a way to keep the mind open to what comes through, because this is important for the generation of creativity, imagination, and their reflective practice.

Additionally, the researchers found that by establishing a learning environment where the participants felt comfortable and accepting that there is no right or wrong, they were free to not be corrected. This creativity and reflective practice workshop experience centered around having fun and learning through a 'spirit of play'. By opening oneself up to really enjoying the experience, participants gained insights into 'being' present in the moment and working with uncertainty and challenges.

DISCUSSION

The Need for Systemic Change to the Academy

Changes to educational teacher standards, re-modeling of institutional structures and legislative changes are combining to shift the academy as we know it. Imperative in these change processes is that we embrace the opportunity to do things better. The increasing emphasis on transformational learning requires addressing the significant gaps that exist in developing graduates with the level of confidence and self-efficacy to teach and learn in exacting and potentially constantly changing environments.

The challenge for teacher programs in higher education is to support their own graduating students' teaching connected to quality learning standards (O'Brien et al., 2017), currently threatened by:

- teaching in an overcrowded curriculum—limited time and space allowed for self- knowledge & self-care.
- education standards and programs that restrict developing the valuable skill sets of critical, creative, and reflective thinking.

Arts-based inquiry research applied in this study shows how creativity and reflection can foster creativity and reflective practice in higher educational teacher programs through experiential learning. As Dewey (1933) asserts, we don't simply learn from experience. He points out that it is through reflection on experience that learning occurs. The restrictive tendency of academic silos has stifled creativity and reflective practices. Efland (1990) substantiates the growing evidence of the impact that art education courses are having on pre-service practitioners in their higher education programs.

Despite the push by ACARA (2020), the arts in Australia are not considered an important curriculum key learning area and as a result, pre-service practitioners are not valuing the relevance of creativity and reflective practices. It is also well documented that pre-service practitioners express they have limited prior knowledge of the arts (Wade-Leeuwen, 2016a) as the teaching programs in higher education allocate inadequate time and space for experiencing the arts through any meaningful way during their teacher education programs. It is also well documented that pre-service practitioners tend to have inconsistent scaffolded experiences of the creative process leading to a superficial discipline of knowledge and teacher disengagement.

Connecting to Palmer, (2017) in support of integrative education, we urge an ontological and epistemological shift to understanding the relational, interdependent nature of our being and becoming, in the world. A renewed system of education supports higher order thinking skills, including reflection and creativity (McLachlan, 2014; Wade-Leeuwen, 2016a). Disrupting the focus of knowledge acquisition, we support Dewey's (1933) notion of experiential learning, whereby learning happens through the doing.

Additionally, Greene (2010) advocated for an educational system where learners are effective and productive in their various modes of expressions and that learning requires a space of playful relaxation, where imagination is an important component of heightening self-awareness, demanding both reflection and praxis. Dewey (1934, p. 336), claims that "works of art are the most intimate and energetic means of aiding individuals to share the art of living".

An integrated model supporting transformative learning

This arts-based inquiry research demonstrates how creativity and reflection can be fostered in higher education programs through the creative arts by focusing on different levels of creativity achieved through a spirit of play and continually reflecting on their practice during the process. Interactive processes energize a flow, moving in and out of doing and being, being and doing, supporting transformative learning.

In developing our model, we have aimed to integrate, research, theory, and practice, to explore the questions: how can creativity, critical thinking, and reflection of teacher practitioners, and other professionals, be fostered and evaluated during higher educational workshops? What role does self-care, self-knowledge, and dispositional attributes play in this environment? Feedback from our case studies are evidence of the capacity for higher education students to develop self-care and self- knowledge through exploring diverse levels of creativity and reflection, including:

- various modes of expression
- 5 levels of creativity
- heightening self-awareness
- Ongoing reflection (Schön, 1987) and influence on praxis

The studio-based workshops encouraged specific dispositions such as risk-taking attitudes, an increased sense of curiosity, an ability to break boundaries, more understanding of how to be flexible and fluid in the creative process, the possibility of making artifacts that are unique with attention to detail when the learners are given an opportunity to play. And finally, through scaffolded arts experiences the learners can become more mindful and reflective of their actions.

The typology provided a model for scaffolding the development of the participants' skills, knowledge and capacity through the experiential learning process. The focus on the participant's inward journey is conceptualized as moving through (in and out of) levels of participation and reflection. Connecting to head, heart, and hand, draws on inner wisdom and knowledge in the discovery of "who am I?".

Participants in the creativity and reflective practice workshop are encouraged to develop and apply personal skills and dispositions such as self-discipline, goal setting, and working independently, and show initiative, confidence, resilience, and adaptability. The importance of inwardness in teaching and learning has been achieved by specific focus on experiential learning and teaching how to identify and work with different levels of creativity, which can be achieved through a spirit of play and continually reflective practice during the process.

Participant feedback showed a range of cultural similarities and differences between the workshop participants' in both countries. Particularly interesting was the diverse responses associated with factors and influences on individual dispositions, such as a deeper awareness of the deeper levels of reflective practice and using creativity to transform their learning.

The importance of encouraging teachers' self-care and self-knowledge informs the best pedagogy. Appreciating diverse perspectives through dialogue and deep listening during the workshop, leads to a deeper understanding of different ways of relating, which are fostered when the focus is on creativity and reflective practice.

Conclusion

As reflective practitioners/educators we have challenged traditional academic views of teaching and learning in higher education. Despite systemic challenges, the development of twenty-first-century skills requires creativity, critical thinking, and reflection skills to be embedded in higher education curriculum. We explored how innovative approaches to integrated education may promote transformation, through the facilitation of two critical and reflective practice workshops utilizing Arts-based inquiry and reflective practice.

Facilitation of skill development through workshops encouraged, scaffolded, and supported participants on their journey of discovery, learning a little bit more about: "who am I?" Our own understanding of transformational learning, occurring in rich, complex situations that challenge beliefs, assumptions, and attitudes, was strengthened. As was our belief in a dialogical, scaffolded, multi-dimensional process that offers real connection to body, mind, and spirit.

Findings from participant feedback informed future workshops, providing important reflections on what is required to enable transformative learning.

- Fostering the capacity of participants/students in higher education, to engage with creativity, critical thinking, and reflection skills for developing in all domains of learning.
- Reflective practitioners are better equipped for dealing with the complexities, contradictions, and paradoxes of contemporary society.
- Embedding Arts-based practices in teacher education curriculum improves the scope of creative experiential learning activities.

For us, disrupting traditional approaches means amplifying Arts-based and reflective practices as valid and authentic approaches for interpreting the world as we see it. The more we open to differing perspectives that challenge our beliefs and values, the more we transform our cultural learning towards an integrative education. The dispositions of self-care and self-knowledge, risk-taking, curiosity and boundary breaking, are essential for developing transformative pedagogical approaches to teaching and learning.

REFERENCES

ACARA (2016). Cross-curriculum priorities. Australian Curriculum Assessment and Reporting Authority: Educational Services Australia. Retrieved on 28 January, 2021 from https://www.australiancurriculum.edu.au/crosscurriculumpriorities.

ACARA (2020). The Australian curriculum: The Arts. Retrieved on 28 January, 2021 from https://www.australiancurriculum.edu.au/f-10-curriculum/general-capabilities/.

Acton, R., & Glasgow, P. (2015). Teacher wellbeing in neoliberal contexts: A review of literature. *Australian Journal of Teacher Education*, 40(8). https://doi.org/10.14221/ajte.2015v40n8.6

Autry, L. L., & Walker, M. E. (2011). Artistic representation: Promoting student creativity and self-reflection. *Journal of Creativity in Mental Health*. 6(1), 42–55.

Barone, T., & Eisner, E. W. (2011). *Arts based research*. Los Angeles: Sage.

Bloom, B. S. (1956). Taxonomy of educational objectives. Vol. 1: Cognitive domain. *McKay, 20(24)*.

Burnard, P., Dragovic, T., Jasilek, S., Biddulph, J., Rolls, L., Durning, A., & Fenyvesi, K. (2018). The art of co-creating arts-based possibility spaces for fostering STE(A)M practices in primary education. In T. Chemi & X. Du (Eds.), *Arts-based methods on education around the world* (pp. 247–282). Rivers Publishers. https://doi.org/10.13052/rp-9788793609372

Coulson, D., Harvey, M. (2013). Scaffolding student reflection for experience-based learning: A framework. *Teaching in Higher Education, 18*(4), 401–413.https://doi.org/10.1080/13562517.2012.752726

Department of Education. (2015). *Wellbeing Framework for Schools.* https://education.nsw.gov.au/student-wellbeing/whole-school-approach/wellbeing-framework-for-schools.

Dewey, J. (1933). *How we think: A restatement of the relation of reflective thinking to the educative process.* D.C. Heath.

Dewey, J. (1934). *Art as experience.* G. P. Putnam's Sons.

Eisner, E. W. (2017). *The enlightened eye: Qualitative inquiry and the enhancement of educational practice.* Teachers College Press.

Efland, A. D. (1990). *A history of art education.* Teachers College Press.

Freire, P. (2018). *Teachers as cultural workers: Letters to those who dare teach.* Routledge.

Greene, M. (2010). Resisting plague: Pedagogies of thoughtfulness and imagination. In J. Sandlin, B. D. Schultz, & J. Burdick (Eds.), (pp.28–31), *Handbook of Public Pedagogy.* Routledge.

Hall, M. P., Jones, L. F., & O'Hare, A. (2018). Internal ways of knowing: A case for contemplative practices in preservice teacher education. In K. Byrnes, J. Dalton, & E. H. Dorman (Eds.), *Cultivating a culture of learning: Contemplative practices, pedagogy, and research in education* (pp. 8–24). Rowman & Littlefield.

Harvey, M., Coulson, D., & McMaugh, A. (2016). Towards a theory of the ecology of reflection: Reflective practice for experiential learning in higher education, *Journal of University Teaching & Learning Practice, 13*(2), 1–20.

Harvey, M., Lloyd, K., McLachlan, K., Semple, A., & Walkerden, G. (2020). *Reflection for learning: a scholarly practice guide for educators.* AdvanceHE. https://www.advance-he.ac.uk/knowledge-hub/reflection-learning-scholarly-practice-guide-educators.

Helyer, R. (2015). Learning through reflection: the critical role of reflection in work-based learning (WBL). *Journal of Work-Applied Management, 7*(1):15–27 DOI: https://doi.org/10.1108/JWAM-10-2015-003

Krathwohl, D. R. (2002). A revision of Bloom's taxonomy: An overview. *Theory into Practice, 41*(4), 212–218.

McLachlan, K., Yeomans, L., & Lim, K-Z-G. (2017). Exploring an approach to embedding employability skills in a work integrated learning curriculum.

In R.G. Walker & S.B. Bedford (Eds.), *Research and development in higher education: Curriculum transformation*, 40 (pp. 241–249). Australia.

McLachlan, K. J. (2014). *The role of critical self-reflection in the practice of community development workers: a retrospective analysis of four community development projects in a rural community in Australia suffering social, economic and environmental hardships*, Doctoral dissertation, University of Queensland, Brisbane, Queensland. https://espace.library.uq.edu.au/view/UQ:327806

Mezirow, J. (2006). An overview of transformative learning. In P. Sutherland & J. Crowther (Eds.), *Lifelong learning: Concepts and contexts* (pp. 24–38). Routledge.

O'Brien, M., Wade-Leeuwen, B., Hadley, F., Andrews, R., Kelly, N., & Kickbusch S. (2017). Reconsidering the communicative space: Learning to be. In J. Kriewaldt, A. Ambrosetti, D. Rorrison, R. Capeness. (Eds.), *Educating Future Teachers: Innovative Perspectives in Professional Experience*. 7 (pp.105–121). Springer. https://doi.org/10.1007/978-981-10-5484-614

Palmer, P. J. (2017). *The courage to teach: Exploring the inner landscape of a teacher's life*. John Wiley Sons.

Sachs, J., & Clark, L. (Eds.). (2017). *Learning through community engagement: Vision and practice in higher education*. Singapore: Springer Nature.

Savage, G., & Lingard, B. (2018). Changing modes of governance in Australian teacher education policy. In *Navigating the common good in teacher education policy: Critical and international perspectives* (pp. 64–80). Routledge.

Schön, D. A. (1987). *Educating the reflective practitioner*. Jossey-Bass.

Sternberg, R. J., & Lubart, T. I. (1999). The concept of creativity: Prospects and paradigms. Cambridge University Press.

Trede, F., Macklin, R. & Bridges, D. (2012). Professional identity development: A review of the higher education literature. *Studies in Higher Education*, 37(3), 365–384.

Wade-Leeuwen, B. (2016a). *Out of the shadows: Fostering creativity in teacher education programs*. Common Ground Publishing.

Wade-Leeuwen, B. (2016b). Intercultural arts-based research inquiry: First marks of the reformer's brush. *Australian Art Education*, 37(2), 151–164.

Wenger, E. (2000). Communities of practice and social learning systems. *Organization*, 7(2), 225–246.

Yin, R. (2014). *Case study research design and methods*. Sage.

CHAPTER 12

Law School: Imbuing It with Both Rigor and Support

Justine A. Dunlap

INTRODUCTION

When I started law school in 1979, law schools were not warm and fuzzy places. For instance, at first-year orientation, the Law Dean suggested that students "look to your left, now look to your right, one of you won't be here next year." This statement set the tone quite clearly. Failure—at a one-in-three rate, it appeared—was part and parcel of legal education. It was a necessary thread woven into the fabric of learning the law.

What was then deemed a necessary and perhaps unremarkable component, has turned out to have been an unnecessary evil. I am not just referring to the "look to your left..." remark with its blunt prediction. I am also referring to the belief that the rigor necessary for a sound legal education must contain elements of fear, intimidation, and cruelty.

Law students and lawyers experience higher than average rates of depression, suicide, and substance abuse. Law schools have contributed to

J. A. Dunlap (✉)
University of Massachusetts School of Law, Dartmouth, MA, USA
e-mail: jdunlap@umassd.edu

© The Author(s), under exclusive license to Springer Nature Switzerland AG 2021
M. P. Hall and A. K. Brault (eds.), *Academia from the Inside*,
https://doi.org/10.1007/978-3-030-83895-9_12

this dismal reality by the ways in which they have traditionally conducted their instruction. It now seems clear, to me at least, that rigor does not mean cruelty. Indeed, cruelty is antithetical to the well-being of law students, not a necessary rite of passage. Doctors take the Hippocratic Oath, the classic version of which says that the doctor will do the sick "no harm or injustice" (Marks, 2021). Perhaps the law school professor should pledge likewise.

Luckily, legal education has shifted a bit in the past generation or two, much of it in beneficial ways. The immediate driver of change that may come to mind is, of course, technology. Another recent change is the remote delivery of legal education that resulted from the COVID-19 global pandemic. It is true that technology and COVID have had profound impacts on law school teaching; however, the change to which I refer and write about here is less apparent. That change is legal education's move toward becoming more humane. Professor Larry Krieger has referred to this humanizing legal education effort as "a distinct progressive energy [that] has begun to pervade the landscape of legal education in the past few years" (Krieger, 2008).

The progressive energy toward humanizing legal education is for the greater good. I heartily advocate for its continuation and expansion. This transformation must continue and, indeed, expand if one cares about the new lawyers turned out by law schools every year, the clients they serve, their reputation, and ultimately, the value of the profession. In this chapter, I examine the importance of humanizing legal education by looking at it through my own journey from law student to law professor.

First, what do I mean by humanizing legal education? In part, law professors must not use the Socratic Dialogue to intentionally humiliate students. I also mean that law schools need to be candid by acknowledging the stress and address the particular risks for law students and lawyers. Law schools must also expose students to ways to cope with stress in healthy (or at least health*ier*) ways. According to Professor Krieger, a founder of the movement, humanizing legal education includes concern for, and attention to, the law student's sense of subjective well-being (Krieger, 2008, p. 261).

My Journey from Law Student
to Lawyer to Law Professor

The "look to your left, look to your right" statement communicated the then-dominant fear-infused approach to legal education. I took in the Dean's comment and laughed nervously as I looked to the left and right. But I did not think that it was meant to apply to me. The Dean must be talking to the other students, I thought. I suspect that there were plenty of other law students who believed that they also were not the intended recipient of that comment. No doubt, however, there were many students who internalized that comment and it helped to build their anxiety. Let the terror begin!

Law school comes as a shock to most students. It was definitely a shock to me. No matter how excited and confident I was at orientation, it was soon clear that I had no accurate concept of the terrorizing challenges that law school presented. I could identify with St. Teresa of Avila, who wrote: "There are more tears shed over answered prayers than over unanswered prayers." My "I want to go to law school" prayers had been answered but it was more than hard, more than rigorous. It was brutal.

The first year was the worst. As is often said: First year, they scare you to death, second year they work you to death, third year they bore you to death. Well, in my first year, I was certainly scared to death. I studied hard and over-imbibed harder. At some point in that first semester, I went from being the eager, so-happy-to be-here student to the oppressed and over-whelmed self-perceived underachiever. I nearly dropped out before my fall finals. My experience in my first semester of law school was not, I am sad to say, abnormal. Professor Janet Thompson Jackson reports that she felt as if she "had been dropped into a foreign land" and the "stresses of law school took [her] anxiety to a new high" (Jackson, 2021, 32 and 5).

I managed to stick it out. I had made the decision to become a lawyer at the tender age of 10. There was no plan B. This was my dream. And two professors helped me stay with it. My kind, calm, and centered legal research and writing teacher clearly cared about and took an interest in supporting her first-year charges. The way in which she humanized the first year of law school had an outsized impact. Her humanizing strategy was simple: supply kindness and encouragement in large doses. In other words, she contributed to my sense of subjective well-being.

In addition, I perceived a decency in one particular professor, a decency that other professors hid rather well. Humiliating students was not his goal. Aha, I dared think, there are strains of humanity in this professor, even though he employed the dreaded Socratic method, showcased by Professor Kingsfield in *The Paper Chase* (Paper Chase, 1973 20th Century Fox). His decency demonstrated that not all law professors viewed their student charges as merely a one-in-three statistic of being a law school drop-out.

Should the reader not be familiar, *The Paper Chase* was a movie that immortalized John Houseman as Professor Kingsfield. Kingsfield taught contract law to first-year law students at a top-rate law school. In one scene, Kingsfield, after a hard-charging Socratic interchange with a student, calls the student up to the front of the very large and imposing (and nearly all-male, white) classroom. Kingsfield gives the student a dime and instructs him (in this pre-cell phone era) to go call his mother to tell her that there is a good chance that he will not become a lawyer after all.

When I began my legal education, the emotional toll that law school exacted from its students was largely unacknowledged. When it was acknowledged, it was in a prideful fashion. Legal education boasted of its toughness and, yes, brutality. It was a signifier of the worthy—a form of hazing straight from the educators themselves. The high non-economic costs of law school were just part of the package of becoming a lawyer. It was unquestioned and, some at least claimed, part of the intrinsic value of a legal education.

Fast forward three years ahead, please. I survived law school. I had a job I wanted in a city in which I wanted to live. Thankfully, I passed the bar examination although that stress was mind-numbing. At long last, I had achieved the appropriate developmental milestones for being a lawyer. The dreams of my 10-year-old self were realized.

I worked at the Legal Aid Society of the District of Columbia representing parents in civil court child abuse and neglect proceedings. It was challenging and worthy work. I believed that what I did made a difference and held meaning. It was essential to do it well and I gave it my all. At that nascent stage of my career, being a law professor was not an aspiration. I had not liked law school very much, after all; why would I want to work at one? More importantly, I loved practicing law.

My unlikely path to law teaching began a decade into my legal career when I received a cold-call request to guest lecture to a Washington, D.C. law school class. I was asked to lecture on child abuse laws and practice. That single experience led several years later to my mid-life career change to full-time law teaching.

Now, after being a law professor for over 20 years, I can reflect on what works and what doesn't work for both my students and myself. As part of this reflection, I have become convinced that it is crucial to make legal education more humane. Please note that I am not proposing that we should weaken the rigor of the endeavor. Law school can and must be both rigorous and humane. I will discuss how I have changed my approach to teaching and also say a bit about the slow process of legal education itself becoming more humane. But first, a legal education primer.

Since the 1870s, law school has been taught in largely the same way: A professor employs Socratic Dialogue to grill students on appellate cases collected in a text called a casebook. The curated cases demonstrate a particular legal principle or doctrine and its development, contours, and exceptions. Through the Socratic Dialogue process, students learn to, as the saying goes, think like a lawyer (Rubin, 2007).

This grilling often occurs in cavernous classrooms with many students looking on, thankful that they were not called on yet fearful that they may be next. There are permutations, of course, from this basic structure. Still, though, the Socratic Dialogue/Case Method continues to dominate law school classes, especially in the first-year doctrinal curriculum that consists of Contracts, Property, Civil Procedure, Torts, and Criminal Law. The first year of study likely also includes another substantive (doctrinal) course and a legal research and writing class as well.

Although I now teach Civil Procedure, one of the courses in the first-year curriculum, I began my full-time law teaching in a law school clinic. Clinics are upper-level courses and function as a small law firm within the law school. In clinic, law students represent clients in court or in transactional settings under the supervision of their clinical faculty. Clinics nearly always serve an under-represented clientele. Clinics are a new addition to legal education, relatively speaking, having been developed and adopted by many law schools in the 1970s and 1980s.

My first clinical teaching position was non-tenure track and based on a two-year grant. This was not exactly job security and accurately reflected the ambivalence toward clinical legal education within the legal academy. Clinical law professors have, in my view, a harder and more stressful job than faculty who teach the traditional doctrinal classes. This is true even though clinical positions are often less prestigious, less secure, and less remunerative. The lesser status aspect of clinical teaching has been written about sufficiently elsewhere, but here is why I believe it is harder.

THE CLINICAL LAW PROFESSOR—A TEACHER
WITH SUPERPOWERS

As I note above, clinical law faculty supervise students who are representing real clients. This representation takes place in a variety of fora. For instance, my clinical teaching has been in what is referred to as a litigation clinic, meaning that I supported and supervised students representing clients in court proceedings. To do this well, I needed to know both how to practice law and how to teach students how to practice law.

When I taught clinic, students and I worked together to represent clients, often with the student in the primary role. This collaborative partnership aimed to place students in the professional role they are training for and invest them with capacity and agency. They are no longer just students awaiting the perceived wisdom of their faculty in a large and impersonal classroom or fiercely debating the details of a law school hypothetical with their cohorts.

Clinical teaching is multi-faceted. The coverage includes working with students on how to interview and counsel clients, how to draft legal documents, and how to negotiate. And that is all pre-trial! The learning also includes the many skills needed to conduct a trial. Finally, there are the pervasive skills that are needed throughout any client representation. Those skills include strategy, professional judgment, ethics, and dealing with opposing counsel and other system-wide players.

This is happening with real clients and in real tribunals. During the hearing or other event, the clinical professor, after being heavily involved in the student's preparation, stands back as the student proceeds with all the inefficiencies of a novice. The professor likely has two goals in mind: (1) to prevent errors that will hurt the client and (2) to observe the student's performance and provide feedback afterward.

The learning laboratory that is the courtroom or negotiation accomplishes much for the student's journey from law student to lawyer. Through the trial, or any other student clinical performance in the real world, the student learns that context matters. Learning while doing the actual tasks is richer and more lasting. Real-world activity also provides a sense of accomplishment and pride. But representing actual clients in actual cases is also replete with stress.

Stressful matters are core to the job of the clinic student lawyer. The clinical faculty are there to support the students and help them process what is happening as they develop their lawyer persona in real time. One does not get that kind of faculty-student interaction when discussing a Civil Procedure hypothetical in a first-year class. Or even during an exam review. Take my word for it—I have done both.

Also, clinical faculty see students close up and in demanding conditions. Therefore, they are often the faculty members with whom students talk and in whom students confide. These faculty members may also be more aware of students' maladaptive choices for dealing with stress and/or students' mental health issues. Thus, clinical faculty often possess more knowledge than their doctrinal peers about the struggles students are having. All of these elements of clinical law teaching have contributed, I believe, to clinical faculty developing more humanizing approaches to law teaching.

Humanizing as a Default Pedagogy

I have had many interactions over the years with many clinical law professors. I was on the board of the Clinical Legal Education Association. I presented for years at a conference for new clinicians. As part of co-writing an article on training new clinicians, I read hundreds of surveys from clinical teachers about their experiences teaching clinics. My encounters taught me, and continue to teach me, that most clinicians have, as their default teaching practice, a humanizing educational modality. They probably would not be clinicians if they did not relish the idea of working closely with students to help them become good lawyers. And that alone largely inoculates clinical faculty from using dehumanizing educational practices.

For me, teaching client interviewing and counseling was an especially helpful reminder of the importance of humanizing in general. The rapport-building and active listening skills that are essential to effective client interviewing involve engaging and connecting with another human being. If I espoused one thing in the classroom but practiced otherwise, there would be a glaring discrepancy between my words and my actions. I strove to walk my talk.

In sum, as a clinical law professor, I found myself routinely incorporating humanizing educational practices. I must acknowledge, though, that I was simply swimming with the stream. If I stalled or faltered, I would be carried along by others in the clinical teaching community. Using humane teaching pedagogy is, for most, part of the clinical professor's DNA.

THE MOVE TO THE DOCTRINAL CLASSROOM

After nearly eight years of clinical teaching, in 2003 I started teaching primarily doctrinal classes. I taught two courses in the first-year curriculum: Property and Civil Procedure. I also taught—and still teach—some upper-level courses such as Family Law and Access to Justice.

I found the switch from clinical teaching to more traditional classroom teaching to be a difficult transition. This difficulty surprised me, because I knew from being an adjunct professor when I was practicing law that I enjoyed teaching large doctrinal courses. After all, there is some similarity between courtroom and classroom performance.

I soon realized that one of the challenges of moving to full-time doctrinal teaching was that I had left behind the community of human-izing clinical teachers. Further, I found it to be far more difficult to connect with students in ways that appeared to naturally occur when teaching a clinical course. Lecturing and Socratic Dialogue in a large class-room setting is quite different from working with clinic students closely as they learned how to be lawyers. I missed the latter experience greatly, just as I missed the community of clinical teachers. I found that the absence of that community diminished my teaching experience.

Luckily, I heard about a law teaching conference not long after I started teaching first-year Property Law, a notoriously difficult class that I had never taught before. I was eager to attend this conference since, as a new doctrinal law teacher, I had been having fewer conversations about teaching with doctrinal colleagues than I had enjoyed with clinical colleagues while teaching clinic. I also noticed that the annual national conference for law faculty had significantly fewer sessions on teaching than did the annual clinical law professor conference, which was largely devoted to teaching.

As providence would have it, I discovered this group and its confer-ence, and off I went. *Eureka! Here were my peeps*. I met doctrinal faculty who wanted to improve their teaching and talk with others about what worked and what did not work in the traditional classroom. And although I was unaware of it at the time, I was meeting new colleagues who formed the core of the humanizing legal education movement. They were law faculty who explicitly cared about their students, their own teaching, and the impact that their teaching had on their students. Although I had left the community of clinical teachers, I had found a new community.

My excitement at this teaching conference was palpable. I was likewise excited about the nascent movement to make explicit the connection between good law teaching and humane law teaching, between humane law teaching and high-caliber law student learning.

Within this new community, people were researching and writing about the high rates of law student depression and substance abuse. They were educating the rest of us. It was, indeed, news to me, though I may have been willfully unaware.

Perhaps it was (and still may be) a situation of those who had ears to hear did, and those who did not have ears to hear ignored the message or criticized the methodology or—plain and simple—belittled the efforts. After all, the belittlers had survived and perhaps even thrived under the traditional law school Socratic-Dialogue-style of teaching. What was wrong with this new cadre of students, the belittlers might wonder, that they need such coddling?

One legal scholar described this mode of thinking as follows: "… any stress resulting from a legal education [i]s necessary to prepare students for the demands of a law practice. …[student-centered] protective efforts … interfere[e] with the Darwinian process of 'unnatural selection' [necessary] …in law school to weed out those obviously unfit to practice law, and so, in the long run, [are] a misguided and counterproductive effort" (Schuwerk, 2004). Thankfully, I believe that legal education has come a long way from the notion that student-centered efforts are "misguided and counterproductive."

In the early days of this humanizing movement, the word got out slowly. Or at least more slowly than its proponents would have wished. Its venues were not those generally trafficked by highly influential law faculty. Nevertheless, the movement persisted. The Humanizing Legal Education Association and its listserv gave structure and voice to the emerging effort and were used to disseminate more widely the disturbing information about the ill-effects of law school. The listserv, and the association's meetings at conferences, also helped those of us who were interested in these ideas to connect and collaborate.

Slowly but surely humanizing legal education gained currency and support mounted within the ranks of law teachers. The Humanizing Legal Education Association sought ways to achieve maximum impact and decided to become one of the American Association of Law Schools' (AALS) affinity groups. The AALS is a member-only national group that sponsors both national law professor hiring events and multiple conferences each year. The Humanizing Legal Education Association became the AALS's Balance in Legal Education Section and instantly was better positioned to help law schools know better so that they could do better. The Balance section continues today and sponsors important student-centered programs at AALS's annual conference and other venues.

These humanizing endeavors were occurring synchronistically with other legal education reform efforts between 2000 and 2010. This period coincided with my move away from clinical teaching into doctrinal teaching. In that process, I wrestled with being the kind of doctrinal teacher that I wanted to be. I was searching for the community of teachers that could help me to figure that out and support me. Hence, my delight in finding these colleagues at this conference. And my further delight in connecting with a group of teachers and scholars who were committed to discussing the legal education-related damage that happens to law students and equally committed to lessening that damage.

Finally, lest I be misapprehended, I want to emphasize that many doctrinal faculty care deeply about their teaching and their students. I am lucky enough to work with a faculty that does. But it must be acknowledged that in legal education, scholarship is the coin of the realm. Teaching is second and service comes in at a distant third. Many find value—intrinsic or otherwise—across spheres and diligently try to be productive in all three areas. It is hard to overlook, however, that law schools, many individual law faculty, and meta-legal education groups put more money and prestige into rewarding scholarship than effective teaching or service.

It takes more energy to connect with others interested especially in teaching but it is, I have found, an effort well worthwhile. I have benefited from these efforts over my years of teaching and, by extension, I hope my students have also benefited. A recent example of this for me was an interdisciplinary discussion group on Parker Palmer's *Courage to Teach* sponsored by my university's Office of Faculty Development. A small group of us met bi-weekly over the course of a semester—a pandemic-caused remote learning semester, no less, so we connected over Zoom. We were able to remind ourselves and each other of why we teach—especially important during the stressful pandemic year and a half.

First Humanizing Steps—Encouraging Rather Than Humiliating Students

At the 2004 teaching conference, I attended a session presented by Robert Schuwerk, a law professor at the University of Houston Law Center. Professor Schuwerk described his practice of putting students into law firms and then calling on the law firm rather than on a particular student. He used this technique largely in upper-level courses to help encourage students to read the material and participate, a practice which tends to decrease after the fears of the first year recede.

This approach achieved at least three other student-centered goals, reported Professor Schuwerk. It encouraged collaboration, reduced the pressure of being the student who was cold-called, and fostered both student accountability and mutual support (Schuwerk, 2004).

Listening to Professor Schuwerk describe this practice left me enlightened and relieved. He was suggesting a great solution to a vexing problem. As I describe in a law review article (Dunlap, 2008), I had been struggling with my desire—*or rather with what I thought was supposed to be my desire*—to be a hard-core Socratic Dialogue driller. That was not my authentic self; it was the stereotypical law professor. And truth be told, I was not that good at it, at least not in the manner of the masterful teacher who stays with a student and works effectively with that student through a series of questions that then will result—with a drum roll and swelling horn section—in an epiphany for both the individual student and the class as a whole.

Further, I nursed lingering concern about the level of fear and intimidation that often accompanies Socratic Dialogue. Were these really valuable tools that were needed to help students master the material? Or do they more often interfere with rather than enhance the learning process? As we lawyers often say as part of a legal analysis, did the burden of a Socratic Dialogue outweigh the benefit?

Worse-case scenario, I wondered, might untrammeled Socratic Dialogue, law-school style, lead students to conclude that law professors tended toward the sadistic? One study in the late 1970s indicated that a majority of law students at a particular law school thought that their professors took pleasure in embarrassing them in class (Carrington & Conley, 1977). A more recent article posited that "… law students come to the conclusion that their professors neither like nor respect them …. Indeed, if the truth be told—and it certainly should be—all too often, students are right to come to that conclusion" (Schuwerk, 2004). Please reread those last two sentences. Pretty shocking, no? Law school education, as perceived by both students and faculty, was intentionally hostile to students.

Even if the evidence fully supported the overall benefits of the Socratic method, it wasn't who I was. Just as I encourage students in developing their professional identity to be true to themselves and adopt a style that allows them to be authentic, I had to do the same. I could improve as a Socratic Dialogue questioner and eventually become good at it, but it would never feel right to me.

With this realization firmly in hand, I had to wrestle with and reconcile my belief, which also felt true and authentic, that student preparation is critically important. It is imperative that law students keep up with the material, that they stick with it even when it seems incomprehensible.

The lawyer and novelist Scott Turow wrote in his non-fiction book *One L* that when he was a first-year law student, reading a particular case was like stirring concrete with his eyelashes (Turow, 1977). I certainly read that passage to my own law students. Although I would not have so characterized it then, sharing that passage was a humanizing practice. I was signaling to students it is okay and—yes—normal to struggle. I pulled back the curtain to show that law school is a challenge that all law students experience, even famous and smart ones who went to Harvard Law School.

In the struggle of doing assignments, long hours of reading preparation stack up one upon the other and, horror of horrors, sometimes students do not get everything done. After all, whoever thought that reading ten pages of material could take two hours! Given that I believed preparation is a non-negotiable part of a law student's success, I had to ask myself: Whose work gets finished first and most thoroughly? The answer for many students is that it is the professor most feared: that particular law school's Professor Kingsfield proxy—the professor who will be as relentless as Ahab in Socratic pursuit.

Nonetheless, even if that were true, I could not be that professor. Thus, when reconciling humanizing and student preparation, I learned that, for me, humanizing wins. But perhaps that is a false conflict. It is true only if one accepts that reducing students to fear is the sole or even best way to get them to prepare. And that is not a conclusion that I am inclined to accept, then or now.

Professor Schuwerk's law firm model of class participation provided me with a way to reduce student anxiety, while simultaneously encouraging class preparation. Students would be part of a team and most would not want to be consistently unprepared. This model also reduced my anxiety, which likely made me a better teacher. It certainly made me a more authentic teacher. Fortified by this new knowledge of a humanizing teaching technique, I started forthwith to assemble my large first-year classes into law firms. Borrowing heavily from Professor Schuwerk, I created the groups and gave them law firm rules. The rules, set out below, are distributed to students after we have discussed the law firms and their purpose in class.

Professor Dunlap's Law Firm Procedures—Welcome to Your Law Firms!

1. Select a consensus name for the firm. Be creative, but not embarrassingly so.
2. When called upon, firms cannot pass. But any member of firm may answer.
3. If your firm is called on and another student steps up, be prepared to step in if assistance is needed.
4. If you answer for the firm, *you* are not on the hotseat for the remainder of the class. However, the firm *is* until I move the discussion elsewhere.
5. Every firm member must speak at least three times during the semester.
6. While I am engaging in a colloquy with a firm, other firms should be thinking how they would respond. I *will* move among firms during the class.

In addition to the goals identified by Professor Schuwerk, I saw several other beneficial by-products. Not only is it nice to know someone else is prepared on a day when everything has gone wrong for a particular student, it is also affirming to be the person lending the assist. Finally, the firm model creates structured small groups. Particularly in the isolating and oft-times terrifying fall of the first year, this structure lends itself to further use as a study group or just a few students to hang with, to disclose fears to, or talk to about law school generally.

I still use this law firm model today. As if this were not a sufficiently significant benefit gained from attending the conference, perhaps as galvanizing for me was discovering this community of non-clinical law professors who thought deeply about how best to teach their students without inflicting trauma. This would be the band of merry teachers with whom I would throw in my lot. The 2004 conference was indeed a Eureka experience.

FURTHER HUMANIZING STEPS-DISCUSSING THE RISKS

In my own teaching development trajectory, I also became convinced that it was time to talk candidly with students about the risks magnified by being in law school and to help students discover ways to counteract those risks. The risks to which I refer include the increased level of anxiety and depression as well as the disturbing levels of substance abuse by law students. I believed that simply having the conversation and presenting the topic for consideration and discussion would act as a balm. Students would understand that having this conversation is okay and, even, important.

But how to do it and what, exactly, would doing it look like? I spoke with a friend who also taught law and, with her counsel and a purloined portion of her fortitude, I came up with an exercise that I now do, usually in the late fall of my year-long first-year doctrinal class. It is at this point, after midterms, that many students are discouraged by the results and are looking with acute trepidation to the advent of finals in early December. That this point exists in the late fall is actually a humanizing improvement since, for eons, law school courses had but one test at the end of the semester. Now, many law school courses have midterms and/or some other graded exercise. Thus, the full grade for a course is no longer based on one high-stakes end-of-the-semester exam performance.

The downside of midterms, in that moment at least, is that many students are shocked by the midterm results and may start descending into a deep hole of depression or anxiety, which can continue to build as the pressure of finals looms. I seize this moment as an opportune time for my class session on the dark side of law school.

I devote a 75-minute class to it, barely enough time to scratch the surface. Nonetheless, giving up a whole class initially seemed radical and foolhardy. Because of this, when I first conducted this class, I did so without talking about it with my in-school colleagues. I am not sure what

I thought they would do, but clearly I worried about their disapprobation. On the positive side, devoting an entire class to this topic telegraphs to the students that I take it seriously and perhaps so should they.

The week before the class, I distribute the reading materials and assignment. Traditionally, the only thing that I put in the syllabus for this class is "materials to be distributed" without spelling out what the materials are about. Cowardice? Perhaps.

For reading materials, I assign two law review articles. Many articles would work, but after some trial and error, I settled on articles by Professor Susan Daicoff and the late Professor Peter Cicchino (2001; Daicoff, 1997). I recently reviewed the literature again and decided to stay with these two pieces.

The Daicoff article is a key piece in the area of law student distress. I ask students to focus on two concepts in the article, one of which is Professor Daicoff's discussion of the high rate of depression and substance abuse among law students and lawyers.

The Cicchino piece takes a different tack. It is an essay that employs personal narrative to examine both law school and law practice. Professor Cicchino urges students to examine what matters to them, why they went to law school, and how the law school experience can leave them feeling oppressed. He implores them to reclaim their agency, to realize that although they are doubtless not feeling it in the moment, they, as law students, occupy a space of privilege.

Students respond in writing to questions that I pose in advance, including: (1) Identify the most interesting or surprising part of either article; (2) Name two ways you have changed—or ways that others close to you would say you have changed—since beginning law school; (3) List the four words you would like to be used to describe you as a lawyer; and (4) Identify healthy (and practical) ways you could combat law school stress.

During the class, I start off with some self-disclosure. I share my own law school challenges, especially in the first semester. I talk about my own excessive use of alcohol and about how close I came to dropping out in the first semester. Suffice it to say, this helps set the tone for the class discussion that follows.

This class has proven its usefulness time and again. First, it brings to the fore a topic—law student distress and maladaptive responses thereto—that most students are living, but which generally lurks in the shadows. By introducing this topic and sharing my own experience with law school distress, I validate what students are experiencing. Many students realize for the first time that they are not alone; this knowledge is powerful and reassuring. After naming this phenomenon, we can then move on to think together about ways to combat the negative effects.

Second, the class personalizes their fellow students and me, their professor. Students see that their colleagues who may be strutting and preening are often just engaging in a self-protective act. Because law school often alienates, isolates, and devalues students, this humanizing of the "other" is constructive.

This topic and discussion, even if never formally revisited, remain open throughout the course and, I hope, throughout the students' law school experience. The readings or discussions may be brought up again, either by myself or by the students.

I have been doing this class session for more than a dozen years. I have shared it with other colleagues as I have become more comfortable with it and as the subject matter is much more in the common domain than it was when I started it. I have written a brief description of it for the inclusion of *Techniques for Teaching Law 2* (Hess et al., 2011). If I were starting this exercise anew, would I be braver in sharing about it? Maybe. I hope so. What I have no doubt about is that taking time to discuss student distress and well-being within the law school classroom is a necessary part of a humanizing pedagogy.

As I prepare going forward with the class, I am rethinking my cloak and dagger approach to how I list it in the syllabus. That I did it that way initially shows, I think, how uncomfortable I was even though I believed the topic was critically important. I also probably worried about students' questions and comments in the lead-up to the class. I now believe that it would be useful to be explicit up front, although I am not sure how to summarize the class topic in syllabus-length language.

I also need to alter my private language for this class. I have folders full of material for my "touchy-feely" class. This is a tad embarrassing but worth disclosing, I believe, for what it reveals about the entrenched and dismissive attitudes toward addressing these matters—even by those of us who do address them! A final note of reflection here, though. If I were to start this exercise today, rather than 15 years ago, I think that the law school climate has changed enough that I would not feel the need to be so secretive. The institutional changes and my own progress in being comfortable with the uncomfortable are both positive developments.

HUMANIZING LEGAL EDUCATION
THROUGH AN INSTITUTIONAL LENS

I believe that law schools have an obligation to help students deal with the stress, not add to it through dehumanizing practices. Readily available data documents the harms involved. Starting with the pioneering work of Professor Krieger, multiple studies demonstrate that law students suffer higher rates of depression and anxiety (Krieger, 2002). These elevated rates are compared not just to the general public but also to students in other professional schools, including medical school. These high rates of law student distress also follow law students into the profession (Daicoff, 1997).

Thankfully, this problem is now recognized widely and is being addressed. In addition to the studies about student depression and distress, three broad reform efforts have helped legal education change. These are clinical legal education, the Carnegie Report on Legal Education (The Carnegie Report, 2007), and the Best Practices in Legal Education book (Best Practices in Legal Education, 2007).

The first of these, discussed earlier, is the widespread introduction of clinical legal education in the late twentieth century. The other two institutional reforms were the 2007 issuance of the Carnegie Report and Best Practices for Legal Education book. Among other things, both reports urged law schools to focus more on the professional development of their students.

Also significant is that the Best Practices report urged the de-brutalization of law school. Best Practices cited studies that demonstrated how law school itself harmed students. That merely being a law student would have a negative impact on one's well-being. It was finally being acknowledged that law school's brutality was causing students to have higher rates of depression and substance abuse—higher than either the population at large or students in other professional schools. Or, at the least, the brutality was exacerbating pre-existing propensities. Among the recommendations Best Practices made for law schools was the following: improve the .... professionalism of their graduates; attend to the well-being of their students; do no harm to students; and do not intentionally humiliate or embarrass students. It may seem disturbing that these things need to be said—at least it was disturbing to me. These truths seem self-evident.

As law schools have taken steps to pay attention to the problem and to provide important resources, the American Bar Association (ABA) and the various state entities that license lawyers have also acknowledged that there is a problem within the profession, and are taking steps to address the problem. The state entities have, for instance, some type of counseling or addiction-based services available to their members. In Massachusetts, for instance, the lawyer assistance program is called Lawyers Concerned for Lawyers, and it offers programs and services to law students as well as lawyers.

WELL-BEING IS IN THE HOUSE!

Law schools and the legal profession have started to approach the topic of well-being from a positive perspective rather than just reacting to high levels of depression, anxiety, and substance abuse. In 2016, the profession created a task force composed of organizations, within and without the ABA, to deal with the issue of lawyer well-being (Buchanan & Coyle, 2017). The task force issued a wide-ranging report—The Path to Lawyer Well-Being—with specific recommendations targeted at law schools, local bar associations, judges, liability carriers, and legal employers. Significantly, the task force recommended that the accreditation body for law schools make well-being education a requirement for accreditation. The Council of the ABA Section on Legal Education and Admission to the Bar has taken this advice and a well-being accreditation requirement has been proposed.

The Path to Lawyer Well-Being report contains a sobering recitation of the law student problem. Citing the 2016 Survey of Law Student Well-Being (Organ et al., 2016), the report explains that 42% of students need help for poor mental health, and a quarter are at risk for excessive alcohol use.

The moral argument always has had force, but these data points provide practical utilitarian support for law schools to adopt prevention strategies and "identify aspects of legal education that can be revised to support well-being" (at 35–36). The report's suggestions are carefully phrased with a nuanced acknowledgment that it may be difficult to secure faculty buy-in. This is unfortunate as the report instructs that faculty involvement is critical. Why is it critical? Because, the report states, classroom practices "contribute enormously" to a law student's experience.

Some of the report's specific recommendations for law schools include offering faculty education on promoting well-being in the classroom and discouraging alcohol-centered social events. Many law schools have responded—and indeed many were doing things before the report came out. Schools have added things such as wellness weeks, yoga, meditation, mindfulness courses, counseling, and well-being committees and newsletters. A partial sampling includes UC Berkeley Law School, Seattle Law School, Loyola Chicago Law School, and Washburn (Jackson, 2021).

Occasionally, this can lead to jealous alumni! At my law school, an alumna was on campus during the wellness week that was in progress right before fall finals. She could not believe it and said she wished it had existed when she was in law school.

So, law schools can and have moved along the continuum from being unaware of the issue of massive student distress, to next being aware but largely ignoring the issue, to, at long last, finally paying attention to the deleterious impact that their own practices were having on their students. And now, law schools can and have moved from being concerned about the prevalence of student distress to a broader focus on student well-being. At long last, it is not just illness to be avoided, but rather health that is to be promoted. It is an acknowledgment of Professor Krieger's point: A part of humanizing legal education is concern for students' sense of well-being.

Humanizing on an Individual Scale—Acknowledging the Cost of Racial Inequities

I experienced 2020 as a complicated and challenging year. Among the obvious challenges: the pandemic, remote learning, the decreasing value of facts (which are quite important in the study of law), the increased "othering" of our neighbors, family, and all who believe differently, and the barrage of acts of violence and death against persons of color.

As a professor, I well knew these events were affecting my law students. I was also aware that the support and community that occurs naturally with in-person instruction was painfully absent in the remote classroom. Over the course of the year, I grew in awareness of how these events affected all law students and affected their ability to learn—particularly law students of color.

Legal educators must acknowledge the impact of these difficult external events, strive to understand the impact, and think about how to address it. It is thus good that, in troubling times, beacons of hope and progress emerge. For law schools in 2020, one of those beacons of hope was the Law Deans Antiracist Clearinghouse Project (Conway et al., 2021). Five women law deans of color—Deans Danielle M. Conway, Danielle Holley-Walker, Kim Mutcherson, Angela Onwuachi-Willig, and Carla D. Pratt—created this clearinghouse as a resource for other law deans, law faculty, and staff.

The clearinghouse project website posits that law schools must, through words and actions, "demonstrate a commitment to delivering on an antiracist program of legal education. This antiracist work requires auditing our programs of legal education to assess our progress toward diversifying our faculties, our staff, and especially our student bodies, which in turn diversify our profession." Exhorted and informed by the Deans' Clearinghouse and other resources, legal educators now have multiple materials available to help them to know better and do better in the classroom.

In addition to external events that land with different impact upon different groups, the internal content of legal instruction also inherently plays a role here. Law school classes, for instance, frequently involve sensitive racial and gender topics. Accordingly, a classroom discussion can be more difficult for some students than others.

I can identify multiple cringe-worthy moments of my own classroom ineptitude and thoughtlessness. The moments in which I bungled a sensitive topic. I am still learning. Part of my education process is learning how and where I have blind spots. I must also acknowledge that, despite what I hope are usually best efforts, I do not know what I do not know.

In light of this, I have recently decided to adopt a practice suggested by Professor Susan Kuo of the University of South Carolina law school. In a webinar on teaching sensitive topics, Professor Kuo discussed the good faith statements that she puts in her syllabus and offered an example of how it helped diffuse a difficult classroom comment. Professor Kuo identifies several parts of these statements; there are two that especially speak to me. First, that everyone should feel free to speak their minds in a respectful manner and without fear of judgment from others and, second, listeners should assume good faith on the part of whomever is speaking—especially when they disagree with the speaker.

For many years, I have included in my syllabus statements about speaking civilly and professionally. I tell my students that it is a part of their professional development that they can start to practice their first week of law school. I now resonate with the idea of assuming good faith on the part of the speaker and plan to add it as a regular syllabus component. However, it is important that I do not let offensive statements find cover just because they are cloaked in good faith garb. I hope that by setting forth the good faith statement as a core principle at the beginning of the class, it will not be prone to misuse. As with any new practice, how it will go remains to be seen. But I am learning to be comfortable with the uncomfortable.

Authenticity as a Humanizing Technique

A further means of humanizing law school education is to help students develop and reflect on who they will be as lawyers. This takes many forms, including professional identity discussions, ethics interwoven throughout the curriculum, clinical experiences, and considerations of a student's "lawyering style." Lawyering style is a rather broad landscape, but when I discuss it, I give my students one specific piece of guidance: They will be well-served by making sure that whatever style they choose, it is consistent and comfortable with their own personality and with their own sense of who they are.

That can be a challenging directive, especially for law students who attend directly from college. They are just on the cusp of adulthood. This, though, is what makes it all the more important that the issues of professional development, professional identity formation, and professional responsibility are attended to throughout the students' legal education.

A void in this area, especially in the crucial first year of law school, will be filled with something. Absent guidance, what fills it is less likely to redound to the benefit of the law student, the young lawyer, future clients, the legal profession, or the pursuit and administration of justice. This is not because law students come to law school lacking a moral compass or the desire to pursue justice. In fact, it is just the opposite. My years of teaching inform me that many law students come to law school in order to be the voice of the unheard, to seek justice, to right societal wrongs. However, if law students have, as their template, the morally and ethically challenged lawyers who populate movies, TV and streaming service series, and some John Grisham novels, then their lawyering style and their professional identity will suffer.

How lawyers are portrayed in both fact and fiction comes up in other ways as well. For instance, many daily events involve law and lawsuits. Consequently, teaching law can be a constant Law & Order "ripped from the headlines" episode. Or the professor can decide to ignore what is happening beyond the classroom. It can be a hard decision, but I believe some things are too significant to ignore. Or put differently, to ignore them teaches students another lesson: The law is sterile, the teacher is afraid, or the topic is too difficult. This is not a lesson that I want to teach.

The baseless lawsuits over the 2020 presidential elections serve as a recent example. These suits were dismissed with alacrity by courts of all stripes. They were also generally filed by lawyers who should have known better. This was happening in real time as my students and I were covering material about the obligation of lawyers not to bring lawsuits that lack a basis in law or fact. My classroom messages about lawyerly obligations and ethics radically mismatched the messages from real-life law practice that were plastering headlines, social media, or whatever source serves as the students' news platform.

Students were dismayed, some even wondering if studying law had been the right choice. It was clear to me that I could not ignore these events. Even though I had much mandatory material to cover, a few minutes were necessary here and there to at least acknowledge the reality outside the classroom walls or, in this case, the Zoom platform we inhabited in pandemic times.

My choice to discuss these real-time topics does not need justification. Nonetheless, it is supported by the Carnegie Report on Legal Education's caution that law teaching leaves students confused if it only has a laser focus on the material facts and the law, while jettisoning the moral and justice lenses.

Continuing on the Humanizing Path

Although being set forth here in a linear fashion, there is much overlap and shared content in these efforts. There is a connection, for example, between forming a professional identity and knowing that persons within the profession are suffering negative mental health effects and significantly high rates of drug and alcohol dependence.

The bringing forth of this connection was, for some, new data. For others, it was statistical validation of what they had long known. In any event, it was a catalyst for change. Of course, any change presents a challenge of persuasion, especially in the hoary halls of the legal academy. Add to the challenge the reality that many who have identified or acknowledged this problem, and argued on behalf of its amelioration, are persons with lesser status within the academy. Be they academic support teachers, writing faculty, deans of students, or clinical faculty, these legal educators are more likely to see students in different settings and in smaller cohorts. They are thus privy to the harms students experience in a more direct and personal way. However, they may lack the power with the institution to effect change.

Further, it is time to realize that the individuals occupying these positions already have enough on their plates and work a 12-month contract to boot. They are too often paid less but asked to do more. Deans and individual faculty members must be integrally involved. They must join the deans of students, career development staff, academic support personnel, and clinical faculty in addressing the issues of student distress, well-being, and professionalism. This endeavor should also include students—they are the ones with their lives and health at stake and should have a role in crafting the remedy (Albrecht et al., 2019).

The good news is that many law faculty and administrations are onboard, at least intellectually. The rub is making it happen, particularly when making it happen effectively involves working collaboratively and collectively across the curriculum. Silos are well-entrenched in higher education, and faculty members who do not want to join in the endeavor are generally free to bypass it.

Law faculty and Deans—please step up. Deans, be creative to find ways to make this an institution-wide endeavor, including the faculty. It could be through curricular reform, committee charges, or the dreaded faculty retreat dedicated to this issue. Law faculty must realize the role they had in creating the problem and the position they must occupy in fixing it. Every institution player must turn their attention on how to execute needed changes throughout the life of the law school. Only then will the change that has begun gain the widespread adoption it needs.

As members of one law school's wellness task force noted, faculty by now had knowledge of the problem. But in order to have institutional change, faculty must be made aware (by the others who already knew) that these overstressed law students are not merely dismal statistics but rather their very own students sitting in their very own classes.

REFERENCES

20th Century Fox. (1973). *The Paper Chase* [DVD]. United States.
Albrecht, K., et al. (2019). Wellness as practice, not product: A collaborative approach to fostering a healthier, happier law school community. *Santa Clara Law Review, 59*, 369.
Buchanan, B., & Coyle, J. C. (2017). *National task force on lawyer well-being: Creating a movement to improve well-being in the legal profession.* American Bar Association. https://lawyerwellbeing.net/wp-content/upl oads/2017/11/Lawyer-Wellbeing-Report.pdf.
Carrington, P. D., & Conley, J. J. (1977). The alienation of law students. *Michigan Law Review, 75*(5/6), 887–899.
Cicchino, P. M. (2001). Defending humanity. *American University Journal of Gender, Social Policy & the Law, 9*(1), 1–10.
Conway, D., Holley-Walker, D., Mutcherson, K., Onwuachi-Willig, A., & Pratt, C. (2021). *Law deans antiracist clearinghouse project.* Association of American Law Schools. https://www.aals.org/antiracist-clearinghouse/.
Daicoff, S. (1997). Lawyer, know thyself: Review of empirical research on attorney attributes bearing on professionalism. *American University Law Review, 46*(5), 1337–1428.
Dunlap, J. A. (2008). I'd just as soon flunk you as look at you the evolution to humanizing in large classroom. *Washburn Law Journal, 47*(2), 389–418.
Hess, G. F., Friedland, S. I., Schwartz, M. H., & Sparrow, S. (2011). *Techniques for teaching law 2.* Carolina Academic Press.
Jackson, J. T. (2021). Wellness and law: Reforming legal education to support student wellness. *Howard Law Journal, 65*(1).
Krieger, L. S. (2002). Institutional denial about the dark side of law school, and fresh empirical guidance for constructively breaking the silence. *Journal of Legal Education, 52*(1/2), 112–129.
Krieger, L. S. (2008). Human nature as a new guiding philosophy for legal education and the profession, *Washburn Law Journal, 47*(247).
Kuo, S. (2021, May). *Good faith statements* (email on file with author).
Law deans antiracist clearinghouse project. Association of American Law Schools. (2020). https://www.aals.org/antiracist-clearinghouse/.
Marks, J. (2021). https://www.medicinenet.com/hippocratic_oath/definition.htm.
Organ, J. M., Jaffe, D. B., & Bender, K. M. (2016). Suffering in silence: The survey of law student well-being and the reluctance of law students to seek

help for substance use and mental health concerns. *Journal of Legal Education,* 66(1), 116–156.

Rubin, E. (2007). What's wrong with Langdell's method, and what to do about it. *Vanderbilt Law Review,* 60(2), 609–666.

Schuwerk, R. P. (2004). The law professor as fiduciary: What duties do we owe to our students. *South Texas Law Review,* 45(4), 753–814.

Stuckey, R. (2007). *Best practices for legal education.* CLEA.

Sullivan, W. M., Colby, A., Wegner, W. J., Bond, L., & Shulman, L. S. (2007). *Educating lawyers: Preparation for the profession of law* (1st ed.). Jossey-Bass (Carnegie Report).

Turow, S. (1977). *One L: The turbulent true story of a first year at Harvard Law School* (1st ed.). Putnam.

Xplore. (n.d.). *Saint Teresa of Avila Quotes.* BrainyQuote. https://www.brainy quote.com/quotes/saint_teresa_of_avila_153909.

CHAPTER 13

Embodied Education at Dev Sanskriti Vishwavidyalaya: Narratives from the Field on How a University in Northern India Is Transforming Students

Danielle C. Johansen and Maureen P. Hall

There is need for an educational institution which could mold its students into noble and enlightened human beings: Selfless, warm-hearted, compassionate and kind.

—Pandit Sriram Sharma (1911–1990)

This last chapter of *Academia from the Inside* has been designed to explore for readers the Eastern roots of embodied education, the organizing concept of this book. Readers are invited *inside* the philosophy and pedagogical approaches of Dev Sanskriti Vishwavidyalaya (DSVV), a unique university located in northern India. The ideas and practices at DSVV have been forged from Pandit Srirarm Sharma's vision of a university designed to cultivate the character of individuals and also

D. C. Johansen (✉) · M. P. Hall
University of Massachusetts Dartmouth, North Dartmouth, MA, USA

© The Author(s), under exclusive license to Springer Nature Switzerland AG 2021
M. P. Hall and A. K. Brault (eds.), *Academia from the Inside*,
https://doi.org/10.1007/978-3-030-83895-9_13

prepare them to be global citizens and changemakers. Dr. Chinmay Pandya, Pandit Sriram Sharma's only grandchild, oversees and directs this university and serves to maintain and develop his grandfather's vision.

This chapter captures the educational and global vision of Pandit Sriram Sharma's aspirations, in part through the impact of the daily pedagogical practices that are designed to mold individuals into better human beings. It also captures Dr. Chinmay Pandya's characterization of his grandfather's powerful and universal messages that DSVV brings to the world. In his words that begin this chapter, Pandit Sriram Sharma calls for a new kind of educational institution; DSVV is a manifestation of this idea. It has become clear as the world has struggled to traverse this global pandemic that Pandit Sriram Sharma's vision for global change is needed more than ever. We invite readers to journey inside DSVV, through our lived experiences at DSVV, interviews with Dr. Chinmay Pandya, as well as through personal narratives from other professors and students who have visited this university and experienced embodied education firsthand.

ABOUT THE AUTHORS AND THEIR CONNECTIONS TO DSVV

Dr. Maureen P. Hall, now a full professor of education in Massachusetts, is a teacher educator who earned tenure and the rank of associate professor in 2009. She then applied for a Fulbright in India and was awarded both the Fulbright and her first sabbatical in her academic career.

Danielle Johansen, who holds a Master of Arts in Teaching, is an inclusion special education teacher for eighth graders. She is a mother of two young children, a stepmother of a teenager, and a wife. She is currently working toward a special educator administrator license at Bridgewater State University in Massachusetts.

Maureen's journey to DSVV began in 2010. As she prepared to conduct Fulbright research in India, an acquaintance invited her to DSVV. She couldn't have known that DSVV would become her spiritual education home, one that would be life-changing for her as a person and as an academic. She has since visited the university more than 10 times over the past eleven years.

In 2012, Danielle expressed interest in teaching in India to Dr. Maureen P. Hall at a dinner for graduate students at the University of Massachusetts Dartmouth, where Dr. Hall was a professor of hers. Dr. Hall asked Dr. Chinmay Pandya if there could be an opportunity for

Danielle to travel and live at DSVV for an extended amount of time, and he responded with a resounding yes. During her stay, Dr. Hall encouraged Danielle to write in both a personal journal, and weekly "Indian Reports" to share with family and friends about her experiences; some portions from these Reports are shared throughout the chapter. After spending almost four months at DSVV in 2013, Danielle left the university with new outlooks and understandings of herself as an educator and as a person.

In 2021, Maureen invited Danielle to collaborate in writing this chapter. In that process, both spent time reflecting deeply on their DSVV experiences and on what DSVV has meant to each, as individuals, as professor and student, and now as good friends.

DSVV's Inception: Vision and Location

The spirituality that pervades India is palpable even in the geographical location of the university. DSVV's campus is located in the sacred city of Haridwar in the northern state of Uttarakhand, approximately six hours (by car or train) north of Delhi. The word "Haridwar" translates to mean "gateway to God." The city is one of the seven holiest cities for Hindus, in part because Haridwar is where the sacred Ganges River, beginning in the Himalayas, enters the plains of India for the first time. Nestled between the banks of the Ganges River and the foothills of the Himalayan Mountains, the space creates what local Indians refer to as "vibrations."

Pandit Sriram Sharma, on whose vision DSVV was founded, was a great scholar, freedom fighter, and visionary who lived from 1911 to 1990. He was the architect of a mass transformation that began with the larger movement of All World Gayatri Pariwar (AWGP), an organization dedicated to changing the world through the transmutation of the global consciousness. This change in global consciousness includes uplifting all people, regardless of race, caste, gender, or religion, in order to be the best possible human they can be. Pandit Sriram Sharma's movement continues to grow and flourish: it now has more than 100 million members worldwide. Pandit Srirarm Sharma had the idea of creating a university for students, both national and international, that would contain some of the same founding principles. However, it would not come to fruition within his lifetime, with others going on to found DSVV, in 2002.

Dr. Chinmay Pandya, as the Pro Vice Chancellor of DSVV, gives service by carefully maintaining his grandfather's vision into educational practice. "Creation comes from the creator and Pandit Sriram Sharma was the creator," Pandya notes. He refers to himself as "a torchbearer, a gardener who takes pride in keeping the garden well-maintained" (June 18, 2021, personal communication). That garden has been not only maintained but extended: Pandya's accomplishments and global reach at DSVV are also noteworthy. For example, he has cultivated more than 60 collaborative relationships between DSVV and other institutions of higher education around the world.

EMBODIED EDUCATION AT DSVV: THEORETICAL FRAMEWORK

Dr. Chinmay Pandya extends western notions of spirituality in education, as exemplified in Parker Palmer's work, to a new level of developing global consciousness. This extension informs the theoretical framework of this book, one we refer to as embodied education.

Embodied education, as explored in this book in both theory and practice, is about humanizing education. This humanizing starts with cultivating self-knowledge. There are many routes to self-knowledge, including mantra practice, educational practices, and interventions. Through these practices and others, individuals can uncover their true identities and live in their own truth.

DSVV as an institution describes itself as: "A University for the Global, Cultural & Spiritual Renaissance." The goals of the university show that DSVV aims to:

> unite contemporary education with spiritual training to cultivate well-rounded, competent and personally uplifted graduates, who possess a scientifically grounded understanding and experience of spiritual transformation and a powerful drive to use their gifts to promote the greater good of society. (DSVV Prospectus, 2020–2021)

The emphasis here is on human growth of spirit, rather than on physical or material gains. DSVV graduates should leave with the understanding that being a good person is fundamental to creating global change on an individual level. This emphasis on education as a conduit for becoming a better person is an important part of embodied education. Education becomes much more than just gaining knowledge, instead, embodied education is both a way of being and of living one's life.

Ultimately, two educational concepts underlie DSVV's pedagogies: *Shiksha* and *Vidya*. *Shiksha* refers to a traditional idea of education— achieving abilities to earn a living, which is a common goal of higher education institutions. *Vidya* is education focused on making a person into a good human being through their individual and internal character development. *Vidya* is unique and specific to DSVV. Together, these two intertwined concepts are built into the design of the courses at DSVV.

THE NEED FOR A NEW PARADIGM OF GLOBAL CONSCIOUSNESS

Recent global changes, Dr. Chinmay Pandya notes, constitute "a paradigm shift in the global mindset or consciousness," one that has started to "have a shift in the developmental viewpoint of the humanity— but more towards the technological advances" (Pandya, personal interview, August 2020).

As we make advances in science and technology in the external world, he explains, our internal worlds also change. The world experiences "scenes of internal chaos, confusion and conflict, disillusionment and dissatisfaction." Without a way to anchor the self in reality, this internal chaos is exacerbated through technology. He expands:

> Every single person's mind has become much more tormented than probably a soldier had expected on the battlefield of the last century," Dr. Chinmay Pandya notes. Furthermore, advances in science, technology, and materialism come at a cost: "on the one hand we have huge houses, but on the other hand—we have broken down the families. On the one hand we are reaching for the moon, but on the other hand—we don't even remember who we are," he says. Dr. Chinmay Pandya underlines the drastic increase in anxiety and suffering created by these technological advances. "Now we have means to live but no meaning to live for.

However, because technology makes our lives easier in many ways, it also gives people the opportunities for self-reflection:

> Now people can focus more on their insides. They can focus more on their inner purpose and their reason to be here in this life. Why? 'Am I

here to *only* increase the population of this planet or am I supposed to do something meaningful? 'Am I scheduled to leave a legacy here?' is the question that becomes much more important than ever before.

To combat feelings of anxiety and hopelessness, Dr. Chinmay Pandya urges us to seek out the self-knowledge required to understand our own individual place and purpose in the world:

> This meaning and purpose—behind this adventure in what we call the human life—this is more important than any other thing that we do.... We are born with more capabilities and possibilities for a greater life— than most of us would ever realize. Everyone, in their own moments, can feel the sacred connection. They can perceive this divine potential...and our lives carry an unmanifested purpose, which [Pandit Sriram Sharma] referred to as a 'latent divinity.' He said that everyone has got this latent divinity. And for us to be connected with our true...purpose—this is the purpose of being here. And people need to remember the divine possibility and potential that they carry.

This approach of conveying to students, faculty and visitors of DSVV that every individual carries with them a potential for salient purpose that derives from self-reflection, encompasses embodied education. To find, understand, and honor one's true self is to know and understand one's purpose. Through the unique educational approaches and practices at DSVV, students are given opportunities to manifest Pandit Shriram Sharma's notion of latent divinity. The key, as work at DSVV demonstrates, is to create space for this understanding.

Daily Practices at DSVV: Creating Space for Embodied Education

In order to encourage students to become better humans, DSVV has created spaces within its university with each student having the opportunity to cultivate their internal self (*Vidya*), versus focusing only on the external educational portion (*Shiksha*). Many of the daily practices that occur on campus invoke internal feelings of calm and mental lucidity through their natural courses: there is the daily Yagya of Gayatri Mantra, daily opportunities for meditation, and the expectation that every person contributes some form of daily service to the university. All of these practices in combination create the opportunity for self-reflection which leads to the ability to develop and foster the student's human self, hence creating the opportunities for embodied education.

The Gayatri Mantra Yagya Daily Morning Ceremony

The Yagya Ceremony begins each day at 6:00 a.m. As Danielle describes in an Indian Report from May 2013:

> Yagya is a fire ceremony involving chanting mantras, and throwing a special mixture of wood chips, spices, and herbs into a fire. On average, 6-8 people sit around each fire pit that is made of metal and pyramid-shaped... there are eight pyramids on a built up cement platform. So there is a large cement platform with people sitting in different groupings during the ceremony, and someone guides the ceremony over a loudspeaker. Essentially, the Yagya ceremony is a symbolic selfless sacrifice for God, the earth, and the universe. I enjoy going each morning, and there is something ancient and peaceful in the ceremony. Of course, the ceremony itself is in fact ancient- the directions for the ceremony are contained in the Hindu text Yajurveda, which some estimate was written between 1000 and 600 BC.

In India, "God" is a much more universal concept than in the West. There are hundreds of Hindu deities and demi-Gods, including the God that exists in each living human. Through the chanting of mantras together in groups of forty-eight to sixty-four people, Yagya creates a high level of group meditation.

The Yagya ceremony at DSVV focuses on the Gayatri Mantra. Gayatri Mantra, simplified, is supposed to focus the mind and meditative practice on the central question of "what is my purpose and what is my path?" Gayatri Mantra is an ancient Sanskrit mantra that infuses all practices at DSVV. All Sanskrit mantras are created with what is meant to be the ideal breathing and chanting pattern for meditation. Sanskrit mantras are meant to create specific vibrations through the syllables, breathing, and distinct sounds that are all different and meant to be specific to its goals.

It is also significant to note that mantras are repeated words or phrases that are chanted during meditation, and meditation has been scientifically proven many times over now in Western culture to have phenomenal effects for mental lucidity and overall impact on an individual's well-being. Some people find that by chanting mantras, it keeps the mind able to focus on the chanting, versus "clearing the mind" which is quite difficult to do and maintain for longer than seconds or minutes (depending on the individual's ability to stay clear minded.)

By providing a space for the practice of daily Yagya, DSVV creates the intention and opportunity for students to wake early and begin each day with a clear mind. With focus, the student is more prepared to engage in learning in the educational spaces. In fact, by participating in Yagya the mind is able to also allow for more self-reflection, through the mantra chanting and other meditative practices.

Opportunities for Meditation

A central practice is the Naad Yog, a collective 15-min evening meditation. As the DSVV prospectus describes it: "At 6 o'clock in the evening, after all the classes are completed, the melodious tunes of the flute fill the air, students [and faculty] sit down wherever they are and participate in group meditation" (DSVV Prospectus, 2020–2021). All gates to DSVV are locked; they will be re-opened at 6:15 p.m. and life will resume its buzzing normalcy. But for these fifteen minutes, meditative music "blankets" the campus for all to hear. Near the center of the campus, there is the Shiva temple called Pragyeshwar Mahadev. An amphitheater surrounds the temple, and many of the students and faculty come, alone or together, to sit in silence and absorb the vibrations that occur when so many people sit in collective silence together (Fig. 13.1).

As well, at any time, students and faculty can utilize several spaces on campus for meditation, such as the rose gardens, or the Shiva temple, or they may choose to make the short 7–8 block walk to Shantikunj Ashram. The Shantikunj Ashram, like all ashrams, is a place where people can gather spiritually and temporarily stay at; Shantikunj is also the home-base of AWGP. Specifically at Shantikunj is an air conditioned Himalayan Meditation Room, the focal point of which is the front stage containing a large replica of the Himalayan Mountains. The room has very dim lighting, with Himalayan Mountains illuminated up front. In this room there is no music or noise, just silence in the cool air in front of the impressive range of the highest mountains in the world.

Fig. 13.1 Shiva temple near the center of DSVV campus (photo by Libby Falk Jones)

The Gayatri Mantra: A Guiding Mantra that Infuses DSVV

Gayatri Mantra is fully integrated into all teaching and learning spaces at DSVV; it comes both before and after any educational event. Here is Gayatri Mantra in Sanskrit:

> *Om Bhuḥ Bhuvaḥ Svaḥ*
> *Tat-Savituḥ Vareṇyaṃ*
> *Bhargo Devasya Dhīmahi*
> *Dhiyo Yo Naḥ Prachodayāt*

According to Swami Vivekananda, the meaning of the Gayatri Mantra in English is as follows: "We meditate on the glory of that Being who has produced this universe; may She enlighten our minds" (Vivekananda, 1915). The "she" refers to Gayatri who is a Hindu Goddess with many manifestations; one of which is the Goddess of Vedic Hymns and

Melodies. The Vedas are the oldest Sanskrit text in India and are the oldest scriptures of Hinduism.

Gayatri Mantra finds its origins in ancient sacred Indian texts and is considered one of the oldest known Sanskrit mantras. It is a touchstone to all life at DSVV. Students chant it over and over at yagya, and often before classes begin. When any conferences or seminars are held, mainly populated with international visitors and presenters, Gayatri Mantra is chanted.

A Commitment of Daily Selfless Service

A third unique daily occurrence is the expectation that every student and faculty member volunteer one hour of daily service to the university. This service can range very much from person to person; they may assist in working in one of the many areas on campus (such as the print shop, kitchens, or classrooms). This daily service is in direct correlation with Vidya, as mentioned earlier, that is the focus of developing one's character. By volunteering time, a person becomes an integral part of DSVV, necessary for its continual operation.

The Social Internship: A Requirement for All DSVV Students

Perhaps the most important pedagogical piece of Pandit Sriram Sharma's philosophy of *Vidya* translated into practice is DSVV's Social Internship, which acts as the catalyst for the development of encouraging the betterment of students. Pandit Sriram Sharma said that everyone should contribute to make society a better place and that is the function of the Social Internship at DSVV, one that all students must complete before they can graduate with their degrees.

The Social Internship requires each student to devote a minimum of two months to volunteering and sometimes providing some form of education to others. For example, many students spend time in rural villages, teaching the villagers specific skills that can assist them in the future. In addition, DSVV students also share with them the daily practices used at DSVV, including Yagya, meditation, yogic exercises, and give informational lectures. These efforts often garner interest in village students. Agamveer Singh, one of the elders at DSVV, shared this with Maureen during a recent phone conversation: "Mothers in the villages do not always understand what DSVV students bring to the village, but they encourage their daughters to apply to the university."

Dr. Chinmay Pandya said this Social Internship "is the integral part of this pedagogical model." By requiring students to work toward enhancing someone else's lifestyle or situation, an opportunity is created for gratitude and recognition of one's own situation. Giving time is also a method for creating happiness in the human psyche; by volunteering or helping others, humans feel a level of happiness that is incomparable to simply participating in materialistic or shallow experiences. An equivalent may be something like a student at a Western university spending a semester working for Habitat for Humanity, as a requirement for graduation. Overall, this Social Internship is an important component of embodied education because it gives students a hands-on experience where they can make a difference.

How These Practices Contribute to Creation of Embodied Education at DSVV

These practices that occur at DSVV are congruent with the embodied education that occurs there, and contribute to their growing global reach. Through mantra chanting, meditative practices, and selfless social service, there is the opportunity to reflect on one's self. Meditation creates a space in the mind for growth and reflection naturally, by giving the person who practices the ability to often reflect on one's self and actions in an almost removed and non-judgmental way. By doing so, it opens the self up to growth. Furthermore, daily meditation removes a person from the technology that often pervades our days, creating mental chaos and anxiety.

Therefore, there is quite obviously a global need for these educational approaches, ones that could directly impact others who partake or recreate some of the activities that DSVV incorporates into its pedagogical structure. Although it is true that some Western universities integrate internships and use other initiatives like service learning, the activities at DSVV are outside of any Western norms, such as creating common meditative spaces without technology, including a requirement of a social internship before graduation, and earmarking a daily hour of service toward assisting the university in continual operations. Students who give their time and energy may learn and grow more than when in a traditional classroom. Overall, embodied education practices utilized in

DSVV's approaches help to create a more rounded student and human: an empathetic global citizen practiced in self-reflection.

THE WORLD AS ONE GLOBAL FAMILY: PHILOSOPHY AND PRACTICE

Dr. Chinmay Pandya often underlines and communicates the notion that all people should act as "one global family." He participates in many world forums in which he often reiterates this idea. For example, in October 2019 at the One Young World Global Forum in London, U.K. Dr. Chinmay Pandya was one of the keynotes, and at this particular forum there were faith leaders representing different traditions with him on stage. For context, One Young World Organization (https://www.one youngworld.com/) brings young people together from more than 190 countries worldwide in order to identify new and young leaders in a global society that requires shifts in the paradigm that is leadership, with a particular focus on climate change and impact.

In Dr. Chinmay Pandya's address at the One Young World Forum, he shared a personal story from his teenage years in India when he was a medical student. There were some riots, and he and a group of other students found themselves running for safety and luckily, were able to find shelter together. They were quite terrified, as it was a dangerous and somewhat dire situation. It was then they realized that out of the five of them, there were four different religious traditions represented. Dr. Chinmay Pandya described the situation in this way: "When fear was frightening us, humanity was uniting us." Dr. Chinmay Pandya comes from a Hindu tradition, but he identifies as a global citizen, one who respects all human beings—no matter which tradition(s) individuals may identify with.

There are myriad examples of DSVV's extension of creating "one global family," including through their ongoing crisis response efforts in the face of travesties. DSVV and AWGP continually provide relief to worldwide, and Indian, catastrophes. For example, during the Nepali Earthquake in 2015, they provided people to assist, donated resources, and accepted orphans into the university while providing free tuition and boarding. (https://www.tribuneindia.com/news/archive/features/global-gayatri-family-actively-involved-in-relief-77528).

In 2012, Maureen sent an email to Dr. Chinmay Pandya to inquire about the possibility of sending Danielle to stay and teach at the University; the reply received from Dr. Chinmay Pandya arrived with the subject line, "Absolute Confirmation." In his email, he further expanded on the notion that Maureen was a part of the DSVV family, and therefore could invite anyone to her home. Maureen would go on to invite over a dozen people to visit and stay at DSVV in the coming years, to the present day, and the following section shares some of those guests' and visitors' embodied experiences at DSVV.

Narratives of Westerners' Lived Experiences of Embodied Education at DSVV

Since 2010, Maureen has continued to visit this university and bring her students, colleagues, and friends to experience this unique institution in northern India. In 2012, Danielle Johansen, one of Maureen's graduate education students, showed an interest in visiting India. She would travel there for almost four months and teach an English Communications Class to professors at the university. In 2016, Emily Butler would be another student to travel and teach at DSVV. She would stay for two months and also teach a course, drawing upon a curriculum Danielle wrote and left for other visitors to utilize.

In 2018, several professors from America visited the university; Libby Falk Jones, an English professor from Berea College in Kentucky, visited the university for several weeks starting in February 2018. Jones captures her experiences of what it was like to teach journalism students. In March 2018, Professors Carol Shaw Austad and Kristi Oliver visited DSVV for almost a week. They both presented at the 1st Annual Transforming Education Across East and West: Building Intercultural, Aesthetic, and Interdisciplinary Bridges. Aminda O'Hare, one of Maureen's colleagues in Massachusetts, with whom she researched mindfulness and education, visited DSVV in December 2019 at Maureen's invitation. Although Aminda had never met Dr. Chinmay Pandya in person, she had met him over Skype calls in 2014 and 2015. Aminda and Maureen also made grant submissions for the Obama-Singh grant, which would connect DSVV with their university in Massachusetts.

What follows are reports of how the Westerners named above experienced the day-to-day educational approaches and practices used at DSVV.

2010-Present: Maureen's Embodied Education at DSVV: Finding Her Spiritual Education Home

In July 2010, I found out that I had been awarded a Fulbright in India. At the end of the same month, I met Sanjay Saxena at a local higher education conference. When he found out that I had been awarded a Fulbright in India, he told me about Dev Sanskriti Vishwavidyalaya (DSVV) as it was a learning institution he was very connected to in India. At the end of our conversation, he invited me to stay at this university in northern India for a month before beginning my time as a Fulbrighter in India.

I didn't know then, but Sanjay's invitation to this university in India would go on to change my life in academia as well as my personal life. What I also didn't know was that DSVV would become my spiritual education home, a place that I would share with my students and other educators.

I arrived in India in late September, and after a week each in Delhi and Allahabad, I traveled by train to Haridwar. I had culture shock when I arrived in India, but I started to feel more comfortable after the first few days at DSVV. I was staying at the guest house and started to participate in the day-to-day activities on campus. What follows is a excerpt from my journal from October 2010, written about a week after I arrived at DSVV:

> What a day here! I got up this morning and went to the Yagya ceremony (the bonfires in the morning at 5:45 a.m.—which is a purification ritual). I just received a gift from a professor here who gave me a small book about Yagyas. After the ceremony, I took my walk around campus. I saw the sun come up over the Himalayas....which really struck me. It was as if I had just realized again: I am in northern India!

I connect my time and ongoing relationship with DSVV and Dr. Chinmay Pandya as the key to my route to "living divided no more," to embrace my own spiritual nature, and to continue to develop myself in a range of ways. For example, India taught me patience:

> Today makes my seventh day at Dev Sanskriti University in Haridwar and my sixteenth day in India. Haridwar is located about seven hours north and slightly east of New Delhi (The estimated hours are by train or by car.) This university where I am staying is a bit of heaven. The grounds are beautiful, clean, and inviting. The people are really nice. What am I

learning? Patience is one thing I am learning more and more about. I guess that means I realize that I would see the world a lot more pleasantly at times--if I could cultivate more patience in myself. India is teaching me patience. Things don't always work and plans don't always manifest as they are planned. There are confusing times and miscommunications that can be very frustrating.

I have always been a high-strung person, and, admittedly, patience was never my strong suit. I was living through the culture shock I had in India, and I realized my time at DSVV helped me to develop patience with others and patience with myself.

At the end of my first visit to DSVV in October of 2010, after spending several weeks at the Guest House, Dr. Chinmay Pandya requested a meeting with me on the last day before I left. I remember so clearly the words Dr. Chinmay Pandya said to me because they have and continue to resonate and become true many times since he said them. In that meeting he said this to me: "Dr. Hall—this is your home. You can come here anytime you want, and you can bring anyone you want. And you don't have to let us know when you are coming—because this is your home."

Of any experience I had in India, Dr. Chinmay Pandya's words and message were the most powerful. I was overwhelmed in a good way. He spoke to my heart, as a person and as a teacher. My connection to DSVV makes clear to me just how different various landscapes of academia can be and just how different my home institution in the USA is from my home institution in India! When I use the word "home" the first time, it simply indicates where I teach in terms of geography. When I use "home" in reference to DSVV, it indicates where my heart and soul live at my spiritual educational home in India.

Looking back to another experience, shortly after I arrived at DSVV, I was taken on a tour of Shantikunj. There I saw pictures of Sanjay and Sangeeta Saxena's marriage at Shantikunj. I couldn't have known then that Sanjay Saxena, who was the "acquaintance" who invited me to DSVV in 2010, would go on to become one of my family members.

Later, in 2015, my partner Dan asked me to marry him. I reached out to Dr. Chinmay Pandya to see if I could have a spiritual ceremony at DSVV or Shantikunj in March of 2015, when we were planning our next trip to DSVV. Dr. Chinmay Pandya wrote that he would be so honored to arrange a wedding ceremony for Daniel and me, and that he was happy "that I would be married at my home in India." He helped arrange all of the minute details that go into planning a traditional Indian wedding ceremony. For example, he arranged for a Haldi and Mahendi ceremony the day before the wedding. This was Dan's first visit to India, and he was instantly accepted as a family member. Dan and I were so amazed at the ways in which Dr. Chinmay Pandya "welcomed us home" for this spiritual wedding.

My relationship with DSVV within India deepened and served as a needed healing—following Palmer's model of educational reform. I continue to find ways not to internalize the organizational values of my own academic institution. Drawing on the ideas and practices put forward by Dr. Chinmay Pandya and Palmer identified in the introduction of this work, I resonate on the words of Palmer: "to find a new center for one's life, a center external to the institution and its demands. This does not mean leaving the institution physically; one may stay at one's post. But it does mean taking one's spiritual leave" (2017, p. 174).

A few years after my first visit, a student, Danielle Johansen, approached me about spending some time in India. I sent an email to Dr. Chinmay Pandya to ask if it would be possible to send her there to teach, and he responded with the email title "Absolute Confirmation," and my heart soared. My feelings reflected exactly what Dr. Chinmay Pandya wrote to me: "We have always valued having a very emotional and strong relationship with you and it is wonderful to see that such understanding is now evolving into something significant... let it be this way for the future - that anyone that you support or recommend, we shall be able to host them fully for their duration of stay" (Pandya, personal communication, December 2012).

My transformative experiences at DSVV have been significant in my journey to understanding embodied education as both a concept and a lived reality. In discovering my spiritual education home at DSVV, I found a place that I could regularly travel to, and invite others to join me, in all serving to reconnect me with my purpose and passion for educating teachers and educating all persons. At this university in northern India, I found the balance to offset the disconnect I often encountered within traditional academia. As a member of DSVV's global family, I have followed through and taken seriously Dr. Chinmay Pandya's invitation to my spiritual home. Over the past eleven years, I have invited over a dozen people to visit DSVV since I first found my spiritual education home. In April 2014, I was also awarded visiting professor status at DSVV by Dr. Chinmay Pandya. I have been the keynote of several conferences at

DSVV, brought and socially sponsored several student teachers there for an Indian teaching experience, and even had a wedding ceremony with my husband at Shantikunj in 2015. More recently, my husband, also an educator, was the keynote speaker for two annual international robotics' conferences at DSVV in 2018 and 2019. I continue to visit every year, and I often bring guests along to have their own embodied educational experiences. Dr. Chinmay Pandya has made it clear, both in words and actions over the years, that I am an important member of the DSVV family; DSVV is my spiritual education home.

With the global pandemic, I have not been able to visit my spiritual education home since 2020. I have been worrying about DSVV, as all of the news reports tell of the dire situation in India. However, I have kept in regular touch with Dr. Chinmay Pandya and other members of my spiritual education home. I was heartened to know that both DSVV and Shantikunj (the ashram connected to DSVV) continue to help with relief efforts worldwide. They follow through on taking care of family members, and I am so heartened to be part of this family!

2013: Danielle's Embodied Education at DSVV: Discovering Resiliency

It was December of 2012, and I was at a dinner at the University of Massachusetts Dartmouth sitting next to Dr. Maureen Hall. The dinner was for students who had finished their student teaching that semester, with all of the education professors dispersed at tables throughout with the students. I was seated at a table with Dr. Hall because she had over-seen my student teaching that semester; I had also taken a class of hers previously.

Dr. Hall is an endless energy type of person, and seems to be in a constant state of productivity. She has this incredible ability that when the seed of an idea comes into existence, she will plant it, water it, and create an environment for it to thrive, whether she has to ask others to borrow a pot or dirt or whatever she needs; she doesn't stop to overthink the situation like many others may, but instead will jump in with her spade and start digging. At that dinner, the seed of an idea was created when I turned to her while she was giving us an anecdotal story about her experiences in India, and asked, "do you think there could be an opportunity for me to teach in India?".

She looked at me for several seconds, and the seed was planted at that moment. She told me that she would reach out to a university in northern India that she had a special connection with, a place that she considered as a home, and that she had an idea that perhaps I could spend some time there teaching. The next day she emailed me to say that Dr. Chinmay Pandya had responded to the request with the subject line: "absolute confirmation."

Within a couple of months, Dr. Hall would create a scholarship fund in memory of her parents (who were both teachers) for the purpose of encouraging other students to travel to India, and I was the first recipient of the Ruel J. and Patricia A. Hall Educational Scholarship for India Fund. (See: https://www.umassd.edu/cas/news/maureen-hall.html).

In February of 2013, I boarded a plane in Boston Logan International Airport to travel to Dev Sanskriti Vishwavidyalaya to teach an English Communications Course to the university professors.

Once I arrived at DSVV, I met with Dr. Chinmay Pandya almost daily, usually for a brief five to ten minutes (he's slightly busy being Pro-Vice Chancellor of the university and all of the other work he's doing, but he always made time for me.) During these meetings, I would often express my anxieties ("how will I teach university professors?"), my experiences (he was quite often amused at some of the situations I found myself in, such as when I somehow ended up with the keys to the entire English department on my first day), and sometimes he simply shared wisdom.

Besides my daily meetings with Dr. Chinmay Pandya, I also wrote in a personal journal, and created "Indian Reports," which I would share out with friends, family, and some interested students of Dr. Hall's on a weekly basis chronicling my experiences in a public way. Living in a new culture for such an extended time came with its difficulties for me, and there were times that I truly struggled with being away from family, friends, and the simple comforts of home. In an Indian Report from March 3, 2013, after being at DSVV for just over a week, I shared this struggle:

> I want everyone to think of what they are planning on doing today.
>
> I'm sure many of you are planning on driving to work, being there most of the day. Will you bring your lunch? What will you pack for it? Are you going to go out for lunch, where will you go and with whom? After work maybe you're going home to your family, or hanging out with friends, or maybe you're just relaxing at home by yourself; watching some

TV or reading a book or something. Perhaps you need something from the grocery store or mall, and you're going to go there and pick it up after work. What will you have for dinner? Will it be take-out or cooking tonight? You are all going to be making many choices today; perhaps someone shares those choices with you, but choices you will make.

I cannot do any of these things. I cannot jump in a vehicle and drive to a store to pick up something I want or need. I cannot decide that I want eggs for breakfast, a sandwich for lunch and a burger for dinner. I can't call a friend and ask if they want to run to the mall, or catch a movie. I can't relax tonight on the couch and watch a favorite TV show.

As the newness of being somewhere different wore off, homesickness set in, and it was extremely frustrating for me at points to realize that I didn't have a lot of control over my day-to-day life. As an admitted "control freak" this was by far one of the hardest things for me. I had even arrived with clothes Dr. Hall let me borrow in order for me to fit in a little better, so I wasn't even wearing my own clothes. However, I went on to describe how I coped with it in that moment:

> Sunday morning I felt much better again, and after talking to Dr. Chinmay Pandya I felt even better; he possesses that quality that some people have in which he can soothe all of your worries and concerns and helps me see that whatever I feel, or am going through, is perfectly natural and expected.
>
> I spent some time walking around campus. Then later I went to the gardens that I like, and I listened to some music and wrote in my journal. After discussing these problems in my journal, I ended by saying the following: 'So now I am sitting in my secret garden spot, listening to some relaxing music and writing this entry. I am sitting in the shade, it is the perfect temperature, the sun is shining and I am surrounded by roses in India. Life is good.'
>
> When I returned to my room, Dr. Chinmay Pandya had had some potted flowers brought to my door; I had asked a few days ago if I could have some for my room. I placed the petunias on a table outside on my balcony, in front of my window. Every morning when I wake now, the flowers will be the first thing I see.

By speaking with Dr. Chinmay Pandya, journaling, and spending time in self-reflection, I was able to understand that while at DSVV, I didn't *need* to control every aspect of my daily life. By accepting this and letting go of some of that doubt, worry, and micromanaging that was so second-nature to my being, I was able to understand that there are times to let go and just be in a moment or experience, even if that moment or experience is uncomfortable. This is how we open ourselves to self-knowledge and growth.

While at DSVV, I would find a resiliency I hadn't known I possessed, along with a flexibility I desperately needed to learn. My experience of embodied education was cultivated through meditation, Yagya, my journaling, and my daily meetings with Dr. Chinmay Pandya; these practices accounted for reflection that led to increased self-awareness and knowledge. I learned new ways to approach difficult situations, and to this day, if I am feeling particularly stressed or anxious, I find that chanting the Gayatri Mantra silently still creates a feeling of calmness and lucidity that I have not yet been able to replicate in another way.

DSVV encompasses many things for many people, because each person's life and experience is unique. At DSVV it is this recognition that lends itself to the revolt of simple traditional education (*Shiksha*), and instead incorporates a person's singular experience and journey to assist them in becoming the best person they can be (*Vidya*). The classrooms at DSVV aren't what create the unique learning experiences, it's what each person takes away from the experience of their learning. Ultimately, DSVV provides a safe place for people to create individualized journeys, without pressure or judgment, with the simple expectation that you leave them better than when you arrived. I would like to think that I fulfilled that while there.

2016: Emily Butler's Embodied Education at DSVV: Discovering and Manifesting Purpose

Massachusetts native Emily Butler was another student who was awarded the Ruel J. and Patricia A. Hall Educational Fund for India Scholarship. She graduated from the University of Massachusetts Dartmouth in May 2016 with a bachelor's degree in psychology and had Maureen for one of her last courses at the university. In September 2016, she headed for India to teach at DSVV for two months. Like Danielle, Emily also spent considerable time with Dr. Chinmay Pandya. Emily wrote this about her experiences with DSVV's embodied education:

> I met Dr. Hall during my Spring 2016 semester. It was my senior year of my undergraduate year at the University of Massachusetts Dartmouth. I was looking for some courses to fill my schedule, and happened upon a

200-level education course. I remember Dr. Hall calling DSVV her spiritual home, and how she was welcomed and made to feel like an integral member of the campus community. I spent the semester enjoying Dr. Hall's stories and experiences, imagining what life was like and assuming I would never find out for myself. However, four months, three planes and many apprehensive tears later, I was being greeted at the guesthouse on the DSVV campus in Haridwar, India.

Dr. Hall says I have grit.

If it doesn't challenge you, it doesn't change you.

These were the very words I recited to myself throughout my journey from the East coast of the US to northern India. However, upon my arrival to DSVV, my perspective would be remodeled, reworked and significantly impacted by Dr. Chinmay Pandya and the university.

As expected, the travel had exhausted me in a way I had never experienced before. I had an overwhelming feeling of doubt. I worried about my adjustment and how I would find the emotional strength to regain confidence in my abilities. However, it was in my first meeting with Dr. Chinmay Pandya that I would be ingrained with an invaluable concept: embrace humility.

It was then that I understood the importance of self-reflection and how that translates into being a productive member of a community. Dr. Chinmay Pandya assured me that there was nothing to actually fear. He reminded me that I am supported and don't have to succumb to the unrealistic internal pressures I created in my head. This is where I learned to ask for help when I needed it. At DSVV, I quickly understood that by helping myself, I could then, in turn, better serve others. This lesson is one I have continued to practice throughout multiple aspects of my life and firmly believe that by encouraging such methods, DSVV benefits the members of their community while simultaneously contributing to a greater global cause.

In fact, it was with these learning experiences that I returned to the U.S. and completed a Masters in School Counseling at the University of Massachusetts Boston. The skills that I learned at DSVV assisted me in learning how to recognize the potential within myself to help others, and continue to carry over into my current work.

As Emily described, after meeting with Dr. Chinmay Pandya, and by engaging in reflection, she came to realize that she had to help herself first, so that she, in turn, could support others. Through the embodiment of Dr. Chinmay Pandya's words, Emily stopped doubting her own abilities, expecting the worst, and therefore was able to overcome those situations and thrive at DSVV. It could be argued that Emily in fact reached one of the ultimate goals of DSVV and achieved latent divinity: she was able to recognize and manifest her own potential for helping others, now a continuation of her chosen career of guidance counseling for young students in the USA.

2018–2019: Other US Professors' Visits to DSVV

Several professors who visited the university in 2018 have written about their experiences of DSVV's educational approaches and practices.

Libby Falk Jones's Visit: Interactions with Students

Meeting at a conference in Canada in 2014, Maureen and Libby Jones had discovered common educational interests, particularly in contemplative work. They had collaborated on some articles on mindfulness education. In spring 2018, both were on sabbatical—a perfect time for Maureen to introduce Libby to India and this unique university. Libby came with her husband, Roger, an educator and writer. Connecting with the head of DSVV's journalism department, Libby was able to meet with students. She writes about her embodied education experience:

> This hour-long journalism class is my first focused and probably my only real interaction with the undergraduates at DSVV. I'm a little nervous, quite conscious of difference—of my identity as a 73-year-old Western white woman, not familiar with their language, culture, geography, experience. Not yet fully comfortable with sacred monkeys roaming the campus or sacred cows and sadhus in orange cloaks in the town's streets. Over my western slacks and shirt, I have draped my yellow and red Gayatri scarf, with the Gayatri mantra, guiding principle of the university, scripted around the edges. It keeps slipping off my shoulder.
>
> We have pulled chairs around a long table so we can see one another. To begin: introductions. The students' names are poetry: Juvesh and Kartikeya, Avantika and Bhawna, Jagrutee and Tanushka, Bhrigu and Ruchi. They are from Lucknow, Roorkee, Kanpur, Orissa, Gurugram,

Bhopal, Patna. One is local, from Haridwar. Two are from Delhi. This is everyone's first journalism course. Prior to our meeting, I'd made some notes—distilled wisdom from my years of teaching journalism—of points I hoped we could address. But as always when I teach, I find the most important parts of the conversation are their words, not mine. I begin by asking them why they had chosen to study journalism. They wanted to travel, they told me; they wanted to serve—their families, their communities, country, and the world.

Libby's interactions with these DSVV students provided examples of embodied education because they see learning as something that they need to share with others. The impact of the daily practices at DSVV is palpable. First, students develop self-knowledge and then they understand their roles as change-agents in the world, in service to others. Pandit Sriram Sharma's vision in terms of how each person can develop the divine, what he calls "latent divinity" is evident here.

Carol Shaw Austad's Embodied Education at DSVV: Discovering a New Educational Approach

Psychology Professor Carol Shaw Austad, who teaches at Central Connecticut State University in the USA, was invited by Maureen to visit DSVV and present at an international conference. Carol shared what follows about her visit to DSVV in March 2018:

> I was in awe upon my arrival at DSVV. So much activity, but so much serenity... The Yagya Ceremony was conducted outside my window every day. I found the energy from the chanting to be irresistible. I rose from my bed and floated to the group to participate. Yagya made my day because I was tuned in to asking myself what my purpose and my path is today. I felt as if this was the place in which my personhood could develop with an emphasis on spirituality. I clearly experienced what Dr. Chinmay Pandya speaks of as global consciousness. I was acutely aware of being a member of a global family in this beautiful environment. It is one thing to read about global unity, but experiencing it imbued me with a sense of the global interdependency of the consciousness of all sentient beings. Self-reflection was 'made easy' in this environment.
> I grew during my short stay. I realized I was a small particle in Pandit Sriram Sharma's vision. I know that being a good person can be my contribution to global change. I do not know if I will ever return to DSVV, but I took tools from there [I share] with my students at my University. Along

with encouraging them to earn a degree which helps them to gain employment, I encourage them to be decent and compassionate human beings.
My gratitude to DSVV is long lasting.

Carol would take what she learned and witnessed at DSVV and apply it
to her own teaching approaches at the higher education level in the USA.
Through participating in Yagya and self-reflecting throughout her visit,
she seemed to have experienced what the local Indians refer to as the
"vibrations" at DSVV. Pandit Srirarm Sharma's vision that each person
can enact small changes that lead to larger global ones is present in Carol's
experience and in her attempts to continue to spread the vision of simply
being better to her own university students.

Kristi Oliver's Visit: An Atmosphere Ripe for Deep Connections

Kristi Oliver, former Professor of Art Education at University of
Massachusetts Dartmouth, is now a consultant for Davis Publications
in Worcester, Massachusetts. She and Maureen were good colleagues at
the University of Massachusetts Dartmouth and collaborated on several
peer-reviewed articles, workshops, and conference presentations. Maureen
invited Kristi to come to India and Krist wrote this about her visit to
DSVV in March 2018:

> Just before I left the US, I had spent the day with university level art
> education students at a local museum where we practiced contemplative
> strategies for engaging with artworks in order to connect and forge mean-
> ingful experiences in and through art. Using mindfulness exercises and
> *Lectio Divina*, students struggled to disengage with technology and focus
> on the artworks. Ultimately, the exercises were successful, and the students
> felt more relaxed, connected, and engaged by the end of our session.
>
> Upon arriving at DSVV, we were only there a short time before our first
> session with DSVV students and teachers where we introduced the same
> concepts I had been practicing with my students in the US. What struck
> me was the speed at which they were able to unpack the symbols, concepts
> and spiritual underpinnings of the work we were studying. The connections
> were deep, rich, and profoundly connected to their spiritual beliefs and
> their personal experiences. The DSVV students and teachers did not seem
> to have any trouble focusing, without distractions or other commitments,
> they were simply present and ready. This contrast made me think about
> DSVV in terms of what makes a prime environment for this kind of deep
> connection – having only spent a short time there, it is immediately evident

that the philosophy of DSVV is deeply integrated into everything, the way of life, the way they educate, the experiences they have, all leading to a place of personal and communal spiritual transformation.

The sentiments and reflections offered by the DSVV students and teachers related to the *Lectio Divina* experience was completely aligned with the motto, mission and vision of DSVV as a whole. In teaching, they do not see spirituality and life as separate but one and the same, so that their education for life, spirituality, and academics run through every experience. In this place, everyone is supported and encouraged, everyone teaches and is taught, everyone and everything is integrated in such a way to support the greater good and to think within and beyond ourselves.

Kristi's experiences exemplify the setting that DSVV creates for students, faculty, and visitors that overall encompasses the capacity for creation of embodied education. Embodied education is difficult to achieve in distracted environments; the human self cannot fully reflect or transform if it is distracted. This is another piece of the meditation and Yagya that is offered at the university, as they serve as templates for achieving mental lucidness that then lends itself into focused intentions.

Aminda O'Hare's Visit: DSVV's Generous and Welcoming Atmosphere

Professor Aminda O'Hare is currently the Director of Neuroscience and professor of psychology at Weber State University in Ogden, Utah. Previously, Aminda was a colleague of Maureen's at the University of Massachusetts Dartmouth. Starting in 2013, she and Maureen collaborated on research on mindfulness and education, which resulted in several publications in peer-reviewed venues along with two grants. Maureen invited Aminda to DSVV in 2019. Aminda shares her connection to India and her experience at DSVV:

> During one of my trips to India for the Emory-Tibet Science Initiative, I was able to visit a friend and colleague, Maureen Hall, who is often staying at DSVV in northern India as a visiting professor. This was my first trip to India where I was not staying at the site of a Buddhist monastery in Southwest India. I soaked up the new culture as Maureen and I were driven to campus. After a short stay at DSVV, two things stood out to me that made this university unique. First was the presence of deep traditions of spiritual practice and compassion toward others – we were greeted, fed, and cared for everywhere we went, from individual residencies to the president's office. The second was the intentionality and purpose of the campus design and building structures. This was a campus that was built to enable you to inhabit a contemplative and present mind. These two aspects of the

university were experienced together when we attended Yagya early in the morning. This is a practice where offerings are made around a sacred fire while mantras of healing for the self, others, and the world are offered. Despite not knowing the language or rituals for this practice, we were greeted and gently led through the ceremony by other attendees.

The Experiences that Show Theory in Practice

All of the above experiences are testimonies of the philosophies put into practice at DSVV, as shown from Westerners' perspectives. The atmosphere at DSVV, as shown through Kristi's narrative, encourages embodied education to be achieved through focused intentions, in an environment that eliminates distractions. Maureen's and Carol's experiences were of a more spiritual growth while in the ultimate location for such to occur. Danielle and Emily both grew to recognize their own capacities for resiliency which carried into their lives when they returned to the USA; Danielle has been able to utilize practices she learned to continue to combat stressors when they occur, and Emily recognized her potential for helping others. Libby and Aminda both experienced community through interacting with students and participating in the morning Yagya. Clearly, the Eastern philosophies that Dr. Chinmay Pandya continues in his grandfather's stead are important and useful to Westerners as well as to Indian students and faculty (Fig. 13.2).

CONCLUSION

This final chapter of *Academia from the Inside* reveals that embodied education has global implications. Pandit Srirarm Sharma's vision for Dev Sanskriti Vishwavidyalaya centers on the path to self-knowledge and the transmutation of global consciousness. By creating a space to encourage students to develop the internal self, specifically the educational approaches and the daily practices at DSVV, the students are expected to leave better than when they arrived. The narratives of Western perspectives illustrate several students' and professors' lived experiences of their visits to DSVV.

Pandit Sriram Sharma believed that times of trouble could be the catalyzing times for real change. The implications, challenges, and outcomes of the COVID-19 global pandemic are still emerging, but DSVV and Shantikunj continue to support people as part of their global

Fig. 13.2 DSVV student in meditation (photo by Libby Falk Jones)

family. Specifically, during COVID-19, the Shantikunj Ashram and DSVV became Critical Care Units for any people in the area who had the virus and needed care. Furthermore, they have offered free tuition and lodging for any young person who has lost a parent to COVID-19. Perhaps one thing that COVID-19 has made clear is that we need to think and act as members of a global society, where we as global citizens work collectively to make a better, more humane world.

As the global mindset continues its seismic shifts, there is hope and evidence of progress for manifesting Pandit Sriram Sharma's vision of latent divinity. With its unique approach to education, DSVV offers educational approaches that can help to uncover the salient purpose that exists within each of us and share it with the world. These small changes that occur on the individual level can act as a conduit for changing the world for the better, one individual at a time, and these embodied approaches can be found at this unique university in northern India.

References

Dev Sanskriti Vishwa Vidyalaya. (2020). *Prospectus.* http://www.dsvv.ac.in/reg ular-admissions/prospectus-english-2020-21-revised.pdf

Dev Sanskriti Vishwa Vidyalaya. *The vision of the Dev Sanskriti Vishwa Vidyalaya.* http://www.dsvv.ac.in/dev-sanskriti-university/vision-mission/

Palmer, P. J. (2017). *The courage to teach: Exploring the inner landscape of a teacher's life.* Wiley.

Shantikunj. (2019, November 7). *One young world: The global forum for young leaders. A talk by Dr. Chinmay Pandya* [Video]. Youtube. https://www.you tube.com/watch?v=L5uS4BR-LKU

Tribune India. (2015, May 7). *Global Gayatri family actively involved in relief.* https://www.tribuneindia.com/news/archive/features/global-gayatri-family-actively-involved-in-relief-77528

University of Massachusetts- Dartmouth. (2010, August 2). *Fifth UMass Dart-mouth professor wins prestigious Fulbright.* https://www.umassd.edu/news/2010/fifth-umass-dartmouth-professor-wins-prestigious-fulbright.html

University of Massachusetts- Dartmouth. (2017, January 27). *Professor Maureen Hall creates and endows scholarship for students to teach and study in India.* https://www.umassd.edu/cas/news/maureen-hall.html

Vivekananda, Swami. (1915). *The complete works of Swami Vivekananda* (p. 211). Advaita Ashram.

INDEX